# Christian Spirituality
# God's Presence through the Ages

Richard Woods, O.P.

THOMAS MORE PRESS
CHICAGO
1989

Calligraphic brush, quill and drawn versals by Noreen Monroe Guzie. Initials for chapters 17 through 20, courtesy of Carol Belanger Grafton, ed., *Historic Alphabets and Initials, Woodcut and Ornamental* (New York: Dover Publication, Inc., 1977).

Design by Steven Plane-Taylor.

ISBN 0-88347-246-5

# CONTENTS

# Introduction

L IKE A RIVER, a great theme runs through the years of Christian history, bringing life and hope to wastelands of conflict and speculation, flooding away the heartbreak of failure and loss. This theme is the progressive realization of an ineffable but undeniable Presence in the depths of all experience, a sense of God as the compassionate origin, unfailing guide, and infinite destiny of the whole human tribe.

In the following pages, we will explore how the sense of God's abiding presence arose from its Jewish sources, developed and slowly spread from the time of Jesus through the major periods of Christian history down to our own troubled era, adding size and strength to its own inherent force from a network of other religious tributaries. In particular, I hope to show how ordinary men and women possessed of extraordinary faith and courage created a vision of life far exceeding the wildest ambitions of their culture as well as those of our own politics, science, and technology. For through all the centuries of persecution, expansion, forgetfulness, and eventual renewal, they believed that the silent, untroubled Spirit among and within us wills and works to fashion the human race as a whole into a true People of God — just, peaceable, loving, and ultimately immortal.

Many women and men believe it still. It is they — the saints and mystics — who thus most fully realize the divine potential of humankind and bear the promise and burden of a truly humane future. Such a person stands at the spiritual center of history, already possessing the fullness of the great promise, joining humanity at the deepest core of its nature to infinite being, life and consciousness, linking past to future beyond the limits of time and space, death and failure.

Any story is necessarily limited by its author's point of view. This account of the spiritual history of the Christian people has been undertaken from a consciously Catholic perspective. Because of the age and extensiveness of the Roman communion throughout the world, as well as its spiritual richness and vitality, such a viewpoint provides several advantages in addition to the familiarity of personal adherence. But other Christian traditions are as old or even older. Many have long existed in parts of the world only recently touched by Roman Catholicism and possess an incomparable wealth of spirituality. Orthodoxy and Protestantism, as well as Middle Eastern and Asian Christianity, have also made essential contributions to the history of Christian spirituality. It will be necessary to include all of these traditions in our story, even at the expense of doing so too briefly and inadequately.

Several histories and handbooks of Christian spirituality have been published within the past few years. Most of them provide excellent overviews and resources for further study.[1] The present effort differs from the others in at least one major respect. In order to provide a useful textbook for adults, I have attempted to situate in a single volume the development of Christian spirituality in the life and history of the Church as a whole as well as in view of major events in the wider world.

It can be argued that Christian spirituality has its own rich, inner history possessing a meaning and value independent from events in secular society. Most surveys seem to be written under the influence of that presupposition. Today, however, the significance of that history must, I feel, be measured against the wider backdrop of cultural and social developments that contribute to the worldview of epochs as well as that of ordinary people, for it is within that world and *for* it that Christian spirituality exists in the first place.

Of course, only an encyclopedia could do full justice to such an undertaking, and what I have provided as context is necessarily limited to immediately relevent events in the larger society.[2] Further, no survey can hope to offer more than a coherent sketch even of Catholic spirituality, much less that of the Christian people as a whole. Accordingly, these essays are offered by way of an introduction and an invitation for fuller investigation. (For those who wish to explore more deeply, references in English have been added to this edition in the form of endnotes, and a resource list has been appended.)

In order to limit the present work to a single volume, I have resisted the considerable temptation to cite passages from the writings of spiritual masters, which can, however, be found in a number of excellent anthologies.[3] It would be well to remember, moreover, that all authentic spirituality is first of all the product of life, not merely or even primarily of study. The Word became flesh and blood, not paper and ink.

*Spirit and Presence*

At this early point, the question may legitimately be raised, 'What do you mean by "spirituality"?' Today, people can mean almost anything when they use the word — from the study of the lives and teachings of the saints (especially those from the seventeenth to the nineteenth centuries) to the mental and attitudinal "stance" of football teams and automobile dealers. In what follows, I shall take it to mean the intrinsic, self-transcending character of all human persons and everything that pertains to it, including, most importantly, the ways in which that perhaps infinitely malleable character is realized concretely in everyday life situations. For, drawing on ancient metaphors for "breath" in Hebrew, Greek, and Latin, "*spirit*" itself refers to the essential human capacity to receive and transmit the life of God, our unlimited openness to being, life, and conscious relationship.[4]

Spirituality is therefore primarily concrete and real, since it encompasses all the ways, beliefs, and attitudes people have ever had regarding the development of the human spirit in its collective as well as particular forms. And, like experience itself, spirituality always has an essential social dimension. For each of us acquires our characteristic spirituality in an on-going dialogue with the communities that nurture, support, and challenge us throughout our lives. We are likewise involved spiritually in the life of the world by our practical, everyday contributions to those around us, whether we (or they) recognize it or not.

Of course, "spirituality" can also refer to the organized study and teaching of the varieties of personal and communal spiritualities that have appeared in history and are appearing at this moment. Generally, however, I will use the term in this book to indicate the particular ways in which Christian men and women have come to understand, value, and direct their lives as disciples of Jesus of Nazareth in their own worlds.

We remain ignorant of much of the detail that made up early Christian spiritualities. But one thing seems clear. From the beginning, Christian spirituality as a whole always focused on awareness of and faith in the abiding presence of God, *the* Spirit of being, life, and relationship that grounds and supports all human experience. In fact, Christian spirituality originated and developed as a growing consciousness of the special reality of God's presence as companion and friend in Jesus and his first disciples. Subsequent Christian experience testifies that as such a vital personal presence, God is no merely passive partner in some interior dialogue, but acts within both individuals and the community. More often patiently, but at times abruptly, the Divine Spirit is thus transforming persons and human society itself, together with the natural world, into a new creation.

Recalling the story of this transformation — the formation and reformation of the People of God, "saint-making" — reveals something of the mystery of that Abiding Presence, providing the foundation of at least spiritual theology and, again, the underlying thematic of this book.

Thanks are certainly due to a number of persons who have contributed to this work. Among them, I would especially mention Todd Brennan of the Thomas More Association, who conceived the idea and patiently supported the long process of research and writing, Steven Plane-Taylor for his assistance in production and design, Noreen Guzie for her wonderful calligraphic contributions, and my confreres at Blackfriars, Oxford, whose hospitality and wisdom have sustained my quest for so many years. I dedicate the book to my parents, Margaret and James, who patiently nurtured the earliest roots of my own spirituality, and whose lives are now hidden with Christ in God.

## NOTES

1. Among them, I would single out the following: Jordan Aumann, O.P., *Christian Spirituality in the Catholic Tradition* (San Francisco and London: Ignatius Press/Sheed and Ward, 1985), Michael Cox, *Handbook of Christian Spirituality* (San Francisco: Harper and Row, 1985 ed.), Cheslyn Jones et al., *The Study of Spirituality* (Oxford and New York: Oxford University Press, 1986), and Frank C. Senn, ed., *Protestant Spiritual Traditions* (New York: Paulist Press, 1986). The three-volume set by Louis Bouyer, Jean Leclerq, François Vandenbroucke, and Louis Cognet, *A History of Christian Spirituality*, trans. by Mary P. Ryan, Barbara Wall, et al. (London: Burns and Oates, 1968), remains an indispensable classic in the field.
2. For a fuller exploration of the historical and cultural context of Christian and other spiritualities, see the twenty-five volume series being published by Crossroad (New York), "World Spirituality: An Encyclopedic History of the Religious Quest," under the general editorship of Ewart Cousins. Of major and lasting importance to the study of Christian spirituality is the "Classics of Western Spirituality" series being published by the Paulist Press, New York, which focuses on critical translations of individual writers with ample introductory material and notes.
3. Among recent volumes, see David Fleming, S.M., ed., *The Fire and the Cloud: An Anthology of Catholic Spirituality* (New York: Paulist Press, 1978), and Louis Dupré and James Wiseman, O.S.B., *Light from Light: An Anthology of Christian Mysticism* (New York: Paulist Press, 1988).
4. In formulating this holistic understanding of spirituality, I am indebted to the writings of J. A. T. Robinson, William Ernest Hocking, Kenneth Leech, Reginald Garrigou-Lagrange, and Gerald Hughes, among others, whose works will be found listed in the bibliography at the end of this book. In his last book, the lay theologian William Stringfellow offered this elegantly comprehensive description: "whatever else may be affirmed about a spirituality which has biblical precedent and style, spiritual maturity or spiritual fulfillment necessarily involves the *whole* person – body, mind, soul, place, relationships – in connection with the whole of creation throughout the era of time. Biblical spirituality encompasses the whole person in the totality of existence in the world, not some fragment or scrap or incident of a person." (*The Politics of Spirituality* [Philadelphia: Westminster Press, 1984], p. 22.)

# The Abiding Presence  *1*

NE DAY A MAN APPEARED from nowhere — an itinerant preacher of sorts. He was not a fanatic, nor was he a member of any priestly caste or professional prophetic fraternity. A craftsman by trade and inheritance, his schooling was meager, his financial resources minimal. He lacked influence among the religious and civil authorities, addressing his message of reliance on God and love of neighbor mainly to the lower classes. Something of a mystic and miracle worker, he healed the sick, the blind, the lame and those afflicted with mental and spiritual disorders. His preaching of love, peace, and justice eventually earned him the suspicion and enmity of the ruling class, who for a variety of reasons seem to have engineered his condemnation and execution as a religious heretic and social revolutionary.

Although his immediate circle of followers was completely cowed by this catastrophe, some time after his burial they regrouped under the unshakable belief that their former leader had in fact risen from the dead. Gradually the numbers of those who accepted the story grew into a sizable sect. Some claimed that God had been uniquely present in him, others that he was himself somehow divine. Ritual meals and rites of ablution were held to honor his memory and initiate new members into the growing body of believers. Through these ceremonies the mysterious founder was said to be somehow present himself.

Measures were taken by the religious and civil authorities first to discourage and then to suppress the new sect. But despite even the draconian efforts of state officials, the cult of the young Immortal spread throughout the known world. His teachings were recalled, passed on by word of mouth, and finally committed to writing, which with letters and other writings of the earliest disciples were widely circulated. Similar writings by later disciples were also collected and preserved. Eventually under the influence of powerful leaders, structures and procedures developed which slowly, sometimes painfully integrated the growing mass of disciples into a network of communities which they called *ekklesia*, the "Convocation" or "Assembly." We call it the Church.

Today after some nineteen and one-half centuries, one out of four people on earth professes to be a Christian. Half of those — one out of every eight persons on the planet — belong to a single denomination, called for approximately the last four hundred years the Roman Catholic Church. It is apparently the fastest growing religious body in the world today, particularly in the Third World — Latin America, Africa, and Southeast Asia. It is also the second youngest of the major world religions, next only to Islam. With the exception of Japan, the most highly developed nations on earth are historically and sometimes nominally associated with Christianity. Roman Catholicism in particular is politically the most influential religious institution on the planet. Economically, it is also the richest, demographically the most widespread, linguistically and culturally the most diversified.

Any of these characteristics would provide a point of departure for an extensive and fascinating investigation. All of them rest, however, on the persistence of belief in the meaning of the life and teaching, death, and risen presence of that itinerant preacher and healer, the man named Jesus.[1] More particularly, they point to a few fundamental assertions attributed to the mendicant teacher — that it is possible not only to draw close to God, but to become one with God, sharing in the divine being, life, and consciousness itself and so to follow a way of living based on hope-filled faith, effective and universal love, and compassionate justice.

*The Sense of Presence*

Central to the message of Jesus as cherished and developed by generations of followers is the notion of *presence* — God's presence in Jesus himself, God's presence in the body of believers who unite in Jesus' name and teaching, and God's presence in each person not only as a Christian, but indeed as a human being. Thus, the goal and meaning of human existence is the recognition and enhancement of the sense of Divine Presence, which in all three forms — the person of Jesus as the risen Christ, the community of believers, and the individual human creature as a child of God — is at once both hidden and manifest, which in religious terms is to say a *mystery*.

The subsequent development of Christian spirituality may therefore be best understood in terms of the particular forms in which the abiding presence of God was brought to ever fuller manifestation in the consciousness and activity both of individual persons and collectively.

*The Inheritance from Israel*

Long before the Christian centuries, the history of the Jewish people and the language of the scriptures already testified to the centrality of Presence both as belief and experience.[2] Moreover, early Christian spirituality itself did not arise full-blown on the day of Pentecost or even from the teachings of the first generation of disciples. It emerged in conflict and confusion from a mustard seed of faith and stamina and grew slowly over decades and centuries. Both seed and soil were Jewish. Other cultural and even religious traditions influenced its growth — Greek, Syrian, Roman, even Egyptian. None, however, could imaginably approach the determinative force of Judaism. In form and content, Christian spirituality arose within the Jewish spiritual tradition with its heritage of covenant, remembrance, and blessing, but above all, Presence. It cannot be understood outside the context of that ancestry and that sense of intimate communion.[3]

Unlike the religions of the peoples surrounding ancient Israel, her faith habitually resided in a divine Presence immune from confinement to sacred places and times. Nor was the cultic worship of God restricted to a priestly caste who alone possessed the secret knowledge of expiation, propitiation, and intercession. These elements slowly and perhaps inevitably infiltrated Israelite cult and culture after the monarchy was established in the tenth century. But it had been otherwise "in the beginning," and the heart of biblical spirituality always tended toward freedom from institutional containment and hierarchical control.

*The Abode of God*

The God who spoke to Abraham, Moses, and the prophets professed to dwell among the people chosen to perform a priestly ministry for the nations. In that abiding presence, God was revealed from the beginning as the origin and destiny of all humankind: "by you all the families of the earth shall bless themselves" (Gen. 12: 3). God was also held to be present through all of nature, yet fully transcending the very creation which yielded obediently as a medium of that presence. Neither cave nor mountaintop, desert sanctuary, nor sacred grove could contain the spirit of the living God. The Spirit blew freely where it would, hallowing the site of its manifestations during a moment of revelation, but leaving it afterwards as it had been before.

Nor could time and history limit the everlasting presence that passed effortlessly through the veils of nature: "The Lord, the God of your ancestors, the God of Abraham, the God of Isaac, and the God of Jacob... this is my name forever, and thus I am to be remembered throughout all generations" (Ex. 3: 15). God ruled all times and all seasons with sovereign freedom, eluding with ease the nets of festal celebration and the episodes of solar and lunar crisis that dominated the calendars and consciousness of the "gentiles." Although beyond history, the same God nevertheless freely entered history, shaping it to ends far above all human reckoning and control. Every day was the Day of the Lord.

Thus, Israel's faith primarily lay in a God who would be with her on her journey through history, going before her, following after, bringing her back when she wandered from the path. Israel's spirituality came to embody a host of concrete elements that served to remind her collectively and individually of that presence and the saving acts of "God-with-us" — *Emmanuel*.

Great feasts commemorated historical events such as the Passover, Esther's deliverance of the Jews, and the cleansing of the Temple as well as the peoples' continuing dependence upon God during the yearly agricultural cycle. The living word of God present in the scriptures was constantly before her eyes, as it is today, enshrined in scrolls which are read and chanted in synagogue service. From about the third century before the Common Era,[4] select passages tucked into *tefillin* or phylacteries were worn on the forehead and arms. The *mezuzah*, a small box containing miniature scrolls, is still tacked to the jambs of doorways by many Jews and even some Christians.

Restrictions regarding food, clothing, and sexual practices, like circumcision, the sabbath rest, and other observances, similarly brought God's abiding presence to mind during the round of everyday life. Daily prayer was a continual dialogue with God in the mind and heart. Standards of high ethical behavior were enjoined on all the people so that through works of justice and mercy they would become and remain a living sign to the nations of what God intended for all: "Be whole as I am whole" (Lev. 11:44). For the perfection of wholeness is and ever shall be holiness.

Jewish spirituality was always fraught with the desire to see the face of God, to experience the beatifying ecstasy of knowing God's inner being, the *kabod Yahweh* — the splendor or Glory of the Lord. Yet, as Isaiah protested, "Truly you are a God who hides yourself!" (Is. 45:15). The God of Abraham, Isaac, and Jacob, of Moses and the prophets, dwells in heights and depths inaccessible to human abilities of comprehension or portrayal. Thus, the prohibition against making images of God protected Israel from objectification, the religious expedient that ends in idolatry, rendering the divine Presence external, defined, but psychologically opaque.

Israel's God was present to her imagination, rather, in the interior space of spiritual companionship and communion. Nature was only God's servant, architecture and ritual merely convenient occasions for remembrance and worship. Like the burning bush and Horeb's flaming crest, the ancient shrines, the Tabernacle, the Ark of the Covenant, even the Temple itself were only temporary vehicles of God's presence. Each was lost or destroyed without injury to Israel's inner faith. On the contrary, God's "retreat" from such local and physical associations served to heighten Israel's awareness of the interior mode of presence.

Even so, God's self-disclosure to Israel and the world was mediated not so much by strange prophetic visions such as those of Isaiah and Ezekiel as it was by the intimacy of the inner word and dreams. Israel's God chose to inhabit the interior recesses of the human spirit — consciousness, memory, and the attunement of wills. The pinnacle of religious observance thus came to be neither pilgrimage nor sacrifice but recollection — the sharpening of inner and loving attentiveness, the practice of the presence of God.

Thus the great heroes of Israel's history were men and women who knew God in the intimacy of elect companionship, such as Abraham and Sarah, who entertained Divinity under the oaks at Mamre, or Jacob and Joseph, who heard voices in the night and dreamed strange dreams. Moses conversed with Omnipotence face to face and even glimpsed the backside of God's glory. Judges like Deborah, Jael, and Gideon haggled and argued with God like fishwives. Samuel and Elijah heard the whisper of Infinity in the utter silence of the midnight desert. David loved his Lord passionately, singing and dancing and making music on the harp for his Divine Friend. The great prophets and champions were pursued and penetrated by the ardor of that Lover — Amos, Hosea, Isaiah, Jeremiah, Judith, Esther, and the Maccabees. Therefore when Israel wished to remember God, she also recalled

God's friends, those who had *known* God in the immediacy of present experience, an intimacy ultimately meant for all.

Thus, when in 587 B.C.E. and again in 70 C.E., the nations destroyed the first and second Temples and led the Jews into exile, the faith of Israel was not destablized. Rather it was universalized, as the Jewish people were forced to recover the older, deeper sense of the transcendent presence of God among the community of believers and within the heart of the individual believer wherever he or she might be. Ezekiel's vision of the departure of God's glory before the destruction of the Temple had been as much a promise of the availability of that presence to the exiles in Babylon as it was a protest against the introduction of pagan practices in the sanctuary at Jerusalem. The exiled Jews — the *diaspora* — were human seeds of faith and divine consciousness dispersed among the nations of the world. In the subsequent development of the synagogue, "the house of intercession" (*beth tephillah*), and the lay rabbinate, Israel retained what she had learned with the loss of the Temple and the priesthood. The chosen abode of God is the human heart attuned by justice and compassion to the divine Presence.

The story of the Chosen or Elect People is thus an epic chronicle of the discovery, forgetting and often painful recollection of the transcendent presence of a God immanent in natural, social and temporal events. Even more it is the progressive record of the *interiorization* of the human race, not only of Israel or of the West, but universally. For the same divine power that eludes time, space, and matter revealed itself as an indwelling presence accessible to conscious communion in love and mindfulness. Israel's spirituality was, as the Christian era neared, a true but qualified mysticism, a quest to see the face of God and live. Not in ecstatic rapture, but in the world of everyday affairs, in the midst of natural beauty and national destiny. True vision was deferred in faith until the mystery of death removed the final veil of human inadequacy, just as the Day of the Lord was eventually deferred until the Last Times, the end and transformation of cosmic and social history.

"Thereafter," the psalmist sang, "you will lead me into glory" (Ps. 73: 24b).[5]

God's
Presence in
Christ

As God's presence was the heart of Jewish spirituality, so also it formed the heart of early Christian spirituality. The theme is as equally and richly manifest in both early Christian and rabbinic writings of the same period. For example, the gnomic statement of Jesus in Matthew's gospel, "Where two or three are gathered together in my name, there I am in the midst of them" (Matt. 18:20), finds its parallel in the *Mishnah* — "Two who sit together and occupy themselves with the words of the Torah have the *Shekinah* (the divine presence)" (*Pirqe Aboth* 3:3). In this light, the Christian text even more clearly proclaims that God was uniquely present in Jesus. For in later Judaism, the term *Shekinah* (from *shaken*, "to dwell or abide") had taken on all the richness of earlier references to the glorious manifestation of God in the Pillar of Cloud and Fire, over the Ark, and in the Temple.

For the Jews in exile and later in Judea, after the departure of God's presence from the Temple (Ezek. 9:3 - 11: 23), God did not merely disappear from history, but became even more present in a mysterious manner in the cosmos, in the midst of the devout, and especially in the fullness of time, on the Day of the Lord. Similarly for early Christians, the bodily disappearance of Jesus with his Ascension did not mean his sheer absence from history but the expansion of his presence into the very structure of time and space, even to the "End Time," when he would return in the clouds of heaven to judge the living and the dead. Like the Transfiguration on Mt. Tabor, the Ascension expressed Jesus' identification with the "hidden God" of ancient Jewish tradition — a God universally present in that very hiddenness.

Just as Ezekiel believed in the eventual return of the Glory of God to the Temple, Christians likewise believed that Christ's return in glory would restore the Reign of God, set things right. The Greek word they used for that was *parousia*, which means not only "coming" but "presence." Before that Day, they also believed, Jesus would be present in Spirit among us — not only in the community of disciples in Jerusalem or Galilee, but throughout the world. The Jewish feast of Pentecost, too, celebrates the universal presence of Christ's Spirit.

Thus, for the poet-theologians of the early Church, the transcendent Christ of cosmic presence is no less the immanent Christ whose Spirit lives among and within us — the Jesus for whom the apostles and martyrs searched the wide world and found wherever they looked. He is present in the mysteries of baptism and eucharist, but also in the need of the suffering, oppressed, and poor: "Truly I say to you, as you did it to one of the least of my brothers or sisters, you did it to *me*" (Matt. 25:40). He is present also in the hearts of those who profess faith in the mystery of God's presence in Christ's body, the Church, for the Holy Spirit is poured out in our hearts and prays within us with inexpressible longing when we do not even know what to say (Rom. 8: 26). Christ's spirit is present, too, among those who pray and work for the coming of God's reign on earth as it is in heaven. Finally, with the words Matthew uses to conclude his gospel, Jesus promised, "Behold, I am with you always, even to the end of the world" (Matt. 28:20).

*The Legacy of Judaism*

Christianity was divorced from its Jewish identity by the end of the eighth decade of the common era, but not from its Jewish ancestry. The infant Church had fully inherited the spirituality of a divine Presence forever and fully free from sacred precincts, rites, or caste yet also fully free to manifest itself through any chosen medium, including sanctuary, sacrament, and sacerdotal ministry. Thus the history of Christian spirituality only continued in a new and universal way the line of development begun with Abraham, Moses, and the prophets. In faithful hope during centuries of exile and wandering, Judaism also continued her development of God-consciousness along a different but related way.[6]

Christian belief maintains that in the fullness of time, these divergent but interconnected paths of holiness will finally and forever intersect. In the meantime, it is well to remember their common origin and destiny, their witness to the oneness of God, and their confident, expectant devotion to God's abiding presence. The true Israel remains the sacrament of humankind's encounter with God, the anvil on which divine Presence forges human consciousness into ever increasing measure with the twin hammers of natural and social revelation.

## NOTES

1. Among the immense number of works about Jesus, for perhaps the most relevant in the present context as an appraisal of his life and influence, see Hendrikus Boers, *Who was Jesus? The Historical Jesus and the Synoptic Gospels* (New York: Harper and Row, 1989), and Michael Grant, *Jesus: An Historian's Review of the Gospels* (New York: Charles Scribner's Sons, 1977). For further reference, consult Leland Jennings White, *Jesus the Christ: A Bibliography* (Wilmington, DE: Michael Glazier, 1988).
2. See Arthur Green, ed., *Jewish Spirituality: From the Bible through the Middle Ages* (New York: Crossroad, 1988).
3. For a comprehensive and insightful exploration of the biblical theme of presence, see Samuel Terrien, *The Elusive Presence* (San Francisco: Harper and Row, 1978).
4. In keeping with current practice among Christian and Jewish scholars, the period of time since the birth of Jesus will be referred to as "the Common Era" (C.E.), and the period before that as "Before the Common Era" (B.C.E.).
5. For an account of early Jewish mysticism, see Joseph Dan, "The Religious Experience of the *Merkavah*," in Green, *Jewish Spirituality*, ed. cit., pp. 289-311, and Daniel C. Matt, "The Mystic and the *Mizwot*," ed. cit., pp. 367-404.
6. See John D. Zizioulas, "The Early Christian Community," in Bernard McGinn and John Meyendorff, *Christian Spirituality: Origins to the Twelfth Century* (New York: Crossroad, 1985), pp. 23-43. For a detailed study, see Jean Daniélou, *The Theology of Jewish Christianity* (Philadelphia: Westminster Press, 1964).

# Religious Rivalry and
# The Quest for Wisdom    *2*

ARLY CHRISTIAN SPIRITUALITY was given characteristic shape by the reciprocal impact of powerful personalities among Jesus' leading disciples on the strong social and religious forces that moved among the currents of daily life in first century Palestine. Very early in the life of the Church, local communities developed around apostles and evangelists who preached a distinctive understanding of the teachings of Jesus and the meaning of his life, death, and resurrection.[1] There were significant variations in their accounts, many of which are reflected in the writings of the New Testament — itself containing only a fraction of the gospels, acts, apocalypses, and letters written in the apostolic age. Central, however, to all versions later recognized as authentic by the Church as a whole is the message of a spiritual teacher whose life uniquely and definitively revealed the presence of the living God.

Among the outstanding preachers of that message and that Presence as they encountered the array of Jewish traditions in the middle of the first century, two have always been of particular interest to the Christian people — Simon bar Jonah and Saul of Tarsus.

*The
Fisher
of
Sheep*

Blunt, often impetuous, sometimes vacillating and inconsistent, Simon Peter was perhaps surprisingly selected to be the rock on which Jesus would base his infant community of love, the shepherd who would protect and defend the "little lambs" as well as the sheep.  Strengthened after his cowardly denial by Jesus' love and forgiveness and the abiding gift of his Spirit, Peter fulfilled that charge throughout his days, if often in his characteristically erratic fashion.  He boldly proclaimed Jesus as Lord and Redeemer before throngs of Jewish pilgrims and state officials.  He preached loudly in the Temple and suffered for it at the hands of the priests.  But he also hesitated to admit gentiles to full fellowship without their adopting Jewish ceremonial practices as demanded by ultraconservative Jewish Christians, the "Judaizers."

Caught up at Joppa in a mystical vision, Peter immediately changed his mind and thenceforth defended the reception of gentiles (Acts 10: 9-48).  Never as radical, however, as the Greek-speaking Christians like Stephen or even the more moderate Paul, Peter attempted to mediate between the Hellenists and Judaizers. He was accordingly attacked by both sides.  But slowly Peter's moderation prevailed.  After years of apostolic fence-mending, moreover, his apostolic pre-eminence in the churches as a whole seems to have been generally accepted.  Paul, however, could still confront him angrily when Peter seemed to be wavering in his commitment to the freedom of the gentiles.

Tension between Jewish and gentile Christians was particularly acute in Rome, where the local church appears to have been founded by missionaries from the conservative Jerusalem community.  So heated did the arguments become that in one case the Emperor Claudius banished a large number of Jewish Christians from the city — including Paul's friends Priscilla and Aquila. Eventually both Peter and Paul were drawn into the quarrel. Having largely overcome the differences between themselves at the great council of Jerusalem in 49, they were probably attempting to reconcile various factions when the great catastrophe of 64 struck the city.[2]

A fire of unknown origin swept through most of Rome in July of that year.  To divert public blame away from himself, the Emperor Nero accused the Christians of arson and unleashed a fierce persecution against them.  Popular opinion, already hostile because of dissension between Jewish and gentile Christians, at first supported the emperor.  In the frenzied attack on the defenseless if unruly "sheep," the two great shepherds were themselves swept up and executed, Peter on the Vatican Hill, according to tradition, and Paul on the Ostian Way.

Peter's enduring legacy to the Church can probably best be described as a spirit of reconciliation.  He struggled to prevent schism, attempting to bridge differences between factions suspicious of each other's orthodoxy by the precarious art of compromise.  At times an unsteady one, he was nonetheless a prophet of the whole Christ, sovereign above all national and ethnic diversity.  In this, Cephas — "the Rock" — will remain forever, as he was perceived from the beginning, the model of leadership in the Church as a whole, the good shepherd to all the flock.

*The Last Apostle*   Among the first generation of Christians, the personality and spirituality of Paul of Tarsus stand out even more boldly than those of Peter, James, and John, the pillars of the Church in Jerusalem — or "so-called pillars," as he would bristle in a moment of sarcastic impatience (Gal. 2:9).  As profoundly sensitive as he was explosive, the mercurial ex-Pharisee left his stamp forever upon the whole Church.

Reared a strict Pharisee of the diaspora, he studied under Gamaliel the Great in Jerusalem.  But Paul's famous conversion on the road to Damascus was total and final.  While not the most extreme of the radical Hellenists, he nevertheless staunchly resisted the efforts of the Judaizers, and even those of moderates such as Peter and James, to impose Jewish customs on gentile converts.  In the long haul, he succeeded, but only after decades of controversy.

Because of the number of surviving letters he left the local churches he had founded or supported, it is easy to overestimate Paul's influence in the early Church. On the other hand, fixing the liberal, inclusive character of that Church was his undoubted legacy. By the second century, together with Peter, Paul was reckoned by writers such as Clement of Rome and all early historians as one of the two pillars of the Church universal.

Paul's spirituality focused on the presence of the risen Christ in the body of his disciples, both socially and individually. The dramatic event that led to his complete reversal of belief and conduct was nothing less than a direct and immediate encounter with the glorified Christ, who unmistakably identified himself with his followers: "Saul, why are you persecuting *me*?" (Acts 9:4).

Paul in turn so completely identified himself with Christ that he not only claimed to bear the marks of Jesus' crucifixion in his body (Gal. 6:17), but longed more than anything to die in order to be one forever with his Lord (Phil. 1:21-23). Some commentators have wondered over the years whether like Francis of Assisi, Catherine of Siena and other known stigmatics, Paul was speaking literally about the wounds he bore. We cannot tell. But Paul clearly felt that his sufferings, and those of all who were persecuted or experienced hardships for the sake of Christ, were in fact crucified with Jesus. He no less insisted that all who had been baptized into Christ had died with him and were now risen to a wholly new life, one that would eventually flower in immortal glory (1 Cor. 15: 20-28).

*The Human Milieu*

Daily life in the Palestine of Christian origins was as diverse and complex as that of any people caught up in the throes of political oppression, military occupation and religious turmoil.

After a century of resistance against the efforts of Greek-speaking Syrian overlords to eradicate Jewish national and religious distinctiveness, the country fell gradually under the control of Rome — originally for purposes of mutual defense.

Generally tolerant, even respectful of cultural differences, the Romans declared official Judaism a *religio licita* — a legal and therefore protected form of worship. But military governors and lackey kinglets kept a wary eye out for deviations, which could mean anything that threatened to upset the religious balance of power.

For some time before the time of Christ, Jewish religion had in fact been a mixture of often wildly disparate elements rather than the monolithic body of belief and practice portrayed in popular films and novels. Christianity itself began as one of a host of competing factions or *chaburoth*, and in a short time demonstrated the same tendency to pluralism, one which has persisted to the present.

*Varieties of Jewish Spirituality* — Jewish writers of the period such as Philo and Josephus, the Christian scriptures themselves, and early Christian historians such as Eusebius all portray official Judaism in the early decades of the first century as an amalgam of schools and sects, each of which had its own beliefs, customs, traditions, and interpretations of what it meant to be a Jew. But even this picture is apparently far simpler than the actual religious situation at the time.[3]

Known to everyone even indirectly familiar with the gospels, the major Jewish factions at the time of Jesus were the Pharisees, proud and patriotic conservatives, and the more liberal-minded Sadducees, who practiced a political realism that led to outright collaboration with Rome. Descendants of the Maccabean *hasidim* ("the devout") who had helped overthrow the hated yoke of the Syrian successors of Alexander the Great, the Pharisees were bitterly opposed to any such compromise. Laymen and women rather than "clergy," they nevertheless adhered strongly to the traditional beliefs of strict Judaism. They were also more widespread and numerous. Most scribes, the interpreters of the Law, were Pharisees. The Sadducees on the other hand had come to dominate the priesthood and Temple. Rich, worldly, religiously skeptical, and unpopular, they were mainly concentrated in Jerusalem.

Catholic Christianity still bears the doctrinal and liturgical stamp of Pharisaism — belief in the reality of the soul and even of spirits such as angels and demons, the resurrection of the dead, heaven and hell, the efficacy of prayer for the dead, and a tendency to accept the literal word of scripture as it stands. Nonetheless, Pharisees also accepted the authority of oral tradition. Fasting and abstinence, personal devotion, set times for prayer, almsgiving and other ascetical practices were also features of Pharisaical tradition.

As became clear during Paul's struggles later in Jerusalem and elsewhere, however, there were divergences even within Pharisaism, particularly between the northern or Galilean variety, that of Jews like himself from the diaspora, and the southern form in Judea and especially in Jerusalem. Thus although the beliefs and spirituality of Jesus, Peter, and Paul himself as well as most of the apostles and disciples were Pharisaical, they were scorned as far less sophisticated and refined than those of the ruling class in Jerusalem.[4] And although bitterly critical of many scribes and Pharisees there and elsewhere, as well as opposed by them, Jesus and the early disciples were often equally open to them and were on occasion even defended by them against the rich and urbane Sadducees or other Pharisees.

Opposed to both major parties were the *Zealots* — radically and sometimes violently patriotic in their devotion to Judaism. Although more political than spiritual in their beliefs and practices, the Zealots (or Galileans, as they were sometimes called) contributed several members to the band of Jesus' immediate followers, including an apostle, Simon.

Other major movements or *chaburoth* are known to us mainly by name, but they obviously played an important part in the life of the Jewish people and the early Christian Church — the Essenes, Hemerobaptists, Masbotheans, Samaritans, and Nazorenes among them. Recent discoveries of manuscript scrolls at Qumran, near the Dead Sea, suggest that Essene doctrine may have influenced both the preaching of John the Baptist and Christian apocalyptic thinking. Jesus himself could have known Essenes, but his teaching differs on important points, particularly his openness to pagans and less orthodox Jews as well as his preference for the "little ones" of the realm of God — the poor, outcast, and persecuted members of Jewish society.

*Jewish Monasticism*    Like the Zealots, the *Essenes* were extreme messianic nationalists, but expressed their faith in much more spiritual, even otherworldly terms. Although the language of their writings was warlike, they did not believe in armed resistance but retired to the desert to purify themselves, study scripture, pray, and await the coming of the Lord. They rejected the Temple and the official priesthood as hopelessly compromised, but seem to have developed a priestly class of their own.

Something like a religious order, the Essenes extolled celibacy, although women were evidently permitted to join the community, and some members were married. They possessed their goods in common and decided issues by vote. Like later Christian monks, they had a probationary period of three years, took vows, shared a common meal, and performed manual labor. The Damascus Document, an ancient manuscript first published in 1910, indicates that some Essenes had migrated to cities beyond the Dead Sea area, where the Qumran manuscripts were found beginning in 1947. Philo, the great Jewish scholar writing in Egypt at the time of Christ, described them as well as did his Palestinian contemporary, Josephus. The monastic impulse in later Christian times must be interpreted in the light of such movements, including those outside of Palestine such the Therapeutae, whom Philo also describes and we shall encounter later on.

Another group, the *Nazorenes* or *Mandaeans*, originated in eastern Syria and Palestine. "Gnostics," they combined esoteric Judaism with elements of Persian moral dualism and the cognitive bias of later Greek philosophy. Little is known about them and other smaller Jewish movements such as the *Masbotheans* and *Hemero-baptists*, who from their name apparently practiced daily ritual baptism. The *Samaritans* on the other hand were a sizable ethnic and religious sect whom orthodox Jews traditionally despised as heretical. Nevertheless, Samaritans were present in Judea, and some Jews — including Jesus himself — violated ordinary proprieties by traveling through Samaria on the way to and from Jerusalem. Insofar as the Samaritans were generally regarded as inferior even to pagans, the early Christian mission to them testifies to the triumph of the universalist movement in the primitive Church, following the example of Jesus himself.

The calamities of 70 A.D. and 135, when the Temple was destroyed and eventually the Jewish population of Jerusalem deported, brought an end to much of the rich internal diversity of Judaism. The Sadducees disappeared utterly with the Temple and the priesthood. Similarly, the Zealots and Essenes were either destroyed or faded into history along with the Hemerobaptists and Masbotheans. Several hundred Samaritans have managed to survive up to the present in Nablus, their ancient capital on the west bank of the Jordan. The Mandaeans, joined both by followers of John the Baptist and gnostic Christians, migrated in the third century from Palestine to southern Iraq, where they have survived right up to the present. But Judaism as it has come to be known in the common era has descended from the faith of the Pharisees as has Christianity in many respects. Nevertheless, the radical pluralism of Jewish sects in the first century deeply affected the life and nascent spirituality of the infant Church.

*Early Christian Pluralism*

Overall, the Jewish *chaburoth* differed from one another regarding just about everything except the unity of God and the election of Israel. Because of its deep-rootedness in Jewish faith and practice, the early Christian community was similarly and sharply divided on a score of common issues. In both cases, the divisive concerns were those of conflicting spiritualities — how a shared faith could be expressed in differing ways.

Early Christian spirituality was in fact Jewish spirituality with a critical difference — one that eventually mattered more than all the affinities: the meaning and person of Jesus, especially the central matter of God's unique presence in Jesus.[5]   But the fundamental problem, one which nearly split the early Church into irreconcilable factions, concerned the saving will of God for all people.   Could gentiles be incorporated into the Christian community without first accepting Judaism?

At least four groups struggled for spiritual and political supremacy over this issue in the infant Church.   At the extreme right were the radical "Judaizers" as they were called — those who held that all Christians, whether Jews or gentiles, must adopt and practice the fullness of the Law including circumcision.   At the opposite extreme were the radical "Hellenists" or Greek-speaking Christians, largely Jews from the diaspora and gentile converts like Stephen, Apollos, and the author of the Johannine writings, who urged a total break with Judaism. Between these polar opposites stood the moderate conservatives led by James and Peter on one hand and the liberals led by Paul, Barnabas, and their associates on the other.

For years, debates raged in Jerusalem, Antioch, and elsewhere between the Judaizers and the Hellenists, one of whose number, Stephen, was the first Christian martyr.   Faced with schism, the infant Church achieved an uneasy compromise between the parties of James and Paul at the council of Jerusalem.   The issue was more decisively settled by the destruction of Jerusalem by Roman troops in the year 70 and again in 135.

The eradication of the mother church did not mean victory for the extreme Hellenists, however.   Many lapsed into forms of gnosticism such as that of Marcion, who was virulently anti-Jewish. Further, daughter churches of Jerusalem survived and even flourished in Antioch, Rome, and elsewhere.   But the loss of Jerusalem's paramount influence assured that the universalizing mission of the Pauline churches would determine the course of Christianity for all time to come.   As shown in Paul's letter to the Roman Christians, however, the spirituality of that tradition, much like Peter's, recognized the deep bonds between Judaism and Christianity despite Christian rejection of Jewish ritual and legal obligations.

At least one remnant of radical Jewish Christianity did manage to survive the destruction of Jerusalem. Apparently influenced by the poverty and purity of the Essenes, they were called *Ebionites*, "the poor." Like a similar sect, the *Elkasites*, which sprang from the Zealot movement, they endured for a time in the Judean countryside, cut off from the rest of the Christian communities by their unshakable Jewishness. Eventually, however, these early schismatics also vanished across the borders of historical memory, only a fragment of their writings remaining as a sad reminder of the Church's debt to the rich heritage of Judaism.

For several centuries other heterodox Christians continued to threaten the integrity — and spirituality — of the early Church. Almost at the beginning, antagonism erupted between orthodox Christians and converts from heterodox, gnostic Judaism such as Simon Magus, who attempted to insert the Christian event into an elaborate framework of cosmic emanations, speculative theology, and possibly even ritual magic.

In many cases, we know little more about these gnostic groups and their teachings than their names, such as the *Nicolaitans*. In other cases, even their writings have come down through the ages to tantalize and bewilder Christians with their charm, elegance, and sometimes even deep piety: gospels attributed to Thomas, Philip, Mary and James, the Gospel of Truth, the Secret Book of John, a Secret Gospel of Mark, and the Book of Thomas the Contender among them, as well as countless other fragments.[6]

Many of these wild elements, spun off by the disenchantment of the radical Hellenists, blazed for a moment, then disappeared like the Ebionites. Others — the Menandrianists, Marcianists, Carpocratians, Valentinians, Basilideans and Satornilians — remained vigorous for generations, amounting, as we shall see, to the first great inner threat to the Christian Church as it spread throughout the known world.

*The Art
of
Life*

Several varieties of Christian spirituality arose from the complex matrix of Jewish tradition as found in the diaspora as well as in Palestine. But the main current of early Christian spirituality has its source in the Wisdom tradition of later Judaism as it developed among the Jewish faithful in Egypt, particularly as shaped and promoted by one of the most impressive figures of the period, known simply and forever as Philo the Jew.

In the two centuries before the birth of Jesus, wisdom (*Hochmah*) had come to occupy a central place in the religious life of the Jews in Palestine as well as in the diaspora. Broader than *da'ath*, the knowledge of God, it meant practical knowledge — how to behave in such a manner as to enjoy the favor of both God and one's neighbor.

Jewish Wisdom was a prudential art, similar in many ways to the ethics of Confucius. As a distinctly spiritual way of life, the pursuit of Divine Wisdom developed in the scribal schools at the royal court. Its remoter ancestry can be traced to the court schools of Egypt, Edom, and Babylon, which had provided models in other respects for the Jewish monarchy. Eventually, however, the love of Wisdom came to pervade the life of the people as a whole.

The specifically Jewish origin of Wisdom literature is found in *midrash*, the interpretation of scripture. Whether *halakah*, interpretation of the Torah which provided instruction on moral conduct, or *hagadah*, narrative interpretation for purposes of spiritual insight and edification, the goal of scriptural exegesis was always the same — practical application to present situations. The central theme of such biblical instruction is that of the two paths, one of the wise person, the other of the fool. Allegories, fables, and parables as well as proverbs and riddles were used to show the ultimate value of following the path of life, the way in which Divine Wisdom instructed her children.

Early examples of the wisdom tradition are found in the story of Joseph with its significant Egyptian setting (Gen. 41:38) and that of Solomon (1 Kings 3:28 - 5:12). In the Book of Exodus and elsewhere, the practical and decorative arts were celebrated as wisdom (Exod. 31:2 - 4, 6; 1 Kings 7:14). The prophets such as Jeremiah lamented the departure of wisdom, just as Ezekiel will witness the departure of the divine presence from the temple: "Is wisdom no more in Teman?   Has counsel perished from the prudent? Has their wisdom vanished?" (Jer. 49:7).

In post-exilic Judaism, a characteristic body of sacred literature developed around the theme of artful living, including the books of Job, Proverbs, Ecclesiastes (Qoheleth), Ecclesiasticus (Sirach), and Wisdom — the Writings. In the writings of the priestly class such as Deuteronomy, wisdom was to be found in the observance of *Torah* — the Law (Deut. 4:6). But for those authors of the books called the Writings, it was the gift of God, the manifestation of God's own wisdom dwelling among mortals, and the key to happiness and all success.

The purpose of acquiring wisdom was much more than pragmatic — training for personal advancement or diplomatic service. Youngsters were instructed in the path of wisdom in order to develop moral character and spiritual insight into the meaning of life.   Virtues of truthfulness, honesty, and simplicity were inculcated in the home.   For the wise person should know how to confront the serious problems of life rather than merely to study them intellectually or solve them by wile.

Among great poets and thinkers, such concern for understanding and instruction had already led to profound meditation on the meaning and value of human existence such as found in the Books of Job, Sirach, and, above all, the Book of Wisdom itself, in which she is described as the effulgence of God's glory, the sign of God's living presence among humankind. (The Hebrew word *Hochmah* is feminine. From the earliest times, in Christian liturgical celebrations the attributes of Wisdom were applied to both Mary and to Jesus as well as to the Holy Spirit.) In Jewish mystical traditions shortly before the time of Christ, especially that in the great Egyptian city of Alexandria, the figure of Wisdom became personified as a special consort of God, eventually acquiring a status far above all creatures, the very brightness of the divine presence itself.[7]

*Early
Christian
Wisdom*

Like the Jewish spiritual tradition out of which it grew, Christian spirituality begins in the wonder of mystery and ends in the promise of glory. Two great wisdom themes run throughout the earliest writings of the followers of Jesus — first, how to live according to God's will in accordance with Jesus' teaching and witness, and second, the meaning of Jesus himself as God's final revelation, a self-communication felt and interpreted as abiding presence, the brightness of divine glory: "We have seen his glory, glory as of the only son from the Father" (John 1: 14).

Elements of midrashic wisdom are found throughout early Christian scripture, from the gospels to the letters of Paul, Hebrews, and Jude. Wisdom themes are prominent in the infancy narratives (Matt. 2: 1 - 12, Luke 1 and 2). As a young man, Jesus surprised his elders by possessing wisdom beyond his years and without benefit of formal schooling (Matt. 13:54, Mark 6:2). Later, following the tradition of the Book of Wisdom, Jesus himself described divine wisdom as a gift rather than an accomplishment, hidden from those who prided themselves on their learning, and given to mere children (Matt. 11: 25, Luke 10:21). Wisdom proved herself in deeds, not words (Matt. 11: 19, Luke 7:35).

Of all early Christian writers, Paul inherited the greatest enthusiasm for the wisdom themes of later Judaism. He, too, celebrated the connection of wisdom and God's glory and saw in Wisdom the very presence of the hidden God made known (Rom. 16:27, Eph. 3:10). For Paul and his disciples, Wisdom was a gift of grace, not earned or acquired (Eph. 1:8; Col. 1:9; 1 Cor. 12:8). Paul also discerned the wide difference between what the world counts as wisdom and true Wisdom: "Christ did not send me to baptize but to preach the gospel, and not with eloquent wisdom, lest the cross of Christ be emptied of its power" (1 Cor. 1:17). He insisted, "I did not come proclaiming to you the testimony of God in lofty words or wisdom," (1 Cor. 2:1), yet — "among the mature we do impart wisdom, although it is not a wisdom of this age or of the rulers of this age..." (1 Cor. 6).

Ultimately for Paul, as for the authors of the Gospel of John and the Epistle to the Hebrews, Wisdom was revealed most perfectly in Christ and him crucified. Before all ages, as well as in his life, death, and resurrection, Jesus Christ is the *logos*, the eternal Word and true Wisdom of God. The cross of Jesus is a scandal only because the Wisdom of God must appear as folly to those who pit their wisdom against God's. Such merely human logic is the true and lasting folly.

## NOTES

1. See especially Raymond Brown, *The Churches the Disciples Left Behind* (New York: Paulist Press, 1987), his *The Community of the Beloved Disciple* (New York: Paulist Press, 1979), and Raymond Brown and John P. Meier, *Antioch and Rome: New Testament Cradles of Catholic Christianity*.
2. See W. H. C. Frend, *The Rise of Christianity* (Philadelphia: Fortress Press, 1984), pp. 109-10.
3. See Marcel Simon, *Jewish Sects at the Time of Jesus*, trans. by James A. Farley (Philadelphia: Fortress Press, 1967), and Jacob Neusner, "Varieties of Judaism in the Formative Age," in Green, *Jewish Spirituality*, ed. cit., pp. 171-97.
4. See John Bowker, *Jesus and the Pharisees* (Cambridge: Cambridge University Press, 1973).
5. See Jean Daniélou, *The Theology of Jewish Christianity* (Philadelphia: Westminster Press, 1964).
6. The most authoritative edition of gnostic materials is James M. Robinson, ed., *The Nag Hammadi Library* (San Francisco: Harper and Row, 1988 ed). The classic work on the influence of gnosticism on the early Church is R. M. Grant's *Gnosticism and Early Christianity* (New York: Columbia University Press, 1966), A more recent, although more controversial study is Elaine Pagels' *The Gnostic Gospels* (New York: Vintage Books, 1981). For a comprehensive selection of non-canonical Jewish and Christian literature from the ancient world, see *The Other Bible*, ed. by Willis Barnstone (San Francisco: Harper and Row, 1984).
7. An excellent overview of the Wisdom tradition can be found in David Winston's introduction to the Anchor Bible edition of *The Wisdom of Solomon* (Garden City, NY: Doubleday and Co., [Anchor Bible, v. 43] 1979).

# Fire on Earth: Charism and Crisis in the Early Church

# 3

ONFLICT AND CONTROVERSY shaped the spiritual history of the Christian people from the start. Repeatedly, crises from within and danger from outside threatened the bond of unity that blossomed from the community's experience of God's abiding presence in the spirit of Jesus. Even so, through schism, heresy, and often violent persecution, the ideal and often the reality of ordinary Christian life remained communion in peace, love, freedom, and equality.

After the relative victory of the moderate Hellenists over radical Judaizers at the Council of Jerusalem, two new and serious challenges arose from within the primitive Church itself. The first was a spirit of elitism and divisiveness resulting from an emphasis on extraordinary gifts and prophecies. The second crisis found proponents of the "catholic" character of the Church, with its inclusive, far-ranging institutional forms and policies pitted against champions of the freer, more spontaneous but also more exclusive style of life found in often widely separated local communities.

In the years that followed, this tension between the universal and particular aspects of Christian life would become an enduring characteristic in the Church, one that continues to create conflict today. But for all its disruptive potential, it has always imbued

Christian spirituality with a lively sense of all-embracing concreteness. Rule and exception, unity and diversity, wholeness and particularity, letter and spirit, tradition and development – such are the parameters of living witness to the presence of God, not merely the stuff of turmoil and factional debate.

Even while the early Church was embroiled in inner conflicts over gifts and government, external threats appeared first in the form of oppression and then persecution by Jewish leaders and eventually by Roman imperial authorities. A more insidious danger came from the temptation to dilute the open, holistic gospel message with the esoteric speculations and secret rites of *gnosticism*. But just as recognition of the catholicity and openness of the Church and its spirituality emerged from the internal crises, so also the external challenges of martyrdom and doctrinal attack brought to consciousness the Church's spiritual power and theological authority. Each new achievement brought in its wake a host of new difficulties, however. Even martyrdom would produce a century of controversy over matters of loyalty and discipline.

*Come the End:
Millennial
Illusions and
Delusions*
A prefatory crisis that confronted and influenced a very early strand of Christian spirituality stemmed from the belief that Jesus would quickly return in glory and majesty to judge the nations and inaugurate the Realm of God.[1] Jewish apocalyptic speculations and expectations such as found in the *Book of Enoch* and *2 Esdras* undoubtedly shaped such beliefs as seen in the epistles attributed to Peter and Jude. It was rooted in Jesus' own teaching as recorded in the gospels (see especially Matt. 24: 29-30, Mark 13: 24-26, Luke 21: 25-27, etc.). St. Paul's exhortations to the Christians of Thessalonika in Macedonia show that he, too, subscribed at first to an immanent *parousia* – the return of Christ in physical, personal presence. Paul also insisted that such a hope should not prevent anyone from continuing the daily round of work, prayer, and service to the community. Nevertheless, because the days were drawing urgently short, ordinary human activities

and institutions, even marriage, were to be accounted for little. The earthly city was neither abiding nor, especially, absolute. The prayer arising from this joy-filled expectation, *Maranatha!* – "Lord, come soon!" (1 Cor. 16:22, Rev. 22: 20) – would resound in the liturgy for all centuries to come, especially during the advent season.

As the years drew on, Paul and his circle of disciples tempered belief in the immanent Parousia with an emphasis on sanctifying life in the present world to prepare for the life of glory to come in God's own good time. As a whole, the Church followed them. Marriage was no longer to be devalued as a temporary expedient, but recognized as a sacrament of Christ's love for and presence in his body, the Church. For Christians, daily life is not rendered pointless or fearful but hallowed in advance by the brightness of that day. We are therefore urged even more strongly to redeem the times by works of love and justice (Eph. 5: 16).

Despite such cautions, some early Christians (like later believers right up to the present) continued to seize upon the fast-approaching day of Christ's return as the major focus of their faith. Stimulated by the highly symbolic, poetic vision of the *Book of Revelation* (which was recognized as a part of Christian scripture only after several centuries of misgiving and debate), such believers frequently centered their attention on the thousand-year reign of Christ promised in Rev. 20. Most of these "millenarians" or "chiliasts," including the great and orthodox writers Justin Martyr and Irenaeus, maintained that Christ's reign would follow the Parousia. Later, some Christians impatiently came to believe that the millennial epoch of peace and justice would precede and indeed inaugurate the Second Coming.

Although opposed by the keenest theologians from the second to the fourth centuries, notably Clement and Origen in Alexandria and Augustine in Carthage, the millenarian theme recurred among radical sectarians such as the Montanists in the second century and particularly in the Middle Ages, when it was strongly felt around the year 1000 that the End of the World was near. Then, as after the Protestant Reformation in Germany and Switzerland, in nineteenth-century America, and even today, it became all too easy to identify the beginning of the Millennium with what was too often the inauguration of a religious despotism.  The result at Geneva and Münster, as at Jonestown, was a reign not of peace and justice, but of terror.  Fear and subservience replaced love and freedom.  Dissent from the dictates of the leaders became punishable by ostracism, exile, or even death.

Jesus' injunction "not to go out looking" nor to believe too readily remains the wisest advice concerning millenarian propaganda, since "no one knows the day or hour" (Matt. 26, Mark 13: 21, 32).  We are to be ready to meet Christ at any turn of our lives, not forgetting that we can meet him daily in the eucharist, in scripture, in prayer and works of mercy, as well as in the events of history themselves.  Christ is the Lord of Time.  But even angel voices can fail to deflect eyes too easily fastened on the clouds, where if they do not see the Son of Man coming in majesty, they may project their own vision of him – or what they would like him to be.

*The Lure of the Exotic*  Many problems in Christian belief and practice flow from thus seizing upon one aspect or dimension of the faith – often one of only relative significance – and making it the exclusive point of concern.  Pushed to an extreme, such *hairesis* ("selectivity") eventuates in real heresy – a serious departure from the main body of believers in doctrine, or in *schism* – a split from corporate unity with the Church in practice.  Often, it produces both.

Thus it was when devotional exuberance and prophetic enthusiasm appeared early among the Hellenistic communities of the Christian diaspora.  Soon enough, an exaggerated emphasis on extraordinary gifts and spiritual manifestations came to threaten the unity and peace of the local community in Corinth, and probably elsewhere as well.  As would become more evident in times to come, a taste for exotic religious experience can easily imperil the integrity of the greater household of faith.  And yet, such charismatic manifestations were also recognized by Paul and other Christian leaders as true signs of the presence of God.

Sometimes such episodes have figured prominently in the history of God's people. At other times, they recede in frequency and significance. They are still reported today. Despite continuing conflict and controversy, as signs of the presence of God, they warrant consideration with respect to the story of Christian spirituality. The dilemma faced by the first generation of Christians lay not so much in discerning the provenance of these extraordinary events and abilities, for they also recognized the possibility of deception and illusion. Rather, the issue for them was one of discipline and regulation.

*Signs and Wonders*

Since the Enlightenment, many "modern" biblical scholars and theologians have sought to demythologize scripture and thereby reduce the element of miracle to the play of memory and the desire to illustrate and even magnify the significance of religious events.

Nevertheless, there remains an irreducible record of extraordinary happenings in the history of salvation, one which has continued to the present. Faith, as Jesus taught in the Gospel of John, does not depend on miracles, but it can produce wonders of healing, conversion, and forgiveness. The transformation of ordinary human abilities under the influence of grace is, perhaps, the most common of all such signs, and it was by no means absent from the life of Jesus and the infant Church.

The presence of God that broadcast splendor from the darkness of Sinai, filled the cloud-filled temple, and spoke in the "still, small voice" that Elijah heard after the storm had passed Carmel, was again made manifest at crucial moments in Jesus' life and ministry — at his birth and baptism, and especially at the mysterious transformation witnessed by Peter, John, and James on the Mount of Transfiguration (Mark 9: 2-8, Matt. 17: 1-8, Luke 9: 28-36). Matthew and Luke describe the dazzling radiance of the very faces and clothing of the youths who told of his Resurrection. The Power that raised the dead to life in the days of Elisha (2 Kings 4: 32-35) was manifest in the hand that raised the son of the widow of Naim, the daughter of Jairus, and Lazarus. Lepers were cleansed, the lame and blind healed. Demonic agencies were expelled from their victims at a word. Hidden thoughts and the secret intentions of hearts were disclosed.

At Pentecost, at the house of Cornelius, at Ephesus and Corinth, the presence of the Holy Spirit was experienced in sudden marvels of sound, vision, and speech. The "mighty arm" that delivered Israel from Egypt likewise delivered Peter from prison. The divine splendor and voice that Moses discovered greeted Saul on his way to Damascus.

Even though the author of the *Acts of the Apostles* idealized such events in the early days of the Church and adapted them for theological and apologetic purposes, there is no reason to doubt that ecstatic experiences of the presence of God occurred at critical moments in early Christian history. Similarly, we know from the letters of Paul, as well as from later sources, that *charisms* or extraordinary gifts were to be found almost typically in the lives of certain members of the community. Both kinds of phenomena have occurred since then and still do.

The question then as now, as well as at intervening moments in the history of Christian spirituality, is what place do such extraordinary manifestations have in the life of the Church as a whole and in the spiritualities of her members individually? Then as now Christians want and need to know what they mean and how they are to be integrated into the life of faith.[2]

These charisms or *charismata* were simply "gifts" to Paul and "wonders" to other Christian writers. Such manifestations, particularly those associated with the advent of the Holy Spirit after Jesus' ascension, were interpreted as signs of God's favor, special forms of grace intended to strengthen the confidence of the early community. They did not so much realize the presence of God as did the acts of eucharist and baptism, but announced it, rather, in dramatic, often unexpected ways.

*Crisis
in
Corinth*

For the most part, the charisms did not present a problem for the first Christians, who found their faith indeed confirmed by such "signs and wonders," but not founded on them. The first notable exception seems to have been Corinth, the problem child of Paul's early ministry to the gentiles.

A leading Greek port city, Corinth was notorious in the ancient world for its licentiousness and high spirits. It similarly became famous among Christians for the exuberance with which the Corinthians accepted and expressed the faith. In this exciting, even tempestuous climate, the charismatic gifts which had accompanied the preaching of the gospel elsewhere had an especially electrifying effect. While Christians in Jerusalem, Ephesus, and Antioch took these manifestations more or less in stride, the Corinthians were fascinated by them. They also seem to have engaged in some kind of competition over the most important and, by implication, which members of the community manifesting them were therefore to be given greater honor.

Whatever the exact cause, the elders of the community felt obliged to write Paul for advice on regulating the excessive fervor and factionalism of at least a significant part of their membership, among other problems of discipline there. Paul's response immeasurably enriched the Church as a whole, even though he was writing in the first instance (it is well to remember) for a particular group with a specific set of problems. But his advice would prove useful for centuries to come whenever similar disturbances arose over manifestations of extraordinary gifts, experiences, or events in the life of the Church. And there would be many.

Far from berating the enthusiastic Corinthians for their charismatic ardor, Paul wisely congratulated them. For all accounts, he had a particular love for that unruly, volatile young church. Given his own impetuous nature, his enthusiasm and divine madness, it is not hard to see why. The disturbances may even have resulted from too strenuous an effort on the part of his followers to imitate his own ecstatic experiences. But the Apostle, alert to the divisive potential of extraordinary phenomena, did not hesitate to correct them firmly for their excesses, clearly placing the *charismata* in the right order of things.

The gifts they so valued, especially ecstatic speech, were, he insisted, the least important in the scale of ministries and charisms, being preceded by those of apostles, prophets, and teachers – the three earliest ranks of ministry and order. Next came miracle-working, healing, service, administration, and, finally, speaking in tongues (1 Cor. 12: 28). More excellent than all, he continued, was the profound love of true charity (*agape*), which unified all the other gifts just as it bound the entire community and the Church as a whole into a single body of Incarnate Love, manifesting order and harmony among its members (1 Cor. 13-14).

*The Future of Prophecy* — In the first and second centuries, with the community increasingly beset with acute problems of external persecution and internal dissension, it is understandable that more critical energy was not devoted to admittedly subtle questions of mystical psychology.

Nevertheless, the place of prophetic utterance was recognized, for instance, in sub-apostolic writings such as the *Didache* ("The Teaching"), which was probably of Alexandrian origin.[3]

After instructions on giving thanks following the eucharist, the text reads, "In the case of prophets, however, you should let them give thanks in their own way," that is, speaking in a spirit. Simple rules of discernment and discipline augmenting Paul's injunctions in 1 Corinthians are also given. Prophets are not to be examined in the midst of their ecstatic utterances. Nevertheless, their conduct before and after is to be considered along with their message. Thus, "every prophet who teaches the truth but fails to practice what he preaches is a false prophet." If prophets demand money for themselves, they are to be ignored. But if they instruct that it should be given to the needy, they are not to be condemned.

Finally, apostles and travelers are not to stay longer than two days, but if they settle, they must find work. Prophets and teachers, however, are to be sustained by tithes. Evidently, wandering ecstatics occasionally presented a problem for the early Church in Egypt as well as in Greece. Significantly, if none were present, the produce was to be given to the poor; tithing was seen to be of benefit to the giver as well as the recipient.

*Asian Enthusiasms and African Encounters*    Despite his eloquent efforts, not even Paul had been able fully to resolve the crisis at Corinth. At the end of the century, the letter to that church from Clement of Rome indicates that contention had not yet subsided. In the following century, at about the same time that the *Didache* was compiled, another excessive sect of dissident Christians, both ecstatic and morally austere, became a lingering problem for the Church in Asia – *Montanism*.[4] From there it spread to some extent into North Africa, mainly because of its appeal to one of the most brilliant apologists of the period, Tertullian of Carthage. Except for his spirited defense of the "New Prophecy," as the teachings of Montanus were first called, the heresy would probably have been limited to a minor occurrence in Phrygia, a region of southwest Asia already well-known, like Corinth, for its religious enthusiasms. There the ecstatic cultists of the Great Mother, Cybele, had long since danced and gashed or whipped themselves in frenzy until covered with blood.

Montanus was himself a Phrygian and may once have been a priest of Cybele. In any event, about the year 160 he became a Christian convert and proclaimed a new revelation centered on the little town of Papuza. By 175, he had gathered about himself a sizable coterie, including two well-to-do women, Priscilla and Maximilla. The latter in particular was reported to possess the spirit of prophecy. The means by which their "New Prophecy" was granted took the form of ecstatic utterances over which the devotees apparently had no control. Their remarks were copied down by disciples, edited, and circulated.

The central teachings of the Montanists asserted that with their new revelation, the third great age of world history had begun.

Previous ages had been that of God the Father, encompassing the centuries up to the birth of Jesus, and that of the Christian era itself up to the New Prophecy. The fullness of revelation began only with the descent of the Holy Spirit upon Montanus, who is report- ed to have claimed "I am the Father, the Word, and the Paraclete." The previous dispensations had now been rendered null and void.

Such a message would become a familiar prophetic refrain in the centuries to follow. Also like later revivalists, the Montanists were anti-intellectual, opposing themselves principally to the airy speculations of the gnostics. They were, further, millenaristic – proclaiming the proximate return of Christ, the end of the world, and the descent of the New Jerusalem, conveniently enough at Papuza. Finally, the Montanists were not content to preach their new revelation only within the local community. Like true en- thusiasts of all times, they expected, even demanded, that Chris- tians everywhere accede to their teaching.

Understandably enough, orthodox Christians viewed the goings- on in Phrygia with disfavor and ultimately some alarm. Within a few years, Montanus and his prophetesses were excommunicated by a synod of bishops. An untrustworthy legend claims that all three later hanged themselves. More significant is the legacy of rigorous puritanism associated with their sect, a characteristic which may have initially attracted the dour Tertullian in his later years.

*The Wasp of Carthage*

Quintus Septimius Florens Tertullian (c. 160-225) became a Christian after achieving distinction as an orator and possibly a lawyer. He may have been or- dained to the priesthood. A brilliant if not profound defender of Christianity against pagan accusers, he produced a steady stream of apologetic literature, which includes some of the finest prose by any early Christian writer.

Already more Catholic than the pope in matters of ascetical practice and morality, especially the torturous issue of flight from persecution, toward the end of his life this austere Carthaginian and his followers grew even more rigid and demanding under Montanist influence.  Like them, Tertullian and his disciples usurped Paul's terminology, despising ordinary Christians as merely "animal" (*psychiki*) as opposed to true Christians (themselves), the "Spirituals" (*pneumatiki*). Such elitist snobbery, which they also shared with their arch-enemies, the gnostics, would become a characteristic feature of many dissident sects in times to come.

Growing disenchanted even with the puritanism of the Montanists, Tertullian eventually founded his own severe, schismatic sect, one which was reconciled to the Catholic Church by Augustine only after two centuries of mutual hostility.  But remnants of both Montanist and "Tertullianist" influence would remain to haunt the Church for many more centuries, reappearing in a host of puritanical disguises.  Most of them would tend, as did their prototypes, including the gnostics, to extol the invisible, "spiritual" church of true believers over the merely visible, "carnal" church of ordinary, frequently weak members.  Not for the truly "pure" were the common discipline and teaching of the Church, especially those regarding the dignity of the body, sexuality, and hence of the sacramentality of marriage.

But the aged Tertullian's chief targets were Christians who, like St. Cyprian, the bishop of Carthage, had fled their sees during persecution or, even worse, had renounced the faith either seemingly or actually but later desired reconciliation. This issue, which touched the two sensitive nerves of Christian spirituality – fidelity and compassion – split the Church for centuries not only in North Africa but in Rome itself. Ironically enough, Tertullian himself not only died outside the Church he had so ably defended in his younger days, but was even denied the martyr's crown he so cherished.

*Charisms in Crisis*

The Montanist crisis raised another, perhaps more important issue for the early Church. Was the practice of prophecy to be extinguished among later Christians? What of raptures, ecstatic speech, and other minor charisms? No one seriously questioned the authenticity of the gifts described and, more importantly, regulated by St. Paul. But had they, like revelation itself, ceased with the end of the apostolic era?

Prophets had still been recognized alongside teachers and administrators as late as the end of the first century, as we see in the Didache and the letters of St. Ignatius, the martyr-bishop of Antioch. The eruption of prophetic experiences in Phrygia half a century later was so startling, however, that it is difficult not to conclude that such charisms had become rare. The conviction that Montanus' revelations were either mistaken or bogus did not resolve the issue. Nor would it be resolved for centuries to come, as the Montanist drama repeated itself in Europe, Asia, and even the New World. Today, as in the second century, many Christians consider such manifestations to be the result of diabolical influence or psychological delusion. Others see them as proof of the presence of God acting in our midst.

The Montanists' fate at least established a negative criterion by which extraordinary gifts could be evaluated, and in fact have been so appraised in the major Catholic tradition of Christianity. Charismatic experiences which produce lasting dissension and schism must be regarded as at least suspect. Conversely, those that strengthen the common bonds of God's people can at least be granted the possibility of genuineness. No one, however, is bound to accept or to believe any such private revelations nor, especially, to act upon them.

The first divisive eruptions of spiritual enthusiasm sorely tried the stamina and ingenuity of Church leaders as well as the patience and trust of ordinary Christians. For they did not merely raise problems to be neatly resolved by formulating creeds and regulating conduct. Such challenges and dilemmas issued from the character of the Church itself, the living body of Christ, as it met the living world.

Throughout the coming centuries and no doubt for all time to come, Christians would repeatedly have to balance and harmonize the elements of love and knowledge, prophecy and mysticism, authority and freedom, worship and service that define the Christian experience itself. How the People of God in past epochs integrated these dynamic, spiritual forces gave content and expression to their spiritualities. To the extent that we are their children, members of the same body and living in much the same kind of world, we can recognize ourselves in them and our struggle for integration in theirs. We can also profit from their experience.

## NOTES

1. On eschatological expectations of the period and later occurrences, see E. R. Chamberlain, *Antichrist and the Millennium* (New York: Saturday Review Press/E. P. Dutton, 1975). On eschatology in general, see R.H. Charles, *Eschatology* [1898-99] (New York: Schocken, 1963), J. A. T. Robinson, *In the End, God* (New York: Harper and Row, 1968), Edward Schillebeeckx and Boniface Willems, eds., *The Problem of Eschatology* New York: Paulist Press, 1969 [Concilium 41]), D. S. Russell, *Apocalpytic, Ancient and Modern* (London: SCM Press, 1978), and Zachery Hayes, O.F.M., *Visions of a Future: A Study of Christian Eschatology* (Wilmington, DE: Michael Glazier, 1989) and his *What Are They Saying about the End of the World?* (New York: Paulist Press, 1983).

2. On the nature and function of charismatic gifts in the Church, see Karl Rahner, "The Charismatic Element in the Church," in *The Dynamic Element in the Church,* trans. by W. J. O'Hara (London: Burns and Oates, 1964, pp. 42-83), his "Visions and Prophecies," in *Studies in Modern Theology* (London: Burns and Oates, 1965), pp. 87-188, and S. V. McCasland, "Signs and Wonders," *Journal of Biblical Literature* 76 (1957): 149-152.

3. A good translation by Maxwell Staniforth can be found in *Early Christian Writings* (New York: Penguin Books, 1968).

4. See Ronald Knox, *Enthusiasm*, pp. 25-49, and Frend, *The Rise of Christianity*, pp. 253-56, 283-85.

# The Seed of the Church  *4*

URING THE FIRST FOUR CENTURIES, the death of martyrs greatly influenced Christian spirituality and will probably do so always. From Stephen the deacon to Archbishop Oscar Romero, Fr. Jerzy Popieluszko, and the latest missionaries slain in Africa and Central America, an unfailing line of witnesses testifies to the supreme value that followers of Jesus place on fidelity. In whatever era, for the most loyal Christian disciples, life itself is not more precious than the honor of God, the truth of the Gospel, and the integrity of the Church — God's people.

Unlike accounts in popular fiction and films, however, early Christians did not live under constant threat of persecution, much less in constant fear of arrest, torture, and summary execution at the hands of a merciless police state — itself a creation of the modern world.[1]  For instance, when around the year 112 the emperor Trajan replied to his exasperated consul in Bythnia, Pliny the Younger, he prescribed that if Christians were caught, they should be punished, but that they should not be deliberately sought out. When a great persecution did finally break out in 303 under Diocletian, it was after a long interval of comparative peace. By then, unfortunately, Rome *was* growing into something like a modern police state. But before that, except for the brief, intense but selective oppression of Decius in 250 and Valerian in 257, the Church had enjoyed almost a century of immunity.

Some emperors were remarkably favorable towards their Christian subjects. Toward the end of the second century, a concubine of the emperor Commodus named Marcia became a Christian and was able to use her not inconsequential influence at court to alleviate the sufferings of many of her co-believers. Around the year 230, Alexander Severus was sufficiently impressed with the talents of a famed Christian scholar, Julian the African, that he commissioned him to construct his library at the Pantheon. A decade later, Philip "the Arab" was so sympathetic that he was rumored to have become a Christian himself.

Few attempts were made to seek Christians out until the beginning of the fourth century. Even then, informers or civic reaction commonly had to incite magistrates and governors already beleaguered by barbarian incursions and ever-increasing demands from Rome for more taxes and grain before they would impose repressive measures. These, moreover, tended to vary in extent and intensity. On the other hand, a few Christians voluntarily offered themselves for execution, sometimes with disastrous consequences for the local community. For such acts of bravado could easily arouse popular blood-lust, as happened in the case of Quintus the Phrygian, who may have been a Montanist.

While Church leaders themselves agreed that there was no greater honor than to die for Christ, they soon rejected the active pursuit of martyrdom as suicidal folly. There was a note of practical wisdom here. Many volunteers who flaunted their faith, at first bravely surrendering to the authorities, later found it expedient to offer the incense and call Caesar a god when confronted with the grim alternatives of the arena or, as Marcus Aurelius dictated in 177, every refinement of torture and a slow death.

Nevertheless, when summoned before the magistrates, thousands of men and women of every age and class, even children chose often prolonged torture and a horrible death rather than renounce Christ — the obvious implication of the emperor worship demanded by law of all citizens beginning under Decius in 250.

(The death penalty was first imposed throughout the empire in 304.)

Many, perhaps most of the martyrs' names have been preserved in lists known as *martyrologies*. Not all of these accounts are equally trustworthy, especially those written long after the events they narrate. Others, however, such as eye-witness accounts or *Acts* of the martyrs contain authentic details, such as those of the martyrs of Lyons and Carthage from about the year 180.

Often, leaders of the community were particularly singled out for persecution and death, as was the case with Ignatius of Antioch, Polycarp of Smyrna, Justin of Rome, and Cyprian of Carthage, perhaps even Peter and Paul long before. Of the first thirty Roman popes between Peter's death in 64 and that of Eusebius in 309, fully twenty-eight were executed. The average length of their rule was about seven or eight years. (For several centuries, the affectionate Greek title *papas*, "little father" — "pope" in English —, was given to any bishop in the West. Some Orthodox and Coptic patriarchs are still called "pope.")

*The Presence of Christ in the Death of His Saints*

It is well known that the Greek word *martyros* means "witness." To die, often after extreme torture, rather than renounce Christ by offering incense or otherwise rendering divine honor to the emperor or state gods, was perceived by early Christians as the highest profession of faith. Even more, it was an act of profound and mystical union with Christ. For Jesus had died violently at the hands of the authorities because of his profession of faith and the works which confirmed it.

As Christ had died for our sins, so that all who believe in him might rise to new life with him, so too those who died for Christ were joined in a special manner to his death and thus to the deepest sources of life in the Church as a whole. Often, the martyrs' self-sacrifice was accompanied by an intense experience of the presence of Christ himself. As recounted prototypically in the death of the deacon Stephen at the hands of the Sanhedrin in the year 35 (Acts 6 and 7), the dying martyr experienced that living presence with a directness and immediacy that transcend all sacramental emblems of faith in the unseen reality of grace. Similarly, Paul's momentous encounter with Christ on the road to Damascus taught him indelibly that Jesus was in actual fact present in the suffering of those he harried: "Why do you persecute *me*?" (Acts 9:4).

Because the death of martyrs effectively realized the presence of the suffering but risen Christ, it immeasurably strengthened the life of the infant Church, and they quickly earned a place of special honor in memory and ritual.   Moreover, the spirituality that enabled them to endure fear, threats, terrible suffering, and death for the love of Jesus, faith in his promises, and hope to share forever in his glory thus became a model for all Christians.  For all lived under the same danger.

Not surprisingly, early Christian spiritual writing is devoted almost exclusively to exhorting those who are fearful to greater steadfastness.   The letters of Ignatius of Antioch are a sublime example.  Virtually intoxicated with the thought of being torn and devoured by crazed and half-starved beasts for his loyalty to Christ, he enjoins all Christians to emulate his joyful sacrifice.  Nor is it surprising that the cult of such martyrs developed and spread rapidly from Palestine to Syria, Rome, and the world.


*Birth Pains*   At first, the persecution of the disciples of Jesus was a local, indeed Jewish affair, an intrafaith conflict over orthodoxy and the perception of incipient heresy.  It rarely involved the drastic measure of capital punishment.  Even so, a year after Stephen's death, James, the brother of John, was beheaded by order of Herod, as related in the Acts of the Apostles (12: 2).  A generation had almost passed when, in the year 62 according to Josephus, James "the brother of the Lord" and leader of the church in Jerusalem, was stoned by the Sanhedrin as Stephen had been.  Two years later, a truly lethal persecution broke out, not in Jerusalem, but in the very heart of the empire.

During Nero's brief but vicious reprisals for the great fire of 64, thousands of Christians may have perished. Some citizens such as Paul were accorded the dignity of decapitation. Non-citizens such as Peter were crucified or burned, their bodies sometimes lighting the imperial gardens at night. Most were slaughtered by gladiators or ravaged by wild beasts in the arena.

Nero's persecution was a local and mercifully limited reaction, one which significantly earned him the condemnation even of pagan historians for its savagery. Nevertheless, it also fixed in the Roman mind and law the criminal character of the Christian religion. Practicing the faith openly was thus illegal until the rescript of Gallienus in 261 brought the Decian persecution to a close. But despite outbursts of popular antagonism and oppression, nearly two hundred years would pass before an empire-wide effort to exterminate the Church was unleashed.

Writing in the fifth century, the historian Orosius, a friend of St. Augustine, claimed that ten major persecutions occurred between that of Nero and the peace of Constantine in 313. Rightly or wrongly, each was identified with a particular emperor — Domitian in 95, Trajan from 111 to 112, Hadrian and Antoninus Pius in 135 and 156, Marcus Aurelius from 161 to 180, Septimus Severus in 202, Maximin in 235, Decius from 249 to 251, Valerian from 253 to 260 — this being the first general persecution of Christians, cancelled by Gallienus in 261.

Despite his inclusion by Orosius, Aurelian did not greatly disturb the Church in 265. But real and lasting fury was unleashed under Diocletian. That severe and widespread persecution began in 303 and lasted until 311, when an edict of toleration was issued reluctantly by Galerius in the East and by Maximin in the West the following year.

Constantine's letter to the governor of Bythnia in 313, commonly called the Edict of Milan, did not completely end the age of persecution. Short outbursts of oppression under Licinius in 322 and 323 and Julian the Apostate from 361 to 363 added yet more names to the martyrologies. Many were those of soldiers, for by this time Christians were to be found even in the army. Among them were the Forty Martyrs of Sebaste, members of the famous "Thundering Legion," who were frozen to death on an ice-covered Armenian pond in 322. Nor did martyrdom cease even in 363 with Julian's death in battle, although wide-scale persecutions became rare, most of them isolated incidents in the missionary territories of the pagan north and west.

*The Lives of the Saints*
As actual persecutions diminished, the *Acts* of the martyrs became a favorite part of spiritual literature. Despite inevitable exaggerations, genuine testimonials such as those of Ignatius of Antioch, Polycarp, Perpetua and Felicitas, and the Martyrs of Lyons are still capable of moving readers deeply.

Polycarp was bishop of Smyrna in Asia Minor. A disciple of the Apostle John when very young, about the year 110 he met and welcomed Ignatius, the fiery bishop of Antioch, who was being escorted to Rome for execution. The record of Polycarp's own martyrdom, like that of Ignatius, was written much later, but very likely preserves details of the old man's journey to Rome, his efforts to elude capture, and his eventual betrayal, arrest, and execution in 155 or 156.

Through a precious epistle from Polycarp to the church at Philippi, along with the seven letters of Ignatius and the letters of Clement of Rome, we are able to glimpse something of the life and spirit of Christians in the years just after the death of the original disciples. Again contrary to common belief, they did not retreat to the catacombs as soon as the persecutions began in order to live and worship in clandestine underground security. At first, they simply continued to meet privately in house churches, not always secretly, but cautiously avoiding unwanted attention from the authorities.

Justin of Rome, a philosophically trained gentile convert from Samaria, advertised tuition openly, an act of forwardness that eventually cost him his life during the persecution of Marcus Aurelius. But for fifteen years before his death, Justin, the first professional Christian theologian, lived and taught without disturbance at his residence above the house of Martinus near the Timotinian bath. In the year 165, however, he and several companions were denounced to the authorities by a jealous rival — the Cynic philosopher Crescens, according to Justin's disciple, Tatian. Refusing to perform the ritual act of divine homage to the emperor, the company of friends was scourged and beheaded.[2]

Many other martyrs provided models of heroism and constancy during the first three centuries. In 177, a civil disturbance at Lyons in Gaul resulted in the arrest, torture, and execution of some fifty Christians. Among them were the bishop of Lyons, Pothinus, who was over ninety, his deacon Sanctus, and a young slave girl named Blandina, who seems to have been especially singled out for the amusement of the spectators. After being scourged, she was suspended crosswise in the arena to be attacked by wild animals. Somehow still alive after that, she was then burned with metal plates. Finally, she was tied into a basket to be tossed to death by an enraged bull. A letter from the Christians of Lyons to a church in Asia testifies that even the "heathen" admitted that they had never seen a woman endure so many terrible sufferings.

The Acts of the martyrs of Lyons provide the earliest record of the presence of the Church in what is now France. It is worthy of note that Bishop Pothinus was succeeded by one of the greatest of the early Christian theological writers, St. Irenaeus, a priest who had been on a mission to Rome when the persecution broke out. He, too, may have died a martyr, although the date given for his death, about the year 200, occurred during an interlude of comparative peace.

In the year 180, under the proconsul Saturninus, seven men and five women were executed at Scillium, near Carthage in what is now Tunisia. The record of the deaths of these simple Christians, like that of the martyrs of Lyons with regard to France, is the first testimony to the existence of a major Christian community in

Africa, one which would figure prominently in the tempestuous centuries to follow.

*Women of Faith*

In the ancient Roman eucharistic canon, fifteen martyrs were given special mention, including several from Carthage along with popes, presbyters, and the protomartyrs John the Baptist and Stephen. Seven were women, whose lives and deaths were of special importance to the Roman church, not only because several were themselves from that community, but because of their importance to the universal communion of saints.

Among them was Perpetua, an African noblewoman who had become a catechumen in the year 202, just after a law of Septimus Severus forbade further conversion to either Judaism or Christianity in order to restrict the proliferation of what were considered foreign religious sects. After being baptized, Perpetua and her companions were executed in the arena at Carthage in 203.

One of the catechumens, Felicitas, was a slave in Perpetua's household and eight months pregnant. Roman law prohibited executing expectant mothers. Fearing separation from her friends as well as later confinement and execution among common criminals, Felicitas and the entire company prayed for an early delivery. Three days before the games during which they were scheduled to be executed, Felicitas gave birth to a baby girl who was adopted by a Christian woman.

According to the acts of her martyrdom, Felicitas was taunted by a guard because she groaned during childbirth. Her reply eloquently expressed the spirituality of presence shared by the early martyrs: "It is I who am suffering now. But there [in the arena], another will be within me suffering for me, because it is for him that I shall be suffering."

Among the other women mentioned in the Roman canon — Agatha, Agnes, Anastasia, Caecilia, and Lucy — information is less reliable. But the mere witness of their names recalls the lasting importance to Christians of all ages of the heroic faith of these otherwise ordinary people.

**The Cult of the Martyrs**   Because of the intense devotion of the community to its martyred members, the custom soon arose in Rome and other churches of celebrating their "birthdays" with a common eucharist shared in the presence of their bodies prior to entombment. Preserving small personal possessions, fragments of clothing, locks of hair, even pieces of bone as cherished reminders of their lives and deaths grew into the practice of venerating relics, one which would have a long and eventually turbulent history in the Church. The greatest of all such concrete memorials to faith under persecution was, of course, the place itself where the martyrs found their final earthly rest and peace.

The tombs where the martyrs were buried and early mortuary rituals were performed were originally merely cemeteries on the outskirts of Rome which Christian communities bought in order to bury their dead like anyone else. One of the earliest was located on the Appian Way "near a ravine" (*kata kumbas* in Greek), which supplied its name. Entrusted to the care of the young priest and ex-slave Callistus by Pope Zephyrinus, the famed "Catacumbas" cemetery soon loaned its name to other subterranean burial chambers — thus the *catacombs*.

Under Roman law, all cemeteries were sacrosanct. Even those of the outlaw Christians were seldom violated by the police. As a fortunate consequence, not only did many liturgical rites develop in the catacombs, but the earliest examples of Christian art are found in their frescoes. They continued to be used for Christian burial until the fifth century, when they were abandoned because of increasing barbarian attacks near the City.

*Seeds of Dissension*  While the blood of martyrs was indeed the seed of the Church, as Tertullian boasted in the late second century, the cult of martyrdom also occasioned deep spiritual divisions in the Church of the third century, even as the frequency if not the fury of persecution decreased. The first of these conflicts involved the reconciliation of Christians who had broken under persecution and apostatized, however briefly. The second arose partly as a result of the cult of martyrdom itself, plunging the Church into its first major schism.

In both instances, the precipitating element was the rigorous, unyielding attitude of several North African bishops and their supporters, who staunchly opposed the efforts of popes such as Zephyrinus, Callistus, and Damasus, as well as other bishops, to readmit Christians who had abjured under Decius and Valerian.

Both the orthodox Roman and Carthaginian churches agreed to accept the lapsed provided that they undertook severe, sometimes lifelong penance. Some schismatics, however, such as Felicissimus of Carthage, received lapsed Christians after only minor satisfaction had been promised. Conversely, the rigid Roman priest Novatian and his followers simply refused to admit under any circumstances those who had renounced the faith in order to avoid persecution — or had even seemed to.

The Novationists called themselves *Cathari* — "the Pure Ones" — and unflinchingly insisted that apostasy was an unforgivable sin. The group went into schism in 251 when Cornelius, a moderate presbyter who favored reconciling lapsed Christians without so much as rebaptizing them, was elected pope by a substantial majority. Consecrated anti-pope the same year, Novatian was martyred in 258, as was St. Cyprian. The minor schism that bears his name survived in some areas for three hundred years, however. But even in the Catholic community, the conflicts over martyrdom were far from ended.

Cyprian of Carthage, who had gone into hiding during the Decian persecution, also objected to the leniency with which some bishops were reconciling lapsed Christians.[3] Suddenly confronted with a rival rigorist bishop in his own diocese, however, Cyprian found himself in uneasy alliance with Rome on the issue. But when a new pope, Stephen, was elected in 245, Cyprian faced a theology clearly at variance with his. Stephen maintained that neither the lapsed nor even those correctly baptized in schismatic or heretical sects needed to be rebaptized in order to be reconciled. For, the pope argued, the sacraments are acts of Christ, not of the Church as a merely earthly institution. Therefore they do not depend on the worthiness of the minister for their effectiveness.

Several local councils escalated the dispute. A bitter impasse ended only with a wave of renewed persecution. Stephen himself was martyred in 257. Under Valerian's decree, Cyprian was banished, then arrested and finally executed in Carthage in 258. After the rescript of Gallienus in 261, a whole generation passed peacefully enough. But during the great persecution of Diocletian, a new cloud of witnesses presented a new challenge to the order and spirituality of the early Church.

*The Donatist Crisis*

Among other repressive acts, the emperor demanded that Christians surrender all sacred books to be burned. Those who complied with the order became known as *traditores* — "betrayers." Even those who substituted other books for the scriptures and liturgical books were castigated by rigorists for their cowardice and duplicity.

Schism erupted in 305 when Donatus of Casae Nigrae and some other rigorist bishops of Numidia objected to the consecration of an alleged *traditor*, Mensurius of Carthage. He had in fact turned over only some heretical volumes in his possession. But he had also cooperated with the authorities to the extent of cancelling public worship. That alone would have been sufficient to have earned him the undying enmity of rigorists, who considered any collaboration to be apostasy. But he most outraged them by forbidding the veneration as martyrs of those who had invited persecution and death by publicly flaunting forbidden books.

Matters climaxed in 311 when Mensurius died and his arch-deacon, Caecilian, was consecrated to succeed him by three bishops. They were led by Felix of Aptunga, who was also accused of being a *traditor*. The Numidians, schooled in the hard-line theology of St. Cyprian, contested the ordination and at the house of a noblewoman named Lucilla, consecrated a rival bishop, Majorinus.

Lucilla's involvement reveals that the schism was primarily a crisis of spirituality concerning devotion to the martyrs and constancy in the face of persecution. As archdeacon, Caecilian had forbidden her to make a show of producing the bone of a dubious martyr at mass and covering it with kisses just before receiving the eucharist. If not superstitious, her behavior was at least a nuisance to the less "devoted" worshippers.

When Majorinus died shortly thereafter, the schismatics replaced him as Bishop of Carthage with Donatus himself, by whose name the movement now became known. In the meantime Caecilian was duly acknowledged by Rome in exchange for abandoning his Cyprianist view of sacramental validity. The Numidians appealed to Constantine, now emperor. He referred the matter to the Council of Arles in 314. Both the council and the emperor eventually sided with Caecilian and the pope. Moreover, after learning that Felix of Aptunga and Caecilian had been wrongly accused, Constantine subjected the Donatists, as they were now called, to an investigation and a brief persecution in 316 — an omen of sad events to follow.

**The Church Militant**

In 321 Constantine issued another edict of toleration, one which included the Donatists. Conflict over the cult of the martyrs was rekindled by the brief outbursts of anti-Christian persecution under Licinius and Julian. But the embers of smoldering Donatism were fanned into a blaze of rigorist fury when, as the imperial persecutions diminished, the slackening of opportunities for martyrdom led in the eyes of the fiercely loyal Christians of

North Africa to a slackening of faith itself. To them, a Church which had no place for martyrs was gravely in danger of becoming no Church at all.

The situation was aggravated in 347 when Constantine's son, Constans, sent legates to effect a reconciliation between the Catholics and Donatists. In Numidia, the legation was attacked by a rioting mob incited by the bishop of Bagai, coincidentally named Donatus. In the following reprisals, Donatus and several other schismatics were killed. Donatus of Carthage was banished and for several years matters remained superficially calm.

*Downward Christian Soldiers* The Donatists particularly venerated the fanatics called in by Donatus of Bagai who were killed during their ambush of the punitive expedition. Orthodox Christians tended to regard them as homicidal and suicidal lunatics. Called *Circumcellions* because of their tactic of encircling orthodox villages and churches, sometimes slaughtering whole congregations with huge clubs they nicknamed "Israels," these roving peasant bands formed a kind of Donatist shock-troops. They preferred to call themselves *Agonistici* — "Christian soldiers." With cries of *Laus Deo!* ("Praise God!"), they terrorized the countryside, occupying churches, forcing creditors to cancel debts, and freeing slaves by intimidating their owners with by no means idle threats of death. On occasion, they blinded opponents with lime and vinegar or simply murdered them.

Devoted to the cult of the martyrs and attributing their zeal to the presence of the Holy Spirit, they sometimes descended on unwary travelers to demand martyrdom at their hands under pain of death if refused. On occasion, when not attacking the churches and persons of Catholics, these wandering and frequently savage religious terrorists hurled themselves from high cliffs following a lavish banquet held in their honor the night before. Resisting all efforts to pacify or suppress them, the Circumcellions survived as a movement until well into the fifth century.

During the short reign of Julian the Apostate, Donatism flourished briefly under imperial favor. But the schism had already begun to fragment into rival sects in 355 with the death of Donatus of Carthage. Any hope of success ended with the restoration of the Christian empire, especially under Theodosius I, who in 379 proclaimed the first Orthodox State. Strong cells of Donatism survived, however, until both Catholic and schismatic African Christians were conquered by the armies of Islam in the seventh century.

## NOTES

1. See Frend, *The Rise of Christianity*, chapters 8, 9, and 13. Frend's *Martyrdom and Persecution in the Early Church* (Garden City, NY: Doubleday, 1967) is the standard work on the subject.
2. For an account of Justin's contribution to Christian thought, see Henry Chadwick, "The Vindication of Christianity," in *Early Christian Thought and the Classical Tradition* (Oxford: The Clarendon Press, 1984), pp. 9-22.
3. For the views of Cyprian, see his *Letters*, which have been published so far in four volumes by the Paulist Press, New York, (*Ancient Christian Writers*, vols. 43. 44, 46, 49).

# Ordinary Faith and Spiritual Ferment    5

B Y THE FOURTH CENTURY, Christian spirituality had acquired the practical contours that would characterize it for ages to come. But the thoughtful evaluation and formulation of that spirituality required calmer days and more developed mental tools than were available during the age of persecution. Unfortunately, the Age of Constantine was not entirely one which encouraged the placid evolution of either spirituality or theology. Both would develop only out of long and bitter conflict between champions of competing visions regarding the meaning and message of Jesus of Nazareth. In the meantime, daily life found its own pattern.

*Ordinary Spirituality in the Early Church*

Before the fourth century, the faith of the young Church was far from an articulated catechism, much less a systematic theology. It consisted of clusters of beliefs about the person, life, and message of Jesus. Similarly, Christian conduct was governed not by a developed system of ethics but by an effort both individual and collective to acquire and imitate the way Jesus lived and died.

Cultivated and perpetuated by a succession of prophetic teachers and leaders, this attitude toward people and life situations had become a distinctive spirituality, a shared understanding of the way of life expected of anyone who would be a disciple of Christ. Rooted in confident trust in God, expressed in acts of love and social justice, it looked in hope toward the coming of Christ in glory to establish the everlasting reign of God on earth.

In addition to faith, love, and hope-filled service, simplicity or single-heartedness (*aplotes*) was recognized as the Christian spiritual ideal. Its opposite, double-mindedness (*dipsychia*), the attempt to serve two masters, was seen to lead to compromise and catastrophe. Such "purity of heart" covered every dimension of life — family relationships, service to the state, business dealings, and outreach to the poor, suffering, and oppressed.

In an era in which licentiousness and public obscenity were becoming commonplace, Christians esteemed sexual restraint with particular reverence — as the Church's persecutors realized all too well. Such temperance (*egkrateis*) was eventually carried to an extreme in the form of *encratism*, a denial of the sanctity of marriage and sex. "Encratists" attempted to impose absolute celibacy upon everyone. Fortunately for the future of the Church, it didn't work.

Although outlawed and persecuted, by the end of the second century the faith had spread through the empire and beyond, permeating every stratum of society. Christians were found in senatorial families and the imperial court itself. Even the rigorist Tertullian had to admit that Christians could even be found in the military.

Until the fourth century, Christians were forbidden to join the army. But converts from the ranks of the military were regarded differently, especially since it was not possible for an ordinary soldier or even junior officers to resign before their contracted term of duty was over. Such terms could last as long as twenty years or more, as was the case with St. Martin of Tours. But Christian soldiers who subsequently refused to fight or kill, as they were obligated by their baptism, were subject to capital punishment.

Many later martyrs such as Sts. Sebastian and George met death for just this reason.

*Word
and
Worship*

The earliest spirituality of the Church was preeminently liturgical, centered on identification with Christ in the mysteries of baptism and eucharist. The essential forms of that liturgy were adopted from Jewish customs. Sunday, however, was substituted for the Sabbath as the primary day for worship, because of the Lord's Resurrection on the first day of the week. The Sunday after the 14th Nisan, "Easter" as it would someday be called in English, was in all likelihood the first great liturgical feast. Pentecost, originally a Jewish holy day, was also celebrated with particular reverence because of the advent of the Holy Spirit on that day. Only in the fourth century would the feasts of the Ascension and Nativity of the Lord appear in the Christian calendar, the latter celebrated on January 6th in the East and December 25th in the West.

The earliest form of baptism included plunging the candidate into "living" (running) water, followed by a ritual anointing. After the first century, water could also be poured over the head, a necessity in areas without rivers. By the second century, the eucharist or the "breaking of bread" was celebrated weekly, preceded by readings from the writings of the major apostles, the Hebrew prophets, and a sermon. At first the *Anaphora*, the great Prayer of Thanksgiving containing the words of institution, was freely extemporized, followed by the community's "Amen." Communion was then distributed by the deacons, who also took the eucharist to the sick and imprisoned.

Developed from Jewish grace before meals and the *seder* service, the eucharist was originally an evening celebration. It was moved to early morning in Rome and elsewhere because of the large numbers of Christian slaves and gentiles in the community who could not be free to attend after daybreak. Imperial decrees had also been issued which forbade ritual suppers in order to forestall the spread of the cults proliferating at that time, many of them libertine. Many Romans thought that Christianity was one of them.

Private prayer was an important part of each Christian's daily routine. Hippolytus of Rome, an early writer, speaks of praying "seven times a day," in biblical fashion. By the end of the fourth century, public prayer in the morning and evening was a widespread Christian custom. Similarly, Bible-reading in the family group was commonly practiced.

From the earliest period, Christians fasted on Wednesdays and Fridays in distinction from, but also imitation of, the Jews, who fasted on Mondays and Thursdays. The paschal vigil and its fast were observed with particular devotion.

Music was part of the Church's service from the beginning, much of it also derived from synagogue custom. But original hymns were composed very early by both orthodox and gnostic Christians. Many were so lively and beautiful that pagans criticized them for dulling the critical faculties. Early in the third century, Clement of Alexandria attempted to regulate the kind of music appropriate for liturgical use, discouraging in particular songs associated with erotic dances and the theater. Some of these early hymns survived to be incorporated into the Byzantine liturgy by St. Basil in the fourth century.[1]

While pictorial art was not common among Christians before the third century, it was found among gnostic communities a century earlier. But by the end of the second century, images of the Good Shepherd were being inscribed on eucharistic cups, and Clement of Alexandria describes Christian symbols incised on signet rings. Paintings of biblical scenes and symbols such as anchors, boats, and fish appeared in the Roman catacombs at the same time. By the beginning of the fourth century, images of Christ were common and by the turn of the century had become widespread.

Architecture was a later development in Christian worship, which was first restricted to private houses. In 261, however, Gallienus' Edict of Toleration allowed Christians to receive bequests of land and money. Soon, in Rome and elsewhere, house churches began giving way to basilicas, large structures suitable for worship by the growing Christian congregations. Adapted from prevailing pagan forms, these buildings were not ornate nor were they elaborately decorated. But they were "churches." Christianity had emerged from the catacombs daringly enough. The destruction of many basilicas in later outbreaks of persecution was part of the price of that audacity.

*Christian Ministry in the World*    A major part of the spirituality of the ancient Church centered on ministry, especially the work of deacons and deaconesses, who not only took the eucharist to sick or imprisoned Christians, but also distributed food and clothing and otherwise attended to the needs of the community. Even among ordinary people, social action was an integral part of early Christian spirituality. Some of history's earliest charitable institutions were founded in the young Church to provide for the poor, widows and orphans, and the sick. By 251, the Church of Rome was caring for 1500 widows and indigent poor.

Following Jesus' injunctions in the Gospel of Matthew (chapter 25), Christians undertook visits to prisoners and slaves (including those condemned for political dissent), war captives, and religious outlaws like themselves. Relief work was organized in time of famine, earthquake, pestilence, and war. Christians sodalities also provided burial for the poor by donating or purchasing cemeteries, such as the Coemeterium Domitillae, the oldest estate cemetery, and the "Catacumbas," the Roman church's mother cemetery of the martyrs.

Hospitality to travelers was recognized as a major work of charity, especially with large numbers of Christians being driven into exile or taken thousands of miles at their own expense to Rome for trial and execution, as in the case of Ignatius of Antioch.

*Women and Children: Towards Christian Equality*

By maintaining the equality of every person before God, Christianity greatly elevated the position of women religiously and socially in the ancient world. Both women and children enjoyed much less security than men under the law. They were often excluded from the mysteries and cults such as those of Eleusis and Mithra. In order to meet the specific needs of women and children, the order of deaconesses was created at a very early period, although mainly for charitable rather than liturgical purposes.

Christian teaching also upheld the sanctity of marriage in an increasingly licentious society, thus creating a safeguard for married women. Further, unchastity was considered no less serious for husbands than for wives. Divorce was tolerated in certain cases, as seen in the life of the Christian matron, Fabiola, but remarriage was normally forbidden.

As a result of its inclusive attitude, Christianity was very successful among women of all classes. It was mainly through the wives of influential men that the faith first penetrated the higher classes. But virgins and widows were specifically protected and provided for out of common funds. Children had no rights at all under Roman law. As a result, abortion and infanticide by exposure, especially of unwanted baby girls, were common. Both were expressly forbidden by Christians, who often adopted abandoned infants.

*The Church and Slavery*

Although many Christians were slaves, for a variety of reasons slavery was not opposed as an institution until the fourth century. In a society heavily dependent on slavery for its prosperity, agitation to free them would have been considered criminally subversive. It would thus have inevitably worsened the lot not only of the slaves but of the Church itself, which was already looked on as criminal in intent and often in practice.

Christians nevertheless exhorted their masters to treat slaves with kindness and respect as equals before God (cf. St. Paul's

Epistle to Philemon). Slaves were likewise exhorted to faithful and loving obedience. They were discouraged from seeking their freedom at public expense, but Christians themselves financed the manumission of many. Some former slaves even rose to office in the Church, such as St. Callistus of Rome, who became pope in 217. His former status, including punishment in the mines, may have played some part in his later practice of leniency in reconciling Christians guilty of sexual sins and especially of apostasy under threat of execution.

Although severely limited for three centuries by the Church's criminal status, the social activity of ordinary Christians nonetheless inaugurated a spiritual revolution in the name of freedom and equality which eventually transformed the ancient world. In many parts of the world today, that revolution is still in progress. Like ourselves, however, not all early Christians were socially concerned or even well-disposed towards ordinary people, much less the poor and infirm. In the youthful Church, such an attitude nearly wrecked the wholeness of the Faith.

*Elite Spirituality: The Gnostic Crisis*    Despite the sometimes concerted efforts of the Roman empire to eradicate Christianity, the greatest danger to the infant Church and especially to its fledgling spirituality was not persecution, but subversion. *Gnosticism* is the name given to the plethora of both radical and reactionary sects that so threatened the integrity of the Gospel faith for the first three centuries.

Gnostic sects differed greatly and often bitterly opposed each other, each claiming to be the "true Christian way." Dozens of such rival cults flourished from the middle of the first century to the beginning of the third — Naasenes and Ophites (the People of the Serpent), Carpocratians, Nicolaitans, Simonians, and so on. Yet they shared many common features and so can be lumped together uncomfortably in terms of their central common teaching – that salvation can only be attained by means of special knowledge or secret insight into the mysteries of God. Not coincidentally, this information was available, whether by oral instruction or in writing, only within the confines of an inner circle of "initiates." Such esoteric traditions would eventually give rise to reports of "secret gospels" that would last to the present time.[2]

*Gnostic* itself comes the Greek word for knowledge, *gnosis*. It was commonly used in Greek translations of the scriptures for Hebrew terms such as *yadha* and *da'ath*, which meant "direct, first-hand experience," specifically, of God. It was thus familiar to the writers of the Christian scriptures. As it came to be used in the hands of the gnostics to signify special knowledge reserved to a spiritual elite, it acquired a more restricted and misleading meaning. It had become "*gnosis* falsely so-called" as a follower of St. Paul quipped impatiently (1 Tim. 6:20).

Although imbued with a host of "theosophical" speculations, gnostic sects were in fact often stridently anti-intellectual. Their teachings were inevitably based on special revelations, hidden "facts" about the nature of the cosmos and humankind, and how the soul could escape from its confinement in the body to find true immortality in its home beyond the spheres of creation dominated by evil, angelic powers.

An intense moral dualism pervaded their teachings, a vestige of Persian religion that would resurface centuries later in the form of Manichaeism. Sometimes morally loose, gnostics were more often highly puritanical. Sexuality was a serious problem for them. Some would allow initiation only to those candidates who were celibate or virgins. It was commonly held that only the "spiritual," i.e., non-material, part of human persons could be saved. The body was the tomb of the soul. Thus, they tended to deny that Christ's body, the material form of the human Jesus, was in fact real. Similarly, they scoffed at the idea that the living God could have truly become incarnate, most of all by the messy, humbling, painful processes of conception and birth.

Many of these professedly Christian sectarians were extreme Hellenists and rabidly anti-Jewish. Their antagonism (and dualism) extended in many cases to the Hebrew scriptures and even "the god of the old law," whom they regarded as evil and opposed to "the Good God," the true Lord of the universe and Father of Jesus

Christ. Such anti-Semitism denied Christianity's spiritual roots in Judaism, destroyed the integrity of the biblical tradition, including the Christian interpretation of the messianic prophecies, and in particular repudiated Jewish reverence for creation, matter, and the body. Not surprisingly, liturgical worship was regarded as crude materialism.

Early forms of this radical "spiritualism" had already been excoriated in Christian scripture by Paul, his disciples such as the author of 1 Timothy, and the author of the First Epistle of John. Nevertheless, gnostic sects proliferated both in and outside of the Christian community, particularly among the gentile churches of Asia Minor, Greece, and Egypt. In Corinth and Colossae, such false gnosis had presented a formidable problem for the early Pauline churches. Even then the leaders of the gnostic groups were bright, persuasive teachers. Proposing a more profound wisdom than that preached by Paul, Barnabas, Timothy, and Silas, they regarded themselves as having already reached a "perfection" of faith which transcended the simple beliefs of the common folk.

In Colossae, a more Jewish gnosis prevailed, a heterodox inclination towards a worship of angels and the development of special ceremonies and feast days. But again, the promise held out was a superior insight into the meaning of Christ than that available to the multitude and special means of assuring salvation by deliverance from the powers that dominated human existence on earth. The Epistle to the Hebrews was written to combat such views, among others.

*The Son of Satan*

In Syria and Asia Minor, gnostic heresiarchs such as Menander, Satornilus, and Cerinthus fulminated against the Jews and their God, extolling the superiority of the narrow, intuitive insight on which they claimed to have copyright. One of the most interesting and powerful of these early figures was a rich young shipbuilder from Sinope on the Black Sea, Marcion of Pontus.

His father had been the local bishop. But alarmed by his son's radical doctrines, including a wholesale repudiation of the Jewish ancestry of the Church, he excommunicated him. Polycarp, the martyr-bishop of Smyrna already famous for his austerity and asceticism, referred to Marcion as "the first-born of Satan."

About the year 138, Marcion migrated to Rome. At first he was well-received by the Christian community, to which he contributed generous sums of money. But he soon fell under the influence of Cerdo, a Syrian gnostic teacher who confirmed his increasingly dualistic, anti-Jewish, and elitist view of the faith. In 144 he was again expelled from the church, but, undaunted, began extensive missionary voyages to Africa and Asia Minor. His doctrine became very widespread.

A brilliant biblical student, Marcion composed brief prologues to the Pauline epistles and edited the Gospel of Luke. Although his other works were eventually lost, the prologues had an enormous impact on the early Church and were included in the Vulgate Latin translation of the Bible.

*Defenders of the Faith*

Early Christian theological writers were themselves sometimes tainted by anti-Jewish prejudice and "spiritualism," the virulent legacy of radical Hellenism. But the greatest of them, Ignatius of Antioch, Justin Martyr, and Irenaeus, clearly perceived and rejected the gnostic temptation as a lethal threat to the Gospel itself and the Church's understanding of Jesus as Son of God, Lord, and Messiah, the fulfillment of the ancient promise of divine presence.

These *apologists* or "exponents of the faith" upheld the absolute sovereignty and goodness of God, the continuity of biblical tradition, the dignity of the material world, especially that of the human body, and the true humanity of Christ — elements of the first creeds as well as the basis of authentic Christian spirituality.[3]

*Alexandria: Cradle of Mysticism*　During the first three centuries of the Common Era, gnostic heresiarchs such as Simon Magus, Menander, Satornilus, Bardaisan, and Valentinus flourished throughout the Mediterranean basin from Egypt to Gaul. The last and greatest gnostic menace faced by the young Church stemmed from the teachings of the Persian Mani, who was born in Seleucia in 242. But the decisive struggle against gnostic teachings was waged neither in Antioch, Rome, nor Lyons. It occurred, rather, in the great Egyptian city of Alexandria, where Hellenic culture had reached an intellectual zenith and where Christian theology would have its true birth.

Excepting only Jerusalem, the great center of Jewish culture and spirituality lay in Egypt, where the largest concentration of Jews outside of Palestine lived in the huge port city of Alexandria. There the Hebrew scriptures had been translated into Greek – the "Septuagint." There the Book of Wisdom was written and the noble Philo lived and worked, the last of the great wisdom figures of late Judaism. There, according to a tradition accepted by the first Christian historian, Eusebius, the church was founded by St. Mark the evangelist, the cousin of Barnabbas and companion of both Paul and Peter. And there in the second century, not only was an illustrious catechetical school founded, but the mystical spirituality of Christianity would arise out of the conflict with gnosticism.

It would be built on the Jewish Wisdom tradition and particularly on Philo's biblical exegesis and his religious doctrine.[4] A century later at the Council of Nicea, when gnosticism was little more than a bad memory (except for its baneful influence on the Manichaeans), the city would be assigned a rank of patriarchate, second only to Rome. Eventually, Alexandria would be superceded by Constantinople and later fall to the Muslim conquest. But the mystical legacy of Alexandrian Christianity would endure throughout the ages.[5]

*Philo
Judaeus*

Born about the year 30 B.C.E., Philo lived to be an old man, dying between 45 and 50 C.E., but without any evident knowledge of Jesus or the world-changing events occurring in Palestine in his later years.[6] Unlike other members of his aristocratic family, he had few political interests, being content to devote his life to the study of scripture and Greek thought in the hope of demonstrating the philosophical superiority of the Jewish faith to the learned pagans of the great metropolis.[7]

Philo's allegorical method of interpreting scripture would be of particular importance in the development of Christian exegesis and spirituality in later Alexandria. Based on the theme of hidden wisdom, Philo searched for the deeper meaning of obscure and difficult passages in scripture. Symbolic interpretation was not new to the wisdom tradition, but Philo elevated it to greater prominence. His purpose and achievement were essentially and explicitly mystical — discovering the hidden presence of God through contemplation of the Word and faithful obedience in all the events of life.

*Alexandrian
Christianity*

After the destruction of Jerusalem in 70 C.E., and especially with the even greater desolation of the Holy City in 135, several cities far removed from both Jerusalem and Galilee became the focus of Christian organization, belief, and scriptural study. Syrian Antioch and Alexandria became the two earliest and greatest Christian theological centers. Other important Christian centers were Rome, Ephesus, and Damascus, as well as cities in Cilicia and Phrygia.

But the greatest of all the centers of Christian learning and exegesis, and the mother of Christian mysticism, was Alexandria. There, too, in the second century, many of the leading gnostic teachers came to spread their doctrine. Among them were teachers such as Basilides, a gentile Christian intellectual on the leading edge of the chancy dialogue between faith and philosophy.

Like Justin, Basilides possessed a true philosophical spirit. Like Philo, he wished to bridge the gap between faith and philosophy, which is to say Plato. He succeeded in synthesizing elements of Judaism and Platonic thought centered on Jesus as savior into a "way of salvation" based on the acquisition of special intuitive knowledge mediated by himself and similar teachers.

A prodigious scholar, Basilides composed twenty-four books of scriptural exegesis. These would have a lasting influence even on orthodox Christian teaching. His vision of creation was not pessimistic, but he came to believe that the universe was ruled by a vast hierarchy of divine beings, only the last of which was the God of the Jews. While hardly as anti-Jewish in his teaching as Menander, Cerinthus, or Marcion, still Basilides reflected the current anti-Semitism of learned gentile Alexandrians.

Valentinus, another gnostic scholar who was native to Egypt, flourished shortly after Basilides. Probably the greatest of the radical gentile thinkers, like Basilides he taught that the cosmos was ruled by a system of divine beings, the last of whom was Sophia (Wisdom). Her fall brought the material world into being. The God of the Jews was her offspring, whom Valentinus identified with Plato's Demiurge.

In order to bring saving knowledge to humankind of its origin and destiny, the divine being Christ united himself with the man Jesus. Only truly spiritual ("pneumatic") believers — by coincidence, the Valentinians themselves — were capable of receiving this gnosis, however, and ascending to union with the Demiurge. Ordinary Christians ("psychics") might be saved through faith and good works, but the rest of the human race, merely material ("hylic") beings, would perish utterly.

Such teachings, continued by Valentinus' disciple Herakleon and others, greatly influenced Christian thought. It was against them that the first and one of the greatest of the early Christian theologians took up his own pen.

The
Pedagogue
The catechetical school at Alexandria was founded in the late second century. A theological school which addressed itself to the propagation of the Christian Faith among the more cultured classes of Alexandria, it was in fact a Christian *gymnasium*, or college, which also taught the "profane" sciences.

The first known director of the school was a Sicilian Christian convert, Pantaenus, who died about the year 190. He was succeeded by a bright young layman named Clement, who headed the school until 202, when he was succeeded by one of the most brilliant minds of antiquity, the great Origen.

Clement was born around 150 and died in exile in 215. As a Christian philosopher and theologian, he shared many features of the apologists, especially his unremitting opposition to gnosticism, to which he proposed the "true gnosis" of faith. Yet like Philo, his attitude toward Greek philosophy was much more open. Not only did he refuse to characterize Platonic thought as "evil" in the manner of Tatian and Tertullian, he imitated and drew heavily from Philo's program to bridge the chasm between faith and philosophy.[8]

In this, Clement also departed significantly from the anti-intellectual gnostics and laid the foundation for Christian spiritual and dogmatic theology. For him, philosophical questioning was a preparation for faith among the learned. He thus borrowed from Philo and made Christian the famous aphorism that philosophy was the "handmaid" of theology. For the ancient Greeks, he taught, philosophy was of divine origin, a gift from God to be their means of attaining holiness until the Gospel was preached.

In his great, three-part work, the *Protrepticus*, the *Paedagogus*, and the *Stromata*, Clement addressed three groups of critics — pagan philosophers who despised Christians as unlettered bumpkins, the gnostics, who scorned ordinary faith as an inferior form of knowledge, and anti-intellectual Christians who disparaged philosophical thought as a detriment to true belief.

Against the first, he argued that faith is the basis of all discussion and argument and represents a valid, indeed a superior form of knowledge. He rejected the gnostics' elitism and secrecy, maintaining the sufficiency of baptism and faith to assure salvation. He also affirmed the goodness of Creation and the dignity of marriage. Finally, he reminded simple believers that reflection and study are not only good, but even necessary for growth in faith.

Clement's success in establishing a common ground where faith and learning could cooperate in bringing men and women the Gospel of salvation is a testament to his own faith and courage as well as the vision of his great Jewish predecessor and model. For Clement incorporated whole areas of Philo's exegesis and spirituality and passed them on to his own disciples, including the first true genius of the young Church, Origen, whose exegesis and theology would dominate Christian study for centuries to come.

*Spirituality in the Christian Empire*

Gnosticism was not a religion of reason alone, a philosophical Christianity such as Kant would vainly seek in the nineteenth century. It was in fact irrational — an ethereal, heady, snobbish, and ultimately inhuman attempt to salvage the soul from its "imprisonment" in flesh. It promoted a spirituality of mystification, not mystery. It dissolved the revelation of God's presence in the events of everyday life and especially in the material needs of the poor into puddles of esoteric mind-games accessible primarily to the rich and so-called "learned" concerned solely with their own, individual salvation.

The gnostic crisis was a tragic episode in the life of the early Church, but perhaps an inevitable and even necessary one. For the struggle against gnosticism delimited the extreme boundary of the gentile Church. Moreover, the need to combat the gnostics' insidious speculations and secret rites forced Christian thinkers into the arena of public controversy and debate, an arena where in due time the core beliefs of Christian teaching would be articulated — the unity of God's plan of salvation from the "Old" to the "New"

Covenant, the true humanity of Jesus Christ, the dignity of Creation, matter, and sexuality, and the supreme mystery of the inner, triune life of the Divine Persons.

Authentic Christian spirituality was thus disengaged, if never wholly freed, from the perennial lure of elaborate and esoteric rites, anti-intellectualism, secret doctrines, and a rigid caste system of salvation. At the same time, the unity of authentic theology and spirituality, that is, the relationship between doctrine and practice, was recognized as reciprocal and, above all, holistic.

*Towards the New Age*  Right belief and true practice (orthodoxy and ortho-praxis) have never been a gift received freely from on high. They have been, rather, the product of an agonizing struggle to recognize authentic interpretations of the Gospel in an often violent encounter between great personalities. But the Spirit of God was truly present in such memorable meetings, leading God's people through them towards the fullness of truth. We are still embarked on that journey.

It is therefore important to remember the lesson so hardly learned during this formative period of faith and spirituality: dissent and heresy are not the same. Often the doctrine recognized by a later generation as the true expression of the faith was in its own time a despised minority view. Similarly, forms of authentic Christian spirituality such as hermeticism and monasticism were at first a minor and disputed eccentricity in the life of a Church plagued by elitist dissent, error, and downright quackery. Even when tolerated and then revered by the mass of the faithful, such radically authentic expressions of faith were never the "ordinary way," as we shall see next.

# NOTES

1. For a fundamental study of early Christian liturgy, see Johannes Quasten, *Music and Worship in Pagan and Christian Antiquity*, trans. by Boniface Ramsey, O.P. (Washington, DC: National Association of Pastoral Musicians, 1983).
2. For standard works on the gnostic crisis in the early Church, see R. M. Grant, *Gnosticism and Early Christianity* (New York: Columbia University Press, 1966) and Elaine Pagels' *The Gnostic Gospels* (New York: Vintage Books, 1981). See also Frend, *The Rise of Christianity*, chap. 6. and R. M. Grant, "Gnostic Spirituality," in McGinn and Meyendorff, *Christian Spirituality: Origins to the Twelfth Century*, ed. cit., pp. 44-60.
3. The major writings of the Apologists can be found in *Early Christian Writings*, Maxwell Staniforth, trans. (New York: Penguin Books, 1968) and *Early Christian Fathers*, ed. by Cyril C. Richardson (New York: Collier Books, 1970).
4. See the introduction by David Winston, trans. and ed., *The Wisdom of Solomon* (Garden City, NY: Doubleday and Co., [Anchor Bible, v. 43] 1979).
5. See J. E. L. Oulton and Henry Chadwick, eds., *Alexandrian Christianity: Selected Translations of Clement and Origen* (Philadelphia: Westminster Press, 1954) and Andrew Louth, *The Origins of the Christian Mystical Tradition from Plato to Denys* (New York: Oxford University Press, 1981).
6. For excellent introductory studies of Philo, see Erwin R. Goodenough, *An Introduction to Philo Judaeus* (Oxford: Basil Blackwell, 1962), Samuel Sandmel, *Philo of Alexandria: An Introduction* (New York: Oxford University Press, 1979), and David Winston, "Philo and the Contemplative Life," in Green, *Jewish Spirituality*, ed. cit., pp. 198-231.
7. For a representative selection of his writings, see Philo of Alexandria, *On the Contemplative Life, Giants, Selections*, trans. by David Winston (New York: Paulist Press, 1981).
8. For an overview of the life and contribution of Clement of Alexandria, see Henry Chadwick, "The Liberal Puritan," in *Early Christian Thought and the Classical Tradition* (Oxford: The Clarendon Press, 1984), pp. 31-65.

# The Desert and the City   **6**

T HE FOURTH CHRISTIAN CENTURY began explosively. Despite remaining problems, the Gnostic crisis was essentially past. But Donatism was fragmenting the North African churches. Suddenly, imperial persecution broke out with renewed fury, then (except for a brief revival under Julian) abruptly ended with the Church legitimized and stronger than ever. Church leaders, sensing the danger of being co-opted by the same empire that had attempted to stifle the infant community, now had to cope with power politics both in Rome and Constantinople as well as a new threat from within — Arianism.

From an orthodox perspective, the spirituality of the period was dominated by a brilliant ghost from the past and two groups of remarkable Christian thinkers and writers whose bond of friendship was ultimately the link that joined the Church of the Martyrs to the Church Catholic. The story can best be told, perhaps, as a tale of two cities.

*Alexandria's Ghost*

Despite the antiquity and prestige of Athens, Alexandria had emerged in the third century as the intellectual center of the Christian world as well as the cultural capital of the Empire. Central to the role Alexandrian theology would play in the coming controversies, and at the heart of the disputes that would rack the

Church for the next several centuries, was the doctrine and methodology of the most brilliant of all the early Christian scholars and writers — Origen (185 - 254).[1] A defender of orthodoxy against the gnostics and a multitude of both pagan and Christian opponents, he would also come in time to be considered the fountainhead of every heresy.

Origen's name means, oddly enough even for Christian Egypt, "Son of Horus." He was born of Christian parents and reared at Alexandria. When seventeen, his father, Leonidas, was killed in the persecution of 202. Origen himself was prevented from seeking martyrdom only by his mother, who hid his clothes. A year later, Bishop Demetrius appointed him to succeed Clement, who had fled the city, as head of the catechetical school.

Already known for his brilliance, at this time Origen espoused an extremely ascetical form of life. He supposedly even castrated himself in accordance with a literal interpretation of Matt. 19:12. Although such mutilations did occur among the Encratites, the account is probably a later slander, especially because scriptural literalism was foreign to Alexandrian theology and spirituality. In any event, Origen was widely celebrated for his chastity .

It is believed that he studied for a time under Ammonias Saccas, the enigmatic originator of Neoplatonism and the master of Plotinus. Afterwards, Origen traveled to Rome, where he heard Hippolytus, then moved on to Arabia. In 215, he again left Alexandria during the visit of the hostile Emperor Caracalla. In Palestine, he was asked by the bishops of Caesarea and Aelia (the Roman name for Jerusalem) to preach. As Origen was a layman, this breach of ecclesiastical protocol caused him to be recalled in disfavor by the jealous Demetrius.

From 218 to 230, Origen devoted himself exclusively to writing, mainly scriptural commentaries. But on a second trip to Palestine in 231, he was ordained priest by the same bishops. Because of the irregularity of his ordination, Demetrius deposed him from his chair, defrocked him, and sent him into exile. He found refuge at Caesarea where he established a famous theological school. In 250, he was seized during the persecution of Decius, tortured, and imprisoned. He died four years later.

Many of Origen's works have been lost because of later controversies in which almost every side appealed to his authority. His major works were studies, translations, and commentaries on scripture. Without doubt, he was the first great orthodox Bible scholar. His homilies also provide some of the earliest examples of Christian preaching. His theological works, especially the great *Peri Archon* (On First Principles), were profound, extensive, and influential. Here, however, he adopted what many of his later critics in particular took to be much too accommodating a position regarding pagan authors.

Origen's teaching was strongly trinitarian, although strands of subordinationism are clearly present, if not too surprisingly a century before Nicaea. For him, the Son was God (*theos*), but only the Father was *autotheos* (God-himself). In his *Treatise on Prayer*, Origen thus maintained that Christians should pray only to the Father through the Son. (Some of his own prayers, however, were addressed to Christ.)

Among other troublesome ideas, Origen apparently accepted the eternity of world, the finitude of God, and, like a good Platonist, the pre-existence of souls. He was also accused of teaching that on death, the soul may turn into a demon or an angel and that at the end of the world, all creatures would be saved because of the universal love and goodness of God. This, of course, included the devil and other demonic spirits.

His primary theological purpose was, however, anti-gnostic polemic. Thus, what were later construed as concessions to popular conceits and erroneous ideas of the day were in all likelihood only moves in a give-and-take debate.

Among Origen's ardent supporters were saints and scholars such as Pamphilus, Athanasius, Basil the Great, Gregory Nazianzen, and Didymus. His opponents were numerous and vociferous, however, including equally eminent Christian sages and saints — Methodius of Olympus, Epiphanius, Jerome after 395, and, perhaps most potently of all in the sixth century, the Christian Emperor,

Justinian. As a result, Origen's doctrine was condemned in 400 at the Council of Alexandria, in 543 at the Council of Constantinople, which was endorsed by Pope Vigilius and the patriarchs of the East, and again in 553, at the Second Council of Constantinople.

Being an Alexandrian, Origen's approach to the Bible might be expected to have been mystical in the sense that Philo had first used the term. And indeed for him there were three senses of scripture — literal, moral, and allegorical or "mystical." Everything in his universe seems to have a dual aspect, the physical dimension, perceivable by the senses, but also a deeper, hidden, and spiritual dimension which could be penetrated only by enlightened faith. Spiritual perfection entailed rising beyond the sense-world to contemplate and thus be united with the Eternal Word dwelling with the Father.

For Origen, the mystical hermeneutics of scripture did not merely produce general religious truths or ethical principles, but inevitably pointed to particular acts of God with respect to the salvation of the world. His was a true mysticism of the mind, in which the pursuit of knowledge was the way in which rational beings received the Wisdom of God in order to rise towards deification through union with God in Christ.

*Antioch:*
*The Letter*
*and the*
*Spirit*

If Alexandrian theology in the third century became almost synonymous with the name of Origen, it was not so well received elsewhere and for the same reason. The highly symbolic, mystical approach to scripture and theology that typified the Alexandrian tradition, even though moderately so in Origen's works themselves, seemed to engender a need for a balancing viewpoint. It was neither slow nor moderate in coming.

As early as the year 39, the great Syrian capital of Antioch had figured prominently in the story of the infant Church. There, the "Christians" were first differentiated from believers in Jerusalem, the "Nazarenes," with whom they had certain differences.[2] There, toward the end of the first century, the model of the "monarchical episcopate" developed under the powerful influence of Ignatius and soon become the fashion through the growing Christian communities everywhere — a single bishop presiding over the community, assisted by a college of presbyters (elders), deacons, deaconesses, and various "orders" of widows, virgins, acolytes, readers, exorcists, and others.

For more than a century after Ignatius' martyrdom, Antioch would not figure prominently in the development of Christian belief and spirituality. But toward the end of the third century, events catapulted it into prominent controversy with Alexandria. By the end of the age of persecution, these two ancient cities had become the major hinges on which swung both orthodox and heretical interpretations of Christian theology and practice.

Ultimately, the focus of tension between them concerned how God was present in Christ, and through Christ was accessible to believers. The ensuing and bitter Christological controversies culminated in the credal statements of a host of regional synods and the great Ecumenical Councils of Nicea, Ephesus, and Chalcedon.

The first memorable theologian of Antioch was the intemperate bishop, Paul of Samosata, whose views on the Person of Christ propelled the growing schism between the approaches of the two Christian academies into open conflict. Opposed even by Antiochenes, he was condemned in 268 and deposed. The career of the saintly Lucian the Presbyter, master of Arius as well as Eusebius of Caesarea and Eusebius of Nicomedia, was ended by martyrdom in 312. His teaching may or may not have been accurately developed by his students, but the clear tendency was toward the humanist view of Christ that would come to be known as Arianism for its most famous proponent.

During this stormy era of emerging Christian theologies, the Church of Rome — the first of the three ancient patriarchates recognized at Nicea — mainly exercised a moderating influence. The Churches of Caesarea and Jerusalem (the ancient name had been restored by Constantine at the Council) played an even more minor role. There were many other important Christian centers, both new and old — Ephesus, Damascus, Carthage, Nicomedia, Edessa, and Lyons among them. But the dominant poles of theological development and controversy were now clearly in Egypt and Syria.

The Appeal
of
Arianism

A widespread and common-sense interpretation of Christian belief that played down or denied the divine nature of Christ, Arianism was at least partial- ly a reaction against the secret doctrines and airy speculations of the Alexandrian gnostics, which had turned God into a morally ambivalent pantheon and Jesus into a phantom. The simple, rough-and-ready theology of Arius, which he cleverly set to popular tunes and disseminated in street pamphlets, could appeal to both emperors and dock-workers.

Arius was born in Libya about the year 250.[3] After studying under Lucian in Antioch, he traveled to Egypt where he was ordained a deacon by Peter, the bishop of Alexandria. He was later excommunicated for supporting Bishop Melitius in the controversies over readmitting those who had lapsed from the faith. Peter's own martyrdom resolved the issue when his succes- sor, Achillas, reconciled Arius and ordained him to the priesthood in 312.

Although not young, Arius earned immediate success as a dynamic preacher and became renowned for his asceticism. Fundamentally, he held that the Son of God did not exist eternally but was created by the Father as an instrument for the creation of the world. Jesus, moreover, was not God by nature, but had the dignity of the Son of God bestowed on him at his baptism by John. Such in general was the Antiochene Christology.

Arius' teaching was condemned by Bishop Alexander in 320 and he was excommunicated by a regional synod of over one hundred bishops. Nevertheless, his views continued to spread. Constan- tine's attempt at reconciliation failed, and an ecumenical Council was convened by imperial order in order to resolve the dispute.

Convening at Nicea in early summer of 325, the delegates eventually condemned Arius' doctrine a second time, largely because of the eloquence and bartering of Athanasius of Alexandria. Arius was banished to Illyria and the bishops who supported him were exiled.

At court, however, his followers were especially favored by Constantine's sister, Constantia. As a result, in 328 the Arian bishops exiled at Nicea were permitted to return to their sees. Through further intrigue, Arius' enemies were gradually removed. Even Eustathius, the Patriarch of Antioch, was banished in 330 and, five years later, Arius turned the tables on Athanasius himself.

Recalled from exile through the influence of his friend and classmate, Bishop Eusebius of Nicomedia, Arius was received back into the Church and returned to Alexandria. There Athanasius was ordered to receive him. The patriarch refused and was banished to Trier. Arius' full reinstatement was prevented only when, at almost ninety years of age, he collapsed and died in the streets of Constantinople.

*Athanasius: "Old Immortality"* One of the most amazing figures of Christian antiquity, Athanasius appeared at the pivotal moment when the young Church was emerging from the final fury of persecution into the quicksands of imperial favor. Born in 292, he was educated at catechetical school in Alexandria. He composed his first major work, *On the Incarnation*, before he was twenty. Ordained deacon, he became secretary to Bishop Alexander, accompanying him to the Council of Nicea in 325. There, his eloquent and successful anti-Arian campaign earned him the lasting enmity of powerful factions at the court of Constantine.

Athanasius succeeded Alexander as patriarch in 328. But the

life of the new bishop of Alexandria hardly resembled the career of a modern prelate atop an ecclesiastical bureaucracy. In 336 Athanasius' Arian enemies succeeded in having him exiled to Trier. On the death of Constantine in 337, he returned to his see, but again in 339 he was forced to flee to Rome. There he established close and lasting contacts with the orthodox community.

With the aid of Constans, the Emperor of the West, he was restored to Alexandria in 346. But ten years later, the pro-Arian Eastern Emperor, Constantius, exiled him again. Athanasius remained in hiding near Alexandria until the succession of Julian the Apostate in 361. He had hardly begun his efforts to reconcile the more moderate Semi-Arians, when Julian's attempt in 362 to weaken the Church by favoring the Arians led once again to exile.

Athanasius was now seventy. On Julian's death the following year, the old man returned again to Alexandria. Exiled once more in 365 he was restored to his see a year later. The aged patriarch spent the rest of his life in Alexandria building support for the Nicene party and died there in 373.

Despite incredible interruptions, between 339 and 359 Athanasius managed to write a series of defensive works supporting the divinity of Jesus Christ as well as his true humanity and the divinity of the Holy Spirit. He also strongly supported the monastic movement. Among his friends he numbered both Pachomius and Serapion and wrote the biography of the great hermit, Antony. As he had secured orthodox belief through his theological writings, through his spiritual works Athanasius introduced monasticism to the Western Church.

The supporters of Nicea, so long dependent on the brilliance and strength of the aged patriarch of Alexandria, finally triumphed over Arianism at the Council of Constantinople in 381. The victory of orthodoxy would require a century more to consolidate. But Athanasius and his followers had preserved not only the paradoxical belief in both the full divinity and true humanity of Jesus Christ. They also secured forever the central place of worship, especially eucharistic worship, as the Church's response to the abiding presence of God in the mysteries of word and sacrament.

*The Desert Dwellers*   Not only did the conflict between the scholarly urban centers of Alexandria and Antioch shape the form and content of the Church's express belief in the fourth century. In the desert regions around the two cities there developed at the same time the second great force of Christian antiquity — the vibrant monastic movement whose spirituality would vividly illustrate the competing theological visions of the two capitals.

For the first three centuries, Christianity was largely an urban movement, spreading from the lower classes to the imperial court itself. Bishops, teachers, and writers were uniformly called from the ranks of the literate town and city-dwellers. Slowly, however, the message of Christ penetrated the more conservative rural areas, traditionally and staunchly pagan. By the middle of the third century, farming estates and peasant farmers in Egypt, North Africa, Phrygia, Syria, and Asia Minor were firmly Christian. Whether orthodox, Montanist, Donatist, or Novatianist, it was out of these agrarian communities that the first monastic communities emerged.

Monasticism arose not in response to persecution, but in its absence. Men and women intent on proving their love of God to the point of death turned to the natural and psychological testing ground of the spirit — the deserts of Egypt, Syria, and Palestine. Some saw their encounter with the world, the flesh, and the devil as a life-long combat, others as a foretaste of the life of heaven. However they envisioned it, these primitive monks and nuns established a form of life that would leave an indelible impression upon Christian spirituality until the end of time.

Antony, the first recorded hermit and acclaimed Father of Christian monasticism, was a young and wealthy Egyptian farmer. About the year 270, he heard the gospel of the rich young man and felt it directed squarely at himself. He sold his lands and possessions, then went to live alone on the outskirts of his village. Other solitaries, possibly fugitives from persecution, had already congregated there on the border of the desert. Fifteen years later, Antony abandoned even this vestige of community life for the austere Arabian mountain wilderness across the Nile. There his struggles against temptation took visible form as assaults by demons and wild beasts.

Inspired not only by a desire to find a remote place for prayer and fasting and to be alone with God, Antony became the focus of the poor and social outcasts suffering at the hands of the state. In 305, he organized them into a kind of community and gave them a rule. The manifest anti-social sentiment of many of these monks and their successors would have serious implications in the centuries to come.

In 310, Antony retired again into solitude. Twice, however, he reappeared in Alexandria — during the Great Persecution and again to support Athanasius against the Arians during the Nicene controversies. He died in 356 at the age of one hundred and five. His life was written by Athanasius himself and became a model for subsequent forms of monastic spirituality.[4]

As Antony is regarded as the foremost of the solitary hermits, Pachomius established the first *coenobitic* communities - groups of hermits who shared aspects of life in common. Born in Upper Egypt in 290, he was a younger contemporary of Antony and his friend, Athanasius. A pagan soldier, Pachomius was converted in 313 and baptized. He became a disciple of the hermit Palaemon, and in 320 founded the monastery of Tabennisi near the Nile. By the time of his death in 346, Pachomius governed nine monasteries of men and two of women. The rule he composed for his coenobites would greatly influence the later proponents of Christian monasticism in both the East and, through Jerome's Latin translation, the West — Basil the Great, John Cassian, Caesarius of Arles, and Benedict.[5]

As both monks and urban Christians sought advice and direction from these *abbas*, the "Desert Fathers," and their women counterparts, the *ammas*, a profound Christian spirituality began to flourish in the desert near Alexandria. Their stories and pithy sayings or *apothegms* were gathered into collections which represent the first efforts at a specifically Christian spiritual literature.[6]

The tradition of desert spirituality was by no means limited to Egypt. In both Palestine and Syria, similar movements began at about the same time and for many of the same reasons. In Syria especially, the monks were even more hostile to Hellenic culture than their counterparts in Egypt, whose spirituality was moderated by the influence of Clement and Origen. Among the saintly and famous monks of this period are found Diadochus, Evagrius of Pontus, Macarius the Great, and Isaac of Antioch.[7]

John Cassian (360 - 435) occupies a place of singular importance. A Scythian by birth, he founded his first monastery in Bethlehem. An inveterate traveler and student, he appeared in Egypt by 385, where his spirituality was influenced by the writings of Evagrius of Pontus. By 415, he had established two monasteries in Gaul, near Marseilles.

Through his writings, especially the *Institutes* and *Conferences*, he exercised a determining influence on western monasticism, particularly the Benedictine tradition. Although venerated as a saint in the East, Cassian's connection with the fifth-century movement known as Semi-Pelagianism earned him the suspicion of Western church leaders under the sway of Augustine.[8]

Despite the acute, Zen-like wisdom found in the sayings of the desert monks, there was also a kind of world-weariness about many of them that disparaged nature as well as society. Their spirituality was often eccentric and usually otherworldly, far removed from the physical and social demands of the natural world and even the body. Antony, it was said, blushed every time he had to eat or perform any other bodily function. It was sometimes asserted that the body's life was the soul's death. Salvation, therefore, lay in 'mortifying the flesh': "I am killing it because it is killing me," one monk is reported to have said.

*Cappadocian Conquest*

The accomplishments of the unlikely trio of Athanasius, Antony, and Pachomius were matched and in some respects surpassed later in the same century by another trinity of bishops, scholars and saints. Although strongly influenced by the theology and spirituality of the great Alexandrian tradition, they lived neither in

Egypt nor in Syria, but in the central mountainous region of modern Turkey known then as Cappadocia.

Basil, one of the few saints of history later known as "the Great," his younger brother Gregory, later the bishop of Nyssa, together with their close friend Gregory of Nazianzus are collectively known as "the Cappadocian Fathers." But they were part of a larger community of saints that included two illustrious women, Macrina, the sister of Basil and Gregory, and Theosavia, Gregory of Nyssa's wife. Their contributions to theology and spirituality assured the survival of the best elements of the Alexandrian tradition while drawing also upon Antiochene exegesis and the resources of Christian, Jewish, and pagan antiquity.[9]

Gregory Nazianzen (329 - 89), "the Theologian," was the eldest of the group, the son of the Bishop of Nazianzus. When a student at the University of Athens, he met Basil and became fast friends. Retiring and contemplative by temperament, however, soon afterwards Gregory became a monk. Basil later pressured him into being ordained priest, and he was eventually consecrated as Bishop of Sasima in Cappadocia, which he never visited. He remained in Nazianzus as suffragan to help his father until 374, when he retired to a secluded estate in Seleucia.

Called to Council of Constantinople in 381, he distinguished himself as a preacher and worked tirelessly to restore the Nicene faith. Appointed Bishop of Constantinople, he resigned the see, returned to Nazianzus, and finally to his own estates, where he died at the age of sixty. Fittingly, his feast day, January 2nd, is shared with his great friend, Basil. A writer as well as a preacher, Gregory never felt obliged, as earlier Christian thinkers had, to renounce ancient Greek philosophy or even to apologize for his interest in it. Apart from Scripture, he maintained, the Platonists thought best about God and are nearest to the faith.[10]

Basil (330 - 79), a year younger than Gregory, was the leader of the three Cappadocians and no less a student of philosophy and science. He pursued his education first at Caesarea, then at Constantinople and finally at Athens, where he was a fellow student not only of Gregory but also of Julian, later to be Emperor and the most famous Apostate of history.   He may well have studied medicine at some point.

Later, Basil followed the life of a monk in both Syria and Egypt for a while.   At twenty-eight, he became a hermit on the banks of the Isis near Neo-Caesarea.   Nevertheless, he preached missions together with Gregory of Nazianzus.   Julian's efforts to bring him to court failed.   But at the request of Eusebius, the bishop of Caesarea, he left his seclusion in 364 to counter the Arian propaganda of the Emperor Valens.   When Eusebius died in 370, Basil was appointed to succeed him.   More pugnacious as a theologian than either his brother or friend, Basil opposed the teachings of Eunomius and the Pneumatomachian heretics, and allied himself with Athanasius and Pope Damasus to combat the deposition of Meletius, the Patriarch of Antioch.

In his spiritual teaching, Basil followed Origen and the Alexandrian tradition, but was wary of allegorical interpretation.   While not as extreme as the exegetes of Antioch, he was more literal in his approach to scripture than his counterparts in Alexandria.   But he was also more open to pagan authors with regard to philosophy and natural science.   In his *Homilies on the Six Days of Creation*, he drew heavily on astronomy, botany, meteorology, and natural history to defend and explain the biblical account of creation.

As a Christian Platonist, Basil held that the human person was created in the image and likeness of God.   From the intelligible order, however, humankind falls victim to the sensible world. Although destined for eternity, it is trapped in the web of time, and, remote from the presence of God, lies in danger of a final descent into the material dissolution of moral evil.   As with his pagan predecessor, Plotinus, for Basil the task of the true philosopher is to convert the fall into an ascension.   This is achieved by following the right spiritual path.   By purification the passions are quieted and ordered.   By divine enlightenment, the soul rises to the contemplation of divine and natural truth.   Finally, by the grace and love of God, the spirit is drawn up to the heights of divine union, *deification*, in the language of the Eastern Church.

Based partly on the teachings of Philo, Clement, and Evagrius of Pontus, as well as Plotinus, this plan of spiritual and moral development became the classic model of the soul's ascent to God, "the Three Ways of the Spiritual Life." Of great importance to later Christian spirituality, Basil, as well as Gregory of Nyssa, also emphasized the spiritual discipline of mental purification they called *aphairesis*. By this they meant a method of "unknowing" described by the Neoplatonists, but found no less in scripture and the writings of Philo, by which a partial knowledge of God is achieved by the progressive stripping away of every concept that the mind can form about God in the certainty that all are inadequate. For Basil, as for Athanasius, we come nearer to God by "unknowing" than by knowing.

Active throughout his career as a preacher, social reformer, organizer, and builder, Basil never abandoned his love for the monastic life. The rule he composed for his monks left a permanent character on monasticism in both East and West. His early death at forty-nine deprived the Council of Constantinople of one of its staunchest champions of orthodoxy.

Gregory of Nyssa was not even a year younger than his brother, but outlived his comrades by ten and fifteen years respectively, dying in 395 at the age of 65. Alone of the three, he married, although his wife, St. Theosavia, died at an apparently young age. Also a scholar, Gregory first pursued the career of a rhetorician. He entered one of the monasteries founded by his brother, but there is no evidence that he became a monk. Nevertheless, he did become the bishop of Nyssa in 371. Deposed by the Arians five years later, he remained in exile until the death of Valens in 378. He attended the Council of Antioch in 379 and the Councils of Constantinople in 381 and 394, living to see the final overthrow of the great heresy threatening the integrity of the Church as it emerged from the catacombs.

Following Origen and Athanasius, Gregory was also a stalwart defender of the propriety of the title *Theotokos* (God-bearer) for the Virgin Mary, which had been repudiated by the Arians. By the fourth century, devotion to Mary had already become not only a major element in Christian worship and spirituality, but a focus of theological debate between competing factions. Denied strenuously by the Nestorians of Antioch a generation later, the title would be confirmed by the Ecumenical Councils of Ephesus in 431 and Chalcedon in 451.

Gregory of Nyssa was the most mystical of the Cappadocian theologians, drawing even more explicitly on the Alexandrian tradition begun by Philo. His *Life of Moses* is a masterpiece of spiritual literature, using every refinement of allegory to bring his readers closer to the mysterious Presence that, like the Ineffable Power hidden with the divine cloud on Sinai, is at once both near and far, covered from our mortal eyes by the cloud of human imperfection, but alive within us as the very heart of our heart.[11]

*The
Legacy*
The positive, life-affirming spirituality of the Cappadocians provides an able corrective for the often negative tone of the desert monks. What is even more surprising in an era of classical philosophical distrust of nature is the highly positive light in which they regarded the cosmos. Gregory of Nyssa and Basil the Great were filled with wonder at the stars, planets, and comets. They not only showed a deep interest in the natural world. They also enjoyed it.

For the Cappadocians, like the Jews of old from whom they took their model and inspiration, nature was in belief and fact the visible manifestation of divine presence and power, a system of theophanies rather than a merely material product of God's creative activity. Also like the Jews, these early theologians avoided any suggestion of pantheism in their fundamentally mystical attitude toward nature. Creation was ultimately a revelation of Presence, but God and nature were not identical. To encounter the God of creation, the mind and heart had to pass beyond nature.

A lasting tenet of Eastern theology often passed over scantingly by the Western Church Fathers, this mystical vision of creation would find a positive echo centuries later in the poetic spirit of

Irish monasticism and especially the remarkable philosophical and theological system of a ninth-century Irish scholar at the Frankish court, John Scottus. Not by chance, his teaching had developed largely from a study of Maximus the Confessor and the master behind him, Gregory of Nyssa. And from it, the creation-mysticism of the Cappadocians would pass into medieval spirituality through Meister Eckhart and on to St. John of the Cross.

In time, large segments of the leading theological schools of both Alexandria and Antioch would lapse into schism and heresy over doctrinal disagreements — the former into Monophysitism, which fused the divine and human natures of Christ, the latter into Nestorianism, which separated them. The Christian character of neither city would survive the onslaught of Muslim troops that overran the ancient east in 642. But all that still lay far ahead. In the meantime, liberated finally from the vestiges of Roman persecution and Hellenic mystification, Christian spirituality emerged during the fourth century in its first integral form, doctrine and practice together, from the deserts and schools of both Egypt and Syria. Taken from there to Carthage, Rome and Gaul, it would transform the Western world within a century.

## NOTES

1. See Jean Daniélou, *Origen*, trans. by Walter Mitchel (New York: Sheed and Ward, 1955), Henry Crouzel, *Origen*, trans. by A. S. Worrall (Edinburgh: T. and T. Clark, 1989), Charles Kannengiesser and William Petersen, eds., *Origen of Alexandria: His World and His Legacy* (Notre Dame: University of Notre Dame Press, 1988), and Henry Chadwick, "The Illiberal Humanist," *Early Christian Thought and the Classical Tradition*, op. cit., pp. 66-94.

2. See Frend, *The Rise of Christianity*, p. 120. For more comprehensive studies, see D. S. Wallace-Hadrill, *Christian Antioch: A Study of Early Christian Thought in the East* (London: Cambridge University Press, 1982), and Raymond Brown and John P. Meier, *Antioch and Rome: New Testament Cradles of Catholic Christianity* (New York: Paulist Press, 1983).

3. See Rowan Williams, *Arius: History and Tradition* (London: Darton, Longman and Todd, 1987).

4.  See Derwas J. Chitty, trans., *The Letters of St. Antony the Great* (Kalamazoo: Cistercian Publications, 1977).

5.  The *Pachomian Koinonia*, three volumes of writings attributed to St. Pachomius, including the *Life*, the *Rule*, and *Chronicles*, have been translated by Armand Veilleux (Kalamazoo: Cistercian Publications, 1982).

6.  These have been published in several editions. See especially Helen Waddell, *The Desert Fathers* (London: Constable and Co., 1936), *The Sayings of the Desert Fathers*, trans. by Benedicta Ward, S.L.G. (Kalamazoo: Cistercian Publications, 1982), *The Wisdom of the Desert Fathers*, trans. by Benedicta Ward, S.L.G. (Kalamazoo: Cistercian Publications, 1987), and *The Lives of the Desert Fathers*, trans. by Norman Russell (Kalamazoo: Cistercian Publications, 1987). See also Ward's *The Harlots of the Desert* (Kalamazoo: Cistercian Publications, 1987).

7.  The Macarian "homilies" have been edited by George Maloney, S.J., *Intoxicated with God*, (Denville, NJ: Dimension Books, 1978). Evagrius' *Praktikos* and the *Chapters on Prayer* have been translated and edited by John Eudes Bamberger (Kalamazoo: Cistercian Publications, 1981). See also Theodoret of Cyrrhus, *A History of the Monks of Syria*, R. M. Price, trans. (Kalamazoo: Cistercian Publications, 1955) and *On Divine Providence*, Thomas Halton, trans. (New York: Paulist Press, 1988).

8.  For an introduction to Cassian, see *John Cassian: Conferences*, trans. by Colm Luibheid (New York: Paulist Press, 1985).

9.  For a general introduction, see George A. Barrois, trans. and intro., *The Fathers Speak: Saint Basil the Great, Saint Gregory of Nazianzus, Saint Gregory of Nyssa* (Crestwood, NY: St. Vladimir Press, 1986).

10. Toward the end of his life, Gregory also composed poetry, selections being edited and translated by J. A. McGuckin, *St. Gregory Nazianzen: Selected Poems* (Kalamazoo: Cistercian Publications, 1987).

11. For a comprehensive selection of Gregory of Nyssa's writings, see *From Glory to Glory*, selected by Jean Daniélou, S.J., trans. and ed. by Herbert Musurillo, S.J. (Crestwood, NY: St. Vladimir's Seminary Press, 1979). See also *Gregory of Nyssa: The Life of Moses*, trans. and ed. by Abraham Malherbe and Everett Ferguson (New York: Paulist Press, 1978).

# The Age of Augustine    7

B Y THE BEGINNING OF THE FIFTH CENTURY, the pivotal centers of Christian spirituality and theology were shifting from Alexandria and Antioch to Constantinople, the new imperial capital, and Carthage, the capital of Numidian Africa. As usual, Rome and the Church of Italy were caught between.

At this time the official language of both the imperial court and Christian Africa was Latin, not Greek. The spirituality of the North African Church differed from Egyptian and Syrian Christianity, as well as from Italian beliefs and practices, in many other respects. Both Donatism, with its rigorous anti-imperialism and strident asceticism, and Manichaeism, with its dualistic theology and morality, were strong there. In addition, the borders of Roman Africa, like those of Spain, Gaul, and Britain, were overrun with increasing frequency and fury by hordes of barbarians driven west and south by the pressure of population expansion and the need for new lands.

*Darkness from the East*    Donatism was largely restricted to the North African provinces. Manichaeism, a heretical form of Persian Zoroastrianism, was far more widespread. Less successful in Byzantine Christendom than in the West, it found many adherents in North Africa and also sections of Italy, Spain, and Southern Gaul.

Mani, a Zoroastrian visionary and prophet, was born in Persia in 215. He joined an ascetic sect called the Maghtasilah, which practiced celibacy and abstained from all meat and wine. Exiled for his beliefs by Shapur I, he preached through parts of India, China, Tibet, and what is now modern Turkey and Afghanistan. Returning to Persia in 273, Mani was seized, tortured, and executed.

Manichaean doctrine was based on an irreconcilable antagonism between eternal and competing Principles – Light and Darkness. This dualism was also expressed in the polarities of good and evil, spirit and matter, and, to some extent, male and female. Only by freeing oneself from the bonds of material existence, especially sexuality, could the spirit ascend to union with God.

In its Christian interpretation, the Manichees not only elevated Satan, the principle of evil, to equality with God, but held that the individual was not responsible for sins committed in the body, which were the effect of the evil principle operating in the flesh. Manichaean belief in human helplessness in the grip of external and internal forces, coupled oddly with both a strict asceticism and sexual permissiveness (apart from procreation), was to have dire and lasting effects on the West, not least in the career of a brilliant, impressionable young Berber named Augustine.

There were many reasons for the success of puritanical and heretical sects among Christians in North Africa and elsewhere. A major factor was the very legitimation and triumph of Christianity as the new imperial cult. It had suddenly become not only fashionable but prudent for members of the upper classes to convert, even if they deferred baptism until death as a safeguard against having to assume the full weight of commitment. Such mixed success produced some understandably antithetical results in the East and West alike. With social acceptability came spiritual tepidity. But a longing for "real" Christianity also awoke among those who took their religion seriously.

With the rise of Christianity to prominence in the Constantinian 'enlightenment,' many of the social reforms of the previous century, as well as the simplicity of life, care for the poor, and fledgling efforts to end slavery, were replaced by a concern to protect and enhance the status quo. Clerical exemption from the exorbitant taxes of the era and other civil obligations produced an abundance of opportunistic candidates for orders. Bishops' salaries not only rose but were increasingly subvented by the State. For many, power, position, and prestige became more important goals than holiness of life, orthodoxy of belief, or pastoral solicitude. Bishoprics were awarded to political allies and sometimes were even bought and sold.

The effect of such cooptation was a general weakening of the social conscience of the Church as a whole and a loss of spiritual vigor. Recognized by many monks and laity, such slackness produced a counter-effect, the emergence of an uncompromising, sometimes severe asceticism, coupled with *alienatio* – a disdain for urban culture and most forms of civil service.

*The New Asceticism*

Voluntary asceticism had figured in the spirituality of the Church for over a century. Fundamentally, the word *ascesis* means "training" or "discipline," such as that undertaken by athletes or soldiers. Toning and strengthening the spirit, as well as the body and even the mind, were encouraged by St. Paul himself (1 Cor. 9:24-27; cf. Heb. 12:1, etc.). But in the East and Northern Africa, such asceticism soon expressed itself in extreme forms, as monks sought to surpass each other in the rigors of their life-style.

*Dendrites* and *Stylites* achieved physical as well as spiritual heights in tiny cells atop trees and columns. *Adamites* disdained the protection (and modesty) of even minimal clothing. Other ascetics remained standing for prolonged periods, such as Lent, and in some instances on one foot alone. Many eschewed ever washing either themselves or their clothing (more often animal hides), suffering skin diseases and the incessant attacks of vermin as part of the cost of discipleship. Still more allowed their hair and beards to grow uncut, or, conversely, chopped their hair off in deliberately ragged "tonsures" as did Martin of Tours and the Celtic monks of a later period.

Developing later than either Eastern or African asceticism, Western forms did not as a rule favor such public or heroic extremes. Simplicity of life, especially of dress, prayer, and fasting were typical ways in which the ascetical movement expressed itself in the small communities of Martin of Tours, Jerome, Paulinus of Nola, and Augustine.

Ordinary Christians tended to regard even such moderate asceticism as dangerous and possibly heretical, having witnessed the same practices among Manichaeans and Donatists. And when excessive zeal produced tragedy, as in the death from fasting and abstinence of Jerome's young Roman disciple, Blesilla, in 384, public reaction was swift and definitive. The irascible exegete was hounded out of Italy, never to return. But other forms of spirituality had long been developing among ordinary Christians in the Constantinian era.

*Pilgrims and Relics*

As imperial restrictions on the practice of the Faith were replaced with tolerance and eventual preference, pilgrimages and the veneration of relics assumed major proportions in Christian spirituality. Rome, the final resting place of Peter and Paul as well as countless named and unknown martyrs, and Jerusalem, the Holy City, were the chief objectives of devotional journeys. Flourishing in Egypt and Syria, monasticism was quickly established in Palestine as a means of caring for pilgrims and also attending to the Christian shrines.

If Christians were unable to visit the sites of Christ's life, death, and resurrection, relics from the Holy Land and other hallowed places could be brought to them. Already deeply venerated by Donatists, the bones of martyrs and confessors were eagerly sought for the new basilicas and cathedrals rising in the West like wild flowers after a spring rain. Augustine himself would succeed in having the relics of St. Stephen brought to Hippo. But the most famous relic of all was discovered under miraculous circumstances, according to tradition, by the mother of Constantine, the Empress Helena herself.[1]

*Western Monasticism and Ascetical Spirituality*
In the meantime, Pachomian monasticism was slowly gaining ground at the very edge of the Western Empire. Martin of Tours established the first monastery in Gaul in 360. In 410, the year Rome fell to Alaric, St. Honoratus established a monastery at Lérins, an island opposite Cannes. Five years later, John Cassian founded a double monastery at Marseilles. In 417, Bishop Castor founded a community at Apt, seventy miles north of Marseilles for which he asked Cassian to provide a rule. Less formal communities were also proliferating.

Underlying the spiritual vitality of the West at this time was the new ascetical movement shared by both lay and monastic communities. It is the common thread that links the lives and letters of the great figures of the period, whose influence remains strong even today, from Martin of Tours to Augustine and Pelagius.

*Martin of Tours: Soldier and Saint*
Known to posterity as the Bishop of Tours and Patron of France, Martin experienced in his own life the transition from the defensive Christianity of the early fourth century to the imperial cult of Constantine and, finally, the new asceticism that alienated itself from the approved religiosity of the Roman aristocracy.[2] He was the son of a soldier who had risen to the rank of tribune. Born in Pannonia (modern Yugoslavia) in 316, Martin was attracted to Christianity while very young. Inspired by stories of the martyrs of the Great Persecution, he enrolled as a catechumen at the Church of Pavia, where his family had moved. But at fifteen, Martin's father thwarted his dreams of becoming a hermit like Antony by enrolling him for a twenty-five-year tour of compulsory military service.

As a tribune's son, Martin was granted certain privileges which enabled him to assist those in need as he prepared for baptism. One winter, he happened upon a beggar freezing at the gates of Amiens. Having only his military cloak, he divided it with his sword, giving the beggar half in the most famous gesture of charity in the ancient world. For that night, he dreamed that he saw Jesus wrapped in the beggar's portion of the cloak.

Martin was baptized soon afterwards, and the story, as told by his biographer, Sulpicius Severus, entered Christian memory as a paradigm experience of Christ's hidden presence in the world, especially in the suffering of the destitute and oppressed. Much of Martin's life, when he left the military at the age of forty, would be devoted to ministering to the poor, sick, and mentally deranged.

One of the earliest Western ascetics, Martin joined Hilary of Poitiers and founded the first monastery in Gaul at Ligugé (in modern Belgium). Proclaimed by the people of Tours, however, the rustic holy man was consecrated bishop. Unlike many candidates elevated to the episcopacy in the burgeoning new hierarchy, he retained his simple, even unkempt appearance and spartan life-style. He also continued his frequent missionary journeys throughout Gaul.

Martin's monastery at Tours became a center of spiritual life for the Celts and later the Franks. He also influenced many of the great ascetical figures of the next generation, including Paulinus of Nola, Jerome, and Augustine. Nevertheless concerned with the whole Church, Martin kept abreast of developments beyond his own diocese. He vainly attempted to prevent the merciless execution of Priscillian of Avila and his disciples at Tréves in 385. Deceived in this by the usurper-emperor, Maximus Magnus, Martin secluded himself increasingly from the world in the years that followed, confirming the movement already known as *alienatio* — a characteristic of Western asceticism that would have disastrous effects on the Christian empire in the next century.

But even at the end of his life, conscious of the need for evangelizing the pagans beyond Gaul itself, he encouraged the mission in 395 of St. Ninian to the Celts and Picts of southwestern Scotland

and northern Britain. Ninian's church at Whithorn was dedicated to him as were countless other churches and chapels throughout early Christendom.

*Paulinus of Nola: Ascetical Gentleman*

In the Eastern Church, ascetics tended towards active support of the state policies, unlike the monks and holy men and women of the West. In Byzantium, the emperor came close to regaining the divine status of the pagan past; for Ambrose, Jerome, and Augustine, conversely, the court and its business were a necessary evil which too easily interfered with the things of God.

Paulinus of Nola exemplifies the tendency among the members of the nobility of this period to withdraw from civil government for spiritual reasons. He also represents the highest form of cultured Christian life. Classically educated, he shares with Prudentius the distinction of being the first Latin Christian poet. Almost an exact contemporary of Augustine, Paulinus was the son of a senator. A benevolent landowner of vast wealth and influential connections in Rome, Paulinus was a supernumerary consul at twenty-five. In 381 he was appointed provincial governor of Campania. Shortly afterwards, however, perhaps owing to the disruptions following the emperor Gratian's murder and the usurpation of Magnus Maximus, and surely discouraged by the growing callousness and secularism of imperial Christianity, Paulinus withdrew from public life and returned to his family estates in Gaul where he married a Spanish noblewoman, Therasia.

Deeply disturbed by his accidental embroilment in the controversies resulting from the condemnation of Priscillian, the bishop of Avila, Paulinus visited Martin of Tours at Marmoutier in 386. Impressed by the otherworldly asceticism of the monk-bishop and his followers, Paulinus accepted baptism in 389 as a pledge of his commitment not to resume public life. Selling most of his family estates and distributing the money to the poor, he retired with Therasia to her family estate in Saragossa. About this time he established epistolary contact with Jerome.

Narrowly escaping forcible ordination at Barcelona the same year, Paulinus again escaped the clamor of public life and fled with Therasia to the shrine of St. Felix in Nola. There they established a spiritual refuge for monks and the poor. Conditions were relatively austere, but sufficiently comfortable for them and their friends to follow a life of cultured retirement such as that espoused by Augustine at Cassiciacum. A society of spiritual friends, Paulinus, Therasia, and their companions read and discussed Christian and even classical pagan literature, prayed, meditated, and attended to the needs of the distressed as occasion demanded.

From Nola, Paulinus also exchanged letters not only with Augustine, but with a host of cultured Christian leaders from the Mediterranean basin, including Ambrose, Pope Anastasius, and the British expatriate Pelagius, whose quarrels with Jerome and Augustine he attempted vainly to moderate. In 408, Paulinus accepted the office of Bishop of Nola. Twenty-three years later he died there at the age of seventy-eight, possibly the last Christian patrician of the classical era.

*The Problem with Priscillian*    Towards the end of the fourth century, the flourishing ascetical movement ran tragically afoul of church and civil authority in the case of the bishop of Avila, who with his disciples was accused of Manichaeism and sorcery by jealous rivals. In 385, barely fifty years after the Church issued into the freer air of Constantine's "Christian" empire, Priscillian and his principal followers, including several prominent women, were executed by order of Magnus Maximus, the short-lived usurper-emperor of the West.[3]

Evidently one of the more threatening elements of the Priscillianists' doctrine and practice concerned asceticism and prophetic ecstasy. Vegetarian, abstinent from alcohol, given to fasting and vigils, sometimes praying naked like the Adamites, and subject to visionary experience and revelations, Priscillian and his followers displayed many features of both Eastern and Western asceticism.

Extreme advocates of *alienatio*, they held that the world was in the grip of Satanic powers and that baptism required a total repudiation of secular commitments. Not surprisingly, their prosecution and execution were strongly opposed by many ascetical church leaders, including Ambrose and Martin of Tours. After the death sentence had been carried out, Pope Siricius, no friend of the new ascetical movement, also protested lamely. The Priscillianists' accusers were eventually excommunicated at both Milan and Rome.

The trial and executions, along with additional condemnations of Priscillianism later in the fourth century, had a lasting effect on Western Christianity. Priscillian became a popular saint among the dispossessed along the Spanish marches. His memory would survive for hundreds of years, not least at the shrine of Compostello. But a pall of suspicion would also hover for more than a thousand years over charismatic and ascetical elements in Christian spirituality.

More ominously, an important precedent had been established in the bright morning of ecclesiastical liberation. Religious enthusiasm was now capable of incurring a new kind of martyrdom – at the hands of the Christian State itself. Fertilized by Augustine's late endorsement of the employment of civil duress against religious dissenters, the seeds of the Inquisition had already been sown.

*The Perils of Pelagius*

The cultivation of western asceticism produced similarly tragic results in the person of the Romanized Briton Pelagius, a lay theologian and lawyer who served, as had Jerome, as tutor to a noble family, the Anicii. Known at one time or other to Paulinus of Nola, Jerome, and Augustine, Pelagius was on good terms with most southern Italian bishops.

A partisan of the new asceticism, Pelagius led a life of personal austerity. He counseled the rich to renounce their wealth as a hindrance to salvation. But he opposed resignation from society, advocating social action and reform as a moral duty. Pelagius' theology was, moreover, strongly opposed to Manichaeism in any form. His was not only an optimistic, but a heroic vision of human nature, indebted to Stoic ideals but also redolent of his Celtic background.

Pelagius taught that, aided by grace and the example of Christ, it was possible, as Eastern monasticism had long maintained, for a Christian to attain spiritual perfection, even sinlessness in this life. But on this and more personal scores, Pelagius ran afoul of other advocates of asceticism, primarily Jerome himself, whose dim view of human nature was no secret.

A refugee from Alaric's invasion of Rome, Pelagius arrived in Carthage in 411, where his teaching and personal holiness made a favorable impression on Augustine. Pelagius soon moved on to Palestine. A disciple named Celestine remained in Carthage, however, where he antagonized the local clergy and the bishop with his extreme interpretations of Pelagius' doctrine. Even Augustine was alarmed.

In Palestine, Pelagius again collided with Jerome, whose main quarrel at the time was with the monks. Sides were drawn up quickly, and soon Jerome was pelting Carthage, Rome, and Gaul with acrimonious reports about Pelagius and his doctrine. A regional council was convoked to decide the issue under the aegis of the Bishop of Jerusalem. Pelagius was fully acquitted. But the cell of the unpopular Jerome was subsequently looted, an act for which he held Pelagius responsible. His enmity became implacable. The increasingly combative Augustine also rose to the occasion.

Between 416 and 418, councils were convened at Carthage and Rome. A distorted version of Pelagius' doctrine was duly condemned and, as the aged Augustine remarked, the matter was settled. But eighteen southern Italian bishops resigned their sees rather than endorse the condemnation. Pelagius himself vanished into the East, probably finding a spiritual refuge among the Eastern monks whose theology so closely resembled his own. But the Draconian victory of Augustinian theology, while a boon for the Latin West, further imperiled the strained relations between the

Eastern and Western churches, now adding the new tension of opposed spiritualities.

*Women's Spirituality*  Although the "movers and shakers" of the early Christian empire were ordinarily male, women figured prominently in the development of both Eastern and Western Christendom. Helena, Constantia, Eudoxia, Justina, and Pulcheria exercised powerful influence over imperial affairs as well as matters of Christian belief and practice. Similarly, *ammas* shaped the spirituality of both East and West.

Pachomius' sister, Mary, founded the first monastery for women near that of her brother in the upper Nile valley. In the West, several women's communities existed by 350. Jerome formed communities for women in both Rome and Palestine. Significantly, Ambrose, whose faith had been nurtured at an early age by his mother and sister, Marcellina, was the first Western theologian to develop the theme of God's maternal character. In 353, Marcellina became a nun. Within thirty years, Scholastica would be born. And in 415 at Marseilles, John Cassian established St. Savior's monastery for women near that of St. Victor for men.

Mothers and sisters had similarly influenced the spiritual development of Basil the Great and his brother Gregory, as well as John Chrysostom, the great Patriarch of Constantinople whose nemesis was the Empress Eudoxia. And it had been through lay women, particularly the *matronae*, the high-born wives and mothers of the Roman aristocracy, that Christianity penetrated the higher strata of imperial society and ultimately conquered it.

Only legend testifies to the influence of Helena, the Celtic princess and Christian consort of Constantius Chlorus, on her illustrious son, Constantine the Great. But another illustrious son tells us plainly how a remarkable mother's enduring faith not only wrought the conversion of the most brilliant mind of Western Christianity, but in so doing, changed the course of Western history in ways as profound and lasting as the Constantinian revolution.

Monica was a noblewoman born in Tagaste (in modern Algeria) in 332 and reared in a household of
*Formidable*
*Mother*
Catholic believers touched with the rigorous Christianity that informed the extreme spirituality of the
Donatists and their Circumcellion shock troops. She
was married at twenty-two to a member of the lesser
nobility, a pagan *vir curialis* named Patricius, a violent, unfaithful,
but generous husband and father. Monica succeeded in raising her
three children, Augustine, Navigius, and Perpetua, as Christians.
Following African custom at the time, however, she deferred their
baptism.

A woman of uncommon patience and persistence, Monica won
her husband to the faith a year before his death. Augustine was
then sixteen, already involved in the pursuit of pleasure and
worldly success. Patricius applauded and furthered his desire to
study rhetoric at Carthage, which would equip the hot-blooded
youth for a career in law or politics. But Monica feared for his
salvation as he drifted from the faith, taking a mistress and developing a keen interest in the sophisticated teachings of the Christian
Manichees.

Monica was widowed in 371 at the age of forty. By
then she was a grandmother, for Augustine's faithful
*The Son*
*of Tears*
but anonymous mistress had borne him a son, Adeodatus ("Gift of God"). But when Augustine returned
to Tagaste a Manichaean "auditor," she refused to
admit him to her home. A dream convinced her,
however, that Augustine would return to the faith. Encouraged,
she opened her heart and her house to him, his mistress, and their
child. She also attempted to enlist the local bishop to persuade him
of his errors. The old man refused, all too aware of Augustine's
native brilliance as well as his skills in debate and stubbornness.
But moved by her entreaties, he promised her that God would not
permit "that the son of such tears should perish."

After teaching rhetoric in Tagaste for a while, Augustine moved again to Carthage, where he taught for nine years. Still a Manichaean, he was becoming weary of his teachers' inability to resolve the problem of evil. In 383, now thirty years old, he decided to move to Rome to further his career. Alarmed, Monica pleaded with him to stay, pursuing him as far as the coast. Determined to accompany him if he left, she retired to a nearby oratory for the night. Secretly, Augustine set sail that night, leaving a disconsolate mother grieving at the dock the following morning.

Within two years, Monica was in Milan. There, aided by his Manichaean friends in Rome, Augustine had accepted a tutor's position at the court of the Arian empress, Justina. He had, however, already abandoned his adherence to Manichaeism. He had discovered Neoplatonism.

Monica soon involved herself in the life of the Church of Milan, eventually coming to be on close terms with its imposing bishop, Ambrose. She took every opportunity to bring him and her son together. Her strategy was effective. Soon, Augustine decided to accept baptism. More, he sent his beloved mistress back to Africa, for she now stood in the way not only of his career, but of his reception into the Church.

Prudently, Monica found a young woman almost of marriageable age as a suitable fiancée for her son. Surprisingly, Augustine chose to remain celibate. Rather than a recurrence of Manichaeism, this was probably a sign that he had already accepted some of the tenets of the new Christian ascetical movement.

For several months, Augustine, Monica, Adeodatus, Navigius, and several friends retired to a country villa put at their disposal at Cassiciacum. There they enjoyed a Christian idyll such as Paulinus had established at Nola, engaging themselves in prayer, meditation, and leisurely discussions about God and the spiritual life which Augustine later published as the *Dialogues*, including that "On the Blessed Life."

In 387, after his baptism and that of Adeodatus, now fifteen, the family prepared to return to Tagaste. Traveling first to Rome, they stayed at Ostia, the Tiber port. One evening, as Augustine relates in the astonishing tenth chapter of his *Confessions*,[4] he and Monica experienced a simultaneous and ecstatic sense of God's presence as they stood speaking at a window facing the sunset. Five days later, she fell ill and died, surrounded by her beloved sons and grandson.

Heart-riven, Augustine returned to Africa, where he founded a monastic community at Tagaste, probably hoping to recapture the spirit of Cassiciacum. But Adeodatus died the following year, further wounding the sensitive Augustine. Barely two years later, he was surprisingly elected by the people of Carthage and ordained to the priesthood on the spot. Again he founded a religious community, but three years later, was made adjutor bishop to Aurelius of Hippo, whom he succeeded within the year.

Except for journeys necessitated by constant controversies in the thirty-five years left him on earth, Augustine remained in Hippo, refusing to leave even when Gaiseric's vandals lay siege to the city. There he died in 430, the premier Western doctor of the Church.

*Augustine the Mystic*

Augustine's dogmatic theology and aggressive defense of Christian doctrine earned his place in history. But his awareness of the presence of God in the deepest levels of human consciousness also shaped the spirituality of the West. Something new had emerged with his introspective, often tortuous self-analysis. *Feeling* had figured earlier in the teaching of Evagrius of Pontus, but it had never achieved the status in Eastern spirituality as had "objective" descriptions of life and growth in faith.

With Augustine, deep personal experience surfaces as the troubled ground of the human spirit itself, often wrought with desire for total communion with God, but equally bereft of the felt sense of that presence. Confused and tormented by conflicting desires and the downward pull of carnal passion, the Augustinian soul cries out to God for the release that can only come with the divine embrace, beyond all desert and expectation. But it is not mere goodness that attracts the soul to God for Augustine. It is beauty, tenderness, and love.

"Late have I loved you," he writes, "O beauty so ancient and so new! Late have I loved you! You were within me while I had gone outside to seek you. Unlovely myself, I rushed towards all those lovely things you had made. And always you were with me, and I was not with you" (Conf. X).

The presence of God, Augustine knew from his own experience, is so intimate within the believing heart that God is closer to us than we are to ourselves, immediate, but elusive. "Before experiencing God you thought you could talk about Him. When you began to experience Him you realized that what you are experiencing you cannot put into words" (In Ps., 99.6). But what cannot be spoken of can be praised, not so much in words, as in pure jubilation of song (Ibid., 99.5, 32.8). For Augustine, we are the "harp and tabret," the instruments on which God's grace plays divine music: "He Who loves 'a new song' wants to take you to be that harp, that tabret," our human sinews stretched out upon the frame of daily experience so that, like St. Paul, "Christ touches us and the sweetness of truth gives tongue" (Ibid., 149.8).

**The End of the Golden Age**

Ultimately, *alienatio*, the anti-cultural bias of the new Western asceticism, proved disastrous for imperial civilization itself. As the "best and brightest" increasingly turned away from civil participation, government increasingly fell into less capable hands until it collapsed from sheer internal debility and massive external pressure.

Thus, presaged by the execution of Priscillian, the end of the classical era of Western imperial Christianity was ushered in by civil confusion and strife, barbarian invasions from every side, increasing terrorism, and the collapse of the social order. Although recognized as a political catastrophe in the East, the fall of Rome to Alaric in 410, and again to Gaiseric forty-five years later, was interpreted by Western ascetics as the sad but inevitable consequence of original sin, thanks to the widespread acceptance of the sternly pessimistic Augustinian theology of salvation.

In Constantinople, however, the totalitarian vision of the emperor Theodosius would soon be brought to completion by Justinian, bestowing a semblance of law and order, even of peace, upon the East. The Church would continue to prosper, growing ever richer and more powerful under imperial favor. It was still a golden age in Byzantium, if one increasingly tarnished by hierarchical ambition, greed, envy, and political corruption.

Despite intellectual and social bleakness in the West and the moral decay of Byzantium, seeds of renewal were already germinating. With their full flowering centuries later would come a second springtime of Christian spirituality and learning grounded in Italian monasticism and the heroic zeal of missionaries from the very edge of the known world – Ireland and Celtic Britain.

## NOTES

1. The beautiful novel by Evelyn Waugh, *Helena* (Boston: Little Brown, 1950) recreates the early Constantinian era as seen through the eyes of the mother Empress.
2. For an excellent account of the life and teaching of St. Martin of Tours, see Christopher Donaldson, *Martin of Tours* (London: Routledge and Kegan Paul, 1980).
3. The definitive study of Priscillian's condemnation is by Henry Chadwick, *Priscillian of Avila: The Occult and the Charismatic in the Early Church* (Oxford: Clarendon Press, 1976).
4. See Edward Pusey, trans., Harold C. Gardiner, S.J., intro., *The Confessions of St. Augustine* (New York: Pocket Library, 1959).

# Light in the West    **8**

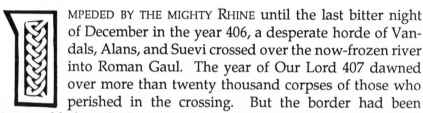

MPEDED BY THE MIGHTY RHINE until the last bitter night of December in the year 406, a desperate horde of Vandals, Alans, and Suevi crossed over the now-frozen river into Roman Gaul. The year of Our Lord 407 dawned over more than twenty thousand corpses of those who perished in the crossing. But the border had been irreparably breached — not only that between Germany and Gaul, but that between Late Antiquity and the Dark Ages. Within seventy years, the last Western emperor would be deposed and medieval Europe would be born amid the labor of centuries of pain, blood, and tears.

Under Alaric their king, the Eastern Goths had plundered the Roman Balkans as early as 397. By 410, in a surprise attack, they had taken Rome itself, and ransacked the city for three days. In a desperate attempt to stave off disaster, the legions were summoned from the edges of the Empire.

In 429, Gaiseric, King of the Vandals, invaded Africa from Spain with eighty thousand of his people. Hippo fell in 431, Carthage in 439. By 450, Britain was abandoned to invading Saxons, Jutes, Angles, Irish pirates, and Picts. Much of Gaul, Spain, and North Africa were controlled by the Arian Vandals, and Attila was again threatening to sack Rome. He failed, but five years later, Gaiseric succeeded in taking the city. Once more the Empire shuddered.

By 473, the Visigoths, once allies of Rome, had seized southern Gaul. Twenty years later, Theodoric I was King of Italy and the Western Empire was dead.[1]

The only institution capable of withstanding the barbarian invasions and preserving even a vestige of ancient civilization in the West was the Church. The instrument of that salvation was monasticism and its spirituality.

Although the roots of that monasticism lay in the soil of Egypt, Palestine, and Syria, the harvest was distinctively Western. Martin of Tours, Cassian, Honoratus, and especially Augustine planted the early shoots. But the followers of Benedict of Nursia and the Irish saints of the distant north nurtured the true and lasting growth. Fed and strengthened by their ministry, Christian Europe would eventually pass from barbarian darkness into the first bright promise of the Middle Ages, a new Empire, and the emergence of medieval Christendom.

*A Gospel Life*

Augustine of Hippo is primarily remembered as a theologian, bishop, and the foremost doctor of the Western church. If recalled today less as a monk, his spiritual influence on Western monasticism during the thousand years following his death was possibly greater than that of his doctrinal authority. Over one hundred religious congregations of men and women adopted the Rule he composed as a way of life for his followers.[2] Among men's communities, in addition to the Augustinian Canons Regular and Friars, these include the Norbertines, Dominicans, Trinitarians, Servites, and Alexians, to name only a few. Among major women's groups other than Augustinians themselves are found the Brigittines, Ursulines, Sisters of the Good Shepherd, and the Visitation Order.

Augustine's Rule gains its unique appeal from its brevity and its solid, scriptural basis. Perhaps recalling the idyllic days of his first monastic retreat with his family and friends at Cassiciacum, Augustine considered the primitive Christian community in

Jerusalem, idealized in the Acts of the Apostles, as the norm of the apostolic life he sought for his disciples.

Like Pachomius and Basil, Augustine promoted coenobitic monasticism, believing that full Christian maturity could best be attained in community. His vision of the perfect society was not, however, that of the "City of Man." As for the first Christians, selfless friendship and its expression in radical justice were the twin pillars upholding the whole edifice of Augustine's spirituality. The Augustinian monastery is a school in which the curriculum, the text, and the educator are all Love itself.

Even a casual glance at the rule can startle a modern reader by its emphasis on evangelical equality — the foundation of both friendship and social justice. Despite obvious similarities with the Pachomian form of common life, authority and organization in Augustinian monasticism differed from that in both Eastern forms and later Benedictine abbeys. Rather than a hierarchical, familial life style in which the monks or nuns were ruled by an *abba* or *amma*, Augustine's leader was a "prior," a member of the community who remained essentially an equal, if first among them for the term of his or her service. Moreover, the leadership role of the prior or prioress was not only less autocratic, but also more restricted in scope. The community largely regulated itself, a consequence of the origins of Augustine's monastic ideal in a society of friends rather than an assembly of "subjects."

As might be expected, the spirituality of Augustine's monasteries emanated from the life and work of the community rather than the vision or doctrine of the leader. Once more, Augustine's revolution clearly drew upon the account of the early Christian community in the Acts of the Apostles. God's presence was mediated by the Holy Spirit operating in the life, love, and service of brothers and sisters equal in dignity and possessed as a group with the grace and gifts of discipleship. Christ's Spirit was the interior guide first of the communal body as a whole and consequently of each member of it.

Spiritual "direction" thus lay in discerning the right path by which the community as a whole made its way toward God. Each member of the community shared a mutual responsibility for the others, both collectively and particularly: encouraging, correcting, healing, and guiding.  As overseer, the prior or prioress orchestrated the process as a whole.

*A Prophetic Way of Life*  Especially when illuminated by passages from his other works, Augustine's Rule provides critical insights into the social situation of his times.  More importantly, it reveals his attitude toward friendship and social justice, which even today remains remarkable for its radical character, psychological depth, and gospel simplicity.

Prevalent even in Christian society in the early fifth century, inequality between rich and poor was to have no place in the monastic community.  All possessions were to be held in common, including clothing.  Such sharing was seen as a means for promoting common life, not inflicting deprivation on its members. Augustine was not a religious romantic, idealizing poverty for its own sake.  He recognized in material want the root of desire, avarice, envy, and violence.  Real poverty was an obstacle to physical and spiritual health, education, and ministry.

*Normal Asceticism*  Augustine had little patience with the isolation and often extreme forms of physical, mental, and spiritual ordeals that had come to characterize the monks and hermits of the East.  This anti-Pelagian legacy of Augustinian moderation would exercise a healthy influence during the Middle Ages and beyond.  But here, too, Augustine's social doctrine was guided by an evangelical criterion. Fasting, he taught, contained no merit unless the food or money saved by abstaining was given to the poor.

His was an asceticism of the mind and heart, an inner discipline which had as its only purpose the development and perfection of love — human and divine.  Although often criticized for his negative attitude toward the body and pleasure, especially in his later writings, in his rule Augustine insisted on proper physical care for all. Health and hygiene constituted an important dimension of spirituality and social justice, especially with regard to the equal treatment demanded for the sick poor. In the later Roman Empire, only surpassing love could provide effective motivation for such a manner of life.

Thus, for Augustine a monastic community was not essentially an institution, especially a juridical or political one. It was first of all a spiritual bond among persons united in all their human characteristics by the power of divine and human friendship. If it was supremely political in the long run, that was because the monastery unmistakably asserted the fundamental dignity and equality of all human beings before God in the midst of a society in which caste, class, and wealth had again become determining factors of human worth.

*The Benedictine Inheritance*  The Augustinian monastery was a model of an ideally egalitarian society, a Christian utopia based on a fundamental democracy of the spirit. The Rule emphasized equal membership and co-responsibility. By contrast, the Rule that would come to dominate Western monasticism for the next thousand years was based on a hierarchical structure more akin to Egyptian coenobitical practice. The monks would be ordered in unequal ranks, and leadership would be invested in the life-long tenure of an *abba* or *amma*: the abbot or abbess.

If the heart of Augustine's Rule had been love, the core of Benedict's was obedience. More aristocratic in tone and authoritarian in principle, the Benedictine approach was also far more painstaking in detailing the daily round of life in the monastic enclosure. And where Augustine's monastery had been found in (if not of) the City, Benedict's abbeys flourished in the Wilderness.

Many of these differences can be understood only in terms of the drastic shifts in culture and society between early fifth-century

Africa and sixth-century Italy. The barbarian invasions had altered the very sense of civilization. The Rule of St. Benedict satisfied a desperate longing for an order and stability that had been taken for granted a century earlier. But it also stood against the social callousness which Augustine's spirituality had so opposed.

Times had changed for the worse. In the Dark Ages, one of the few places where the Christian ideal of social harmony could even survive, much less flourish, was the Benedictine abbey. But this was not some grim fortress where structures of a vanished social system were preserved at the expense of freedom of spirit and gospel equality. At its best, the abbey was a Christian family commonwealth, a humane as well as spiritual city set on a hill, whose light kept both sacred and secular learning alive in the difficult gloaming of the Western empire.

Not only letters, but music, the arts of the scribe and illuminator, even agricultural skills and animal husbandry flourished under Benedictine auspices. Forests were cleared, swamps were drained, orphans were fostered, pilgrims and travelers found rest in safety, and, through increased missionary activity, pagan Franks, Saxons, Angles, Jutes, and Viking Norsemen would be brought patiently and lovingly into the fold of Christ.

**The Patriarch**     Most of Benedict's life will remain forever shrouded in ignorance and obscured by legend. His earliest biographer, Pope Gregory the Great, indicates that he was born of a noble family of Nursia, probably in 480. Sent to Rome for education according to the accepted classical norms of the time, Benedict was repelled by the vice and corruption he found there. Renouncing his inheritance, he sought refuge with an unlikely companion, his nurse, in the Church of St. Peter Affili.

Desiring even greater solitude, he retired to a cave near Subiaco, where he lived for three years. Often kept alive only by the charity of the local shepherds and monks from a nearby monastery, the young man acquired a reputation for holiness and wisdom.

Eventually a group of monks approached him to become their abbot.

But Benedict's austerity soon collided with the lax, worldly life of the monks, who attempted to solve this unexpected problem by resorting to poison. Although spared by divine intervention, Gregory tells us, Benedict took the hint and returned happily to his solitary pursuit of God. As his reputation spread, however, other monks sought his leadership and advice. Finally he grouped them in twelve communities of twelve, each with an abbot. Although still enamored of the solitary life, Benedict assumed the leadership of one of them.

Around 525, the hostility of a local priest forced Benedict and a handful of his disciples to seek refuge on Mount Cassino, where he remained until his death about the year 550. He was buried in the same grave as his sister, Scholastica, who had died seven years earlier. There, blessed by their hallowed remains, over the next five centuries the premier monastery of the West would grow to prominence and power.

*The Form of Life*

In Benedict's early years, the form of monasticism favored in the West was that introduced by John Cassian in the early fifth century. Both the *Institutes* and the *Conferences* are mentioned in Benedict's rule. The Pachomian ideal of the coenobitic community as interpreted by St. Basil also influenced the hermit of Subiaco. But it was from Cassian that Benedict seems to have drawn the pattern of praying the Psalter in common worship at regular intervals during the day.

Benedict's monks, like Cassian's, were also to engage themselves in manual work as part of their spiritual discipline. The Benedictines, too, would emphasize the copying and preservation of manuscripts. With attention to letters came the impetus to foster learning. Daily reading of the Bible and the works of the Fathers were prescribed in the rule. With its unabashed commitment to the spirituality of the mind, later Benedictine monasticism would become

Europe's tutor, as the darkness of the Age of Invasions began to lift.

Although focused on order and discipline in the monastery, favoring the virtues of meekness, obedience, and humility, and organized along strict lines of authority, Benedict's Rule is not severe. From a purely material perspective, given the state of civil life in the sixth century, it provided an attractive alternative to barbarism or peasant subsistence farming. The middle class, from which many of Augustine's and Cassian's monks had come, had disappeared almost entirely. Although great wealth was still amassed in the hands of a few, most of the population of Europe had been reduced to grinding poverty. The monastery offered regularity, security, and sufficiency.

Spiritually, Benedict's Rule was tempered with the same insight into gospel equality that had animated Augustine's Rule. Special consideration was given to the poor, the sick, and the oppressed. Hospitality was recognized as a cardinal expression of charity and justice, and the presence of God was observed in the lives of the monks and nuns as well as the will of the abbot or abbess. If less radical than Augustine's charter of Christian liberty, Benedict's was more practical and its influence far greater. Except for the remote periphery of the Western world, wherever order and civility endured during the dangerous years from the sixth to the eleventh centuries, the sign of Benedict would lie over it.

It was at one of those edges of the known world that the other remarkable monastic movement of the Dark Ages had already begun its long career. For Celtic monasticism predates Benedict's, and perhaps that of Cassian and Honoratus as well. The first small communities were probably established by refugees or pilgrims from Egypt near outposts of Roman and therefore Christian Britain — Cornwall, Wales, and southern Scotland. Thus isolated, many may have survived for centuries in peaceful obscurity. But because of the accidental ministry of a single bishop, a middle-aged man who had no intention of founding a monastic empire, who labored far from Roman outposts, and who never saw Egypt, the unsuspected force of Celtic spirituality would someday burst from such monasteries and drench the southern wastes with Faith.

*Patrick:*
*Light in*
*the North*

In the year of Benedict's birth, Patrick of Ireland was an old man nearing his final days. Over a period of some thirty years, he had worked tirelessly to establish a church where there had been only scatterings of Christian slaves and refugees. He had apparently been preceded to the land called "Eriu" in 431 by another bishop, Palladius, who was sent by Pope Celestine to evangelize the Irish and prevent the spread of Pelagianism there from Britain. We know little more than that about Palladius, except that his mission seems to have ended badly.

Patrick's spirituality is known to us directly from two documents from his own hand, a letter of excommunication sent to an impenitent Christian king in Britain, Coroticus, who had attacked and enslaved some of Patrick's converts; and Patrick's *Confession*, a remarkable testament composed in rusty Latin toward the end of his life as a final statement of fidelity to Christ and the Church.[3]

As with Benedict, Patrick's major contribution to Christian history and spirituality would lie well beyond his own time. Two centuries after his death, the force of his spirit would affect the faith of all Europe. Understandably, later *Lives* of Patrick embroider and exaggerate the events of his life and ministry. But at the time of his death, about the year 491 (although there is serious conflict over dates among Patrician scholars), he was known only to the northern and eastern parts of Ireland itself and the British church of Northumbria, which had commissioned his apostolate.[4]

*The*
*Fugitive*

Patrick was most likely born in northwestern Britain early in the fifth century. His father, Calpurnius, was a deacon and a decurion — a local Roman official. His grandfather, Potitus, was a priest. Although reared a Christian with a smattering of Latin letters and education, Patrick had remained unimpressed until, barely sixteen, he was captured along with several family servants by Irish pirates who raided his father's country estate.

For six years, Patrick tended cattle for his Irish master, probably on the western coast of what is now Mayo. In his solitude, he relates in his *Confessions,* only his faith in God sustained him. Prayer became his constant companion. When about twenty-two, he was alerted in a dream that a means of escape was at hand. He fled overland nearly two hundred miles, perhaps to Bantry Bay, where he finally obtained passage on a trading ship. Landing on the coast of Gaul, now increasingly ravaged by Vandals and Huns, the traders traveled inland some twenty-eight days with their consignment of wolfhounds. Finally, Patrick escaped, and, after several years of wandering, made his way back to his parents' home in Britain.

Patrick may have studied for a time at Auxerre, from where St. Germanus exercised a form of spiritual oversight with regard to southern Britain, or even at Lérins, as some scholars have maintained. In any case, he was ordained a deacon, probably in Britain and possibly in order to succeed his father. But his destiny lay in the west. Again inspired by a dream, Patrick sought and obtained leave to evangelize the pagan Irish, but not without strenuous opposition from some of the British clergy, who objected to his lack of proper training. Towards the end of his life, such opposition would surface again, piercing the old man to the heart and occasioning the rough, magnificent *Confession.* Nevertheless, he was made bishop and, accompanied by several monks ordained as clergy, set out for the land of his former captivity.

Since Patrick was a Celt himself, if a somewhat Romanized one, his spirituality was not alien to the Irish. He had come to know God as Creator in the great natural beauty of the earth. Through dreams and visions, the divine Spirit informed his inner life, which he nurtured by meditative prayer and eventually the study of scripture. Compassionate, zealous, tender-hearted, he knew Christ's presence in the felt assurance of grace: "...again I saw him praying in me," he wrote in the *Confessions,* "and he was as it were within my body, and I heard him above me, that is, above the inner man, and there he was praying mightily with groanings. And meanwhile I was stupefied and astonished, and pondered who it could be that was praying in me. But at the end of the prayer he spoke as if he were the Spirit. And so I awoke, and remembered that the Apostle says, ...'The Lord is our advocate, and prays for us.' "

For almost forty years, Patrick labored to win the Irish to Christ. By the time of his death, about the year 490, the Irish church was established and thriving. Monasteries of men and women were beginning to flower the valleys and mountainsides. Within a century, as a gentle, relentless wave of Benedictines moved up from the south, an intensity of Celtic monks would fling itself across the north. Approaching each other like hands in prayer, they would encompass the pagan tribes of Europe with love and learning. The reconversion of the West had begun.

*Ordinary Spirituality*

Although the development of Western monasticism shines with particular luster in the twilight period after 476, it was then, and always would be, the occupation of a minority of Christians. The lives of ordinary women and men were surely brightened by the presence of the monasteries and the ministry of the monks and nuns. But their own spiritualities continued to be fostered primarily by the local church, with its sacramental life, worship, and community. Throughout the border lands, however, the number of capable bishops and clergy was dwindling. The Christian world had contracted defensively before the pagan onslaught.

Administratively, the center held remarkably firm, especially under Popes of the caliber of Leo I, Celestine, and especially Gregory the Great. Relying mainly on prayer and diplomatic skill, they worked tirelessly to protect the Christian churches from both the Arian Vandals and Visigoths as well as the pagan invaders. At the same time, they were confronted by incessant demands for doctrinal and juridical intervention from the Eastern Church, where controversy and schism threatened from within.

*Troubles in the East* While the West as a whole descended into post-imperial bleakness, Byzantium was approaching the full flower of its golden age. Despite the ordeals of the crusty Patriarch of Constantinople, John Chrysostom, who died of imperial ill treatment in 407, and the devious machinations of various theologians and patriarchs during the great Christological controversies of the fifth century, the spiritual life prospered, if not so noticeably as the material wealth of the Church.

Men wholly dedicated to God, such as the Stylites Simon and Daniel, exercised a profound influence on the lives of common folk as well as the deliberations of councils. At Ephesus in 431 and Chalcedon in 451, the fierce pressure of the wild-looking Egyptian monks provided decisive support for the adherents of Nicean orthodoxy in their struggles against a new threat.

For some time, tensions between the rival traditions of Antioch and Alexandria had been approaching critical proportions. The crisis came in 428, with the imperial appointment of a priest from Persia named Nestorius, a well-known preacher of Antioch, as Patriarch of Constantinople. A series of confrontations followed, eventually leading to the Councils of Ephesus and Chalcedon, Nestorius' downfall, and the estrangement of the East Syrian Church.

*Cyril and Nestorius* Nestorius was a disciple of Theodore of Mopsuestia and heir of the biblical tradition of Paul of Samosata, Lucian, and Arius. He was quickly perceived as a dangerous foe by defenders of the Alexandrian-Nicene tradition. His chief opponent and the architect of his destruction was the Patriarch of Alexandria, Cyril. A powerful politician and brilliant theologian, Cyril did not scruple to resort to intimidation and bribery when reason did not prevail.

A stern critic of Antiochene Christology, which tended to downplay the unity of natures in Christ, Cyril attacked Nestorius by letter and pamphlet. Nestorius was hardly adequate to the requirements of keen theological debate, being "barely literate" according to some accounts. Nor was the new Patriarch skilled at the imperial intrigue in which Cyril found his natural place. Not surprisingly, Nestorius was roundly condemned in 431 by the bishops of the First Council of Ephesus. He was duly deposed by the emperor, whose decision was assured by generous bribes from Alexandria. The theology codified at Nicea had triumphed again.

But the matter of Nestorius was not settled. A second council at Ephesus in 449 attempted to rehabilitate Nestorian doctrines, requiring yet another council at Chalcedon in 451 to set matters straight. The unfortunate consequence was a permanent and bitter estrangement between the Syrian Church and the rest of Christendom, followed by growing tension between Alexandria and Rome, where support for the campaign of Cyril and his successors had been considered lukewarm at best. Nestorius himself died in exile in 452.

Cyril, who had died in 444, was ultimately hailed as a champion of Orthodoxy and recognized in the West as a Doctor of the Church. But in the East, his reputation had been tarnished by his underhanded tactics. In 415, his endorsement of (if not connivance at) the murder of the Neoplatonic philosopher Hypatia at the hands of a Christian mob cast an indelible shadow over his subsequent career.

Although a pagan, Hypatia was the last great philosopher of Roman Alexandria and the teacher of many Christians, including the learned bishop, Synesius of Cyrene. The suspicious circumstances of her death, the memory of Cyril's bullying and bribes at Ephesus, as well as other questionable deeds, prompted Bishop Theodoret of Cyrrhus, one of his many theological adversaries, to celebrate his death as that of someone "born and bred to ruin the churches." Echoing the sentiments of many, Theodoret wrote to Domnus, the Patriarch of Antioch, that a large stone should be placed on Cyril's grave, "lest he come back and show his changeable mind once more."[5]

By the end of the century, both Alexandria and Antioch would have drifted into extreme positions with regard to their dispute over the divinity and humanity of Christ. The heretical tension between Nestorian thought (which eventually asserted two persons in Christ) and the "Monophysite" teaching of Alexandria (which insisted on a single divine nature in Christ) created an intellectual schizophrenia that only a powerful spirituality could bridge. And from the desert, as if on cue, there would soon appear a series of pseudonymous little books and letters that would not only establish a safe ground of the spirit in the midst of the theological wars. Someday, translated into Latin for the West by an Irish monk, they would also inaugurate the mystical revolution of the Middle Ages.

## NOTES

1. For a concise account of the end of classical antiquity, see Solomon Katz, *The Decline of Rome and the Rise of Medieval Europe* (Ithaca and London: Cornell University Press, 1955).
2. For an excellent introduction and translation, see Tarsicius J. Van Bavel, *The Rule of St. Augustine* (Garden City,NY: Image Books, 1986).
3. For a recent commentary on Patrick's spirituality, see Noel Dermot O'Donohue, O.C.D., *Aristocracy of Soul: Patrick of Ireland* (Wilmington, DE: Michael Glazier, 1986).
4. For a discussion of the controversies over the dates and career of St. Patrick, see especially Charles Thomas, *Christianity in Roman Britain* (Berkeley: University of California Press, 1981), pp. 307-46.
5. On Theodoret, see Theodoret of Cyrrhus, *A History of the Monks of Syria*, ed. cit., and *On Divine Providence*, ed. cit.

# From the World's End    9

N Christmas Day, 499, in fulfillment of a vow made to his Christian wife, the pagan Frankish king Clovis and his son, Theodoric, were baptized by Bishop Remegius in the cathedral at Rheims. Like another Constantine, Clovis had attributed his recent victory over the Alemanni to the Christian God. The meaning of that conceit, like that of Clovis' "conversion," had not been missed by imperial and ecclesiastical leaders.

Perhaps more importantly for the future of the Church in Europe, some three thousand of Clovis' troops followed their king into the baptistery at Rheims. For good or ill, the Dark Ages had reached a turning point as significant in the affairs of the City of Man as the wilderness journeys of Patrick and Benedict had been for the City of God. For during the sixth century, the necessary spiritual energy to carry on the long struggle to convert the barbarian invaders while preserving and consolidating remnants of classical Christian culture would come in abundance from the monks of Christian Ireland, the Benedictine movement, and the leadership of greatest pope of the age, himself a Benedictine as well as a saint.

In the East, meantime, even as the Empire began its final, slow descent into bureaucratic rigidity and religious formalism, springs of spiritual renewal were also rising in the deserts of Syria and Palestine.

*The Jesus Prayer*

Advocated for centuries in Egypt by desert monks, sometime in the fifth century short, non-discursive ("monologistic") prayer emerged in Syria as a powerful spiritual practice. It consisted fundamentally of a recollection of the presence of God aided by the repetition of the name of Jesus or a short formula such as "Lord Jesus Christ, Son of God, have mercy on me." In the following century, this *Jesus Prayer*, or "Prayer of the Heart," was especially promoted by St. Diadochus, the Bishop of Photike in northern Greece (ca. 475-550).[1]

Theologically, the background of the Jesus Prayer can be found in the Alexandrian tradition, especially as interpreted by Evagrius of Pontus (346-99) and the Macarian Homilies (ca. 400). It is centered on a profound devotion to the Holy Name of Jesus, the very utterance of which was believed (as in Acts 3:6, 16; 4:10, 12; cf. Mark 9:38 and Phil. 2:9-10) to have saving power. Humility and sorrow for sin (*penthos*) are conveyed by the appeal for mercy, also a scriptural element (cf. Ps. 51, Mark 10:47, Luke 19:38).[2]

Psychologically, these religious attitudes were complemented by a mantra-like repetition, sometimes associated with rhythmical breathing, which focused the mind but simultaneously evoked a pervasive awareness of God's presence. This habit of remembrance, much like the later Sufi practice of *dhikr*, led to a state of blissful tranquillity or rest — *hesychia*. Centuries later, a controversial spiritual school, the Hesychast movement, would take its name from this term.

In the meantime, the contemplative spirituality of the Jesus Prayer would be developed by generations of saints in Syria, Palestine, and Egypt — Barsanuphius and John, their disciple Dorotheus, Abba Philemon, and St. John Climacus, whose seventh-century *Ladder of Perfection* was one of the first attempts to compose a systematic spirituality of the monastic life.

The
Final
Synthesis

At the end of the fifth century, or the beginning of the sixth, a series of short works appeared, also in Syria, that would have an impact on Eastern and Western spiritual theology exceeding even that of the Jesus Prayer on practice. Claimed for one or another reason to have been written by the disciple of St. Paul and first bishop of Athens, Dionysius the "Areopagite" (see Acts 17:34), the works consist of four brief books — *the Divine Names, the Mystical Theology, the Celestial Hierarchy* and *the Ecclesiastical Hierarchy* — and a collection of ten letters.[3]

Pious or otherwise, the fiction was quickly detected by many orthodox theologians, who mistrusted the use of the Dionysian writings by their Monophysite opponents. But the genius and profundity of the doctrine of the "Pseudo-Dionysius" was likewise recognized by both Orthodox and Monophysite.

Endorsed and interpreted by St. Maximus the Confessor later in the sixth century, the Dionysian corpus came to exercise a major and lasting influence on Eastern spirituality. Introduced indirectly into the West by Pope Gregory the Great and more directly in the ninth-century translation by the Irish monk and scholar John Scottus (Eriugena), the Dionysian 'way' came to occupy a place of importance in medieval spirituality second only to that of the Bible itself.

The genius of Pseudo-Dionysius lay in his ability to synthesize the major elements of Alexandrian and Antiochene spiritual theology in a framework based on the Platonic philosophy of Athens. In effect, as a recent commentator has stated, he "absorbed and neutralized" Platonism as a pagan ideology. Far more than that, he revealed a sweeping, even cosmic panorama of creation as the setting for his vision of spiritual development and the manifold relations between God and the human soul.

Still, it is wide of the mark to describe the Dionysian writings as a true theological system. His gift was to articulate a dynamic spiritual structure based on scripture, the classical tradition of Alexandrian theology, and the dominant philosophy of the times. The *summas* of Christian theology still lay centuries ahead.

Overall, Dionysius' great paradigm of creation is an account of the ever more implicate orders or hierarchies that structure God's relationship with the world. These hierarchies exist in the midst of a dynamic movement of the universe out of God's creative energy and the return of all things to their divine origin. In themselves, Dionysius' orders are static. Levels or states of existence, they do not move, nor do human persons ordinarily move from one order to another as on the rungs of a ladder. Angels do not graduate to the rank of archangels. Whether for emperor, monk, or slave girl, spiritual development is a progressive movement towards God *within* the hierarchies. Motivated by love and empowered by grace, the spirit passes through stages of purification, enlightenment, and unification on its return to its eternal home, where, transformed into the image of God by the imitation of Christ, it will be "divinized" in union with God forever.

Controversial but fundamentally orthodox, Dionysius' vision was the logical product of centuries of theological development in Egypt, Palestine, Cappadocia, and Greece. Majestic in its scope, towering in its achievement, it lay at the furthest remove from the simple, almost rustic teaching of the desert monks. Yet there are important areas of convergence. And for centuries to come, the "Corpus Areopagiticum" would hold pride of spiritual place, especially in the West.

## The Negative Way

Although composing a commentary on *the Divine Names* would become a requirement for theological education in the Middle Ages, it was the slim *Mystical Theology* that would have the greatest impact spiritually. Although only one part of a dialectic of "positive," "symbolic," and "negative" approaches to the mystery of God, the *mystical* or "negative" theology epitomized the Way of Unknowing (*agnosia*) that had its roots in ancient Hebrew religion, had been developed by Philo, Clement of Alexandria, and Origen, and further refined by Athanasius and Gregory of Nyssa.

Such "unknowing" means that our truest and best knowledge of God in this life is a non-conceptual experience of God's illimitable, undefinable presence beyond the scope of all discursive reasoning or representation. Such awareness can occur only when the busy mind is still and receptive, having stripped away all its notions of what God is like — the "idols of the mind."

Dionysius thus comes in the end to a position much like that of the Hesychasts, who are so unlike him in other respects. It is this aspect of Dionysius' teaching that galvanized the Christian West when taken over in the fourteenth century by the great preacher and mystic, Meister Eckhart. It also informs the English spiritual masterpiece of the same period, *The Cloud of Unknowing*, the writings of St. John of the Cross, and many other spiritual works before and since.

*Art as Sacrament*

The emphasis on non-conceptual knowledge at this period of Eastern spiritual history stands in significant contrast to two other major developments — positive theology and religious art. Although the *via positiva* or "way of images" is a valid, even prior requirement for a mystical, "negative" theology, the artistic aspect of Byzantine spirituality is even more important, for at this time the art of making *icons*, holy images of Christ and the saints, as well as scenes from the Bible, attained its first and possibly finest perfection.[4]

Significantly, Byzantine iconography avoids graphic representation of God — surely a reflection of mystical *agnosia*. But the fervent belief of the faithful in the power of the visual image to evoke the *presence* of God was not only parallel to that in the power of the Holy Name, but also led to a sacramental veneration of these artistic creations. One result was a severe reaction against icons a century later which led to the destruction of many and a movement to outlaw them — *iconoclasm*. A similar "puritan" movement a thousand years later would deprive the Western Church of some of its greatest treasures of art and literature.

As a defense against such unbalanced reactions, the Christian Church as a whole has not only confirmed the primary place of positive theology but also protected religious art against any mystical or moralistic excess that would attempt to eliminate it. The way of Names and Images is part of the great dialectic by which the human heart as well as the mind approaches the mystery of God.

For Dionysius also, in his recapitulation of the mystical theology of Alexandria and the Cappadocian Fathers in the framework of the pagan mystic, Plotinus, God's nature and presence are revealed to us not only by the negation of images and concepts. All creation is charged with divine wisdom, power, and presence, which makes the universe itself a theophany. The scriptures, rites, and sacraments of the Church, as well as the ministrations of angels, more directly communicate the saving light and life of God to the human spirit. But the encompassing unity of spiritual perfection is attained in the immediate encounter of the soul with God, in depths of experience beyond all images and concepts, much less material symbols. It is attained, moreover, not by human effort, but by the gracious gift of the same unknowable God.

Despite the fundamental orthodoxy of the Dionysian writings, their use by the Monophysites and certain theological deficiencies (for instance, in Christology), as well as their incorporation of Neoplatonist elements, made them suspect to many Christians. The wisdom of this masterful synthesis was preserved for the greater Church largely through the efforts of one of their earliest commentators, a monk-scholar whose own orthodoxy would ultimately cost him his life.

**Maximus the Confessor**

Born around 580 in Constantinople, Maximus was probably educated there at the Imperial Academy, where a revival of Aristotelian philosophy was underway.[5] Having become a monk in 613 after a successful career in the imperial civil service, he moved to Africa in 626 during the Persian invasions. In Rome by 645, his influence at the Lateran Council of 649 contributed to the condemnation of the Monothelite heresy, which proposed that Christ had only a single will, rather than both a divine and a human will.

Monotheletism was designed by imperial officials at a critical moment to bridge the gap between the Alexandrian Monophysites and the Orthodox Church. More a political than a theological solution, it was quickly rejected by the Patriarch of Jerusalem and in Rome. Eventually, the Emperor had to withdraw the position, which was condemned at the Ecumenical Council of Constantinople in 681. Long before that, however, Maximus was arrested for his opposition to the "imperial heresy." In 653, he was flogged, his tongue and his right hand were cut off, and he was sent into exile. He died in 662, a martyr to the orthodox faith.

As a theologian, one of Maximus' major contributions was to interpret the mystical doctrine of St. Gregory of Nyssa and Pseudo-Dionysius in Aristotelian rather than Neoplatonic terms. Thus he avoided some of the pitfalls still associated in the minds of many with the dominant pagan philosophy, while preserving and developing the classical spiritual tradition. Maximus incidentally showed that the fundamental spirituality of the Eastern Church could be disengaged from *any* philosophical frame of reference, which functions as a means of organization and interpretation, but does not determine the teaching as a whole. In any event, because of his sanctity and orthodoxy, Maximus' endorsement guaranteed acceptance of Dionysian spirituality in both East and West.

**The Great Pope**

During the sixth and seventh centuries, isolated saints and scholars of the Western Church, such as Isidore of Seville and the Anglo-Saxon Benedictine monk Bede "the Venerable," kept alive the twin lamps of learning and sanctity. Such figures seem almost exceptional after the great outpouring of the golden age of Byzantium.

Two outstanding instances made all the difference, however. First was the first pope named Gregory, surnamed "the Great," a saint and doctor of the Church and the last of the Latin Fathers. The other was a whole host of saints and scholars from the Celtic churches of Britain and especially Ireland.

Gregory was born to power and privilege as a senator's son around 540.  Made Prefect of the City in 573, he underwent a conversion experience, sold off his inheritance, and, having given the proceeds to the poor, entered one of the seven monasteries he had founded.  Not long afterwards, the pope appointed him one of the seven deacons of Rome, then representative to the court at Constantinople.  On his return to Rome, Gregory was first elected abbot of his monastery, then pope, a position he transformed into that of leader of the Christian West.

A man of endless energy, Gregory devoted himself to vast projects of civil restoration, established "a separate peace" with the invading Lombards, and effectively emancipated the West from Byzantine control.  In 596, he undertook the conversion of England, sending forty monks from his famous monastery under the able if stodgy leadership of Augustine, the first bishop of Canterbury.

But it was Gregory's sermons, scriptural commentaries, and liturgical writings that established his reputation for sanctity and learning.  He accepted and popularized the teachings of Pseudo-Dionysius, although his spirituality was more deeply influenced by Augustine of Hippo and the Benedictine tradition.  Gregory's contribution to spirituality is found not least in his encouragement of church music, the ordinary Latin chant of the Roman Church receiving his name as an enduring tribute of gratitude.

*Celtic Monks and Missionaries*

Gregory strengthened and extended the Church from the Western center.  Meanwhile, at the very edge of the known world, Celtic monks and nuns of Britain, Ireland, and Scotland had inaugurated a centuries' long effort to evangelize Europe from the North.  At least as much the outgrowth of their spontaneous, generous, and heroic spirituality as a planned attempt to spread the Gospel, the Celtic mission was no less successful for that.  Perhaps more. Independent but disciplined and inventive, these evangelists preached, baptized, and established monasteries wherever they went. Columban's monasteries alone dot the map of Europe from Belgium to Italy.[6]

As customary, the Church had traveled to Gaul and Britain along lines chartered by wine merchants and traders. Missionaries, books, and beliefs traveled with tin traders, slaves, and even military and government officials. Legend has it that the Christian faith was first established at Glastonbury (Ynys Witrin) by Joseph of Arimathea himself, who it is also believed was a tin merchant accustomed to the Bristol channel that divides Wales from Cornwall and Britain.

One charming legend found in Somerset holds that Joseph, who was Jesus' great uncle, brought him and his mother to the region of Glastonbury where they lived for several years during the "hidden life" before returning to Judea. The visionary poet William Blake alludes to this belief in his great and famous hymn from *Milton*:

And did those feet in ancient time
Walk upon England's mountains green?
And was the holy Lamb of God
On England's pleasant pastures seen?

However Christianity came, early communities were solidly established in southeastern Britain by the end of the third century, and perhaps even earlier at Carlisle. Monasticism appeared by the end of the fourth century. Connections were strong with the continental and, later, Irish churches, whose influence was felt particularly along the western coast from Cornwall to the Orkneys. The tenor of Celtic monasticism was thus Eastern, and the great abbots were more like Cassian and Martin of Tours than Augustine or Benedict. Although not the earliest, one of the most influential and interesting of them became the Patron of Celtic Britain.

*The Apostle of Wales*

Of St. David (or Sant Dewi, in Welsh), little is known from his own times. But by the early Middle Ages, his reputation as the first archbishop of the British Church had magnified the few known events to the level of myth. His real and lasting achievement was to assure unity and orthodoxy in the midst of disruption and doubt. In the face of political and ecclesiastical encroachment by Irish colonists on one hand and land-hungry Anglo-Saxons on the other, he focused the disparate churches of western Britain into a gathered whole. He also resisted inroads of Pelagianism, which had reappeared as a divisive force in the British church.[7]

David was a descendent of the great Celtic hero Cunedda, who had expelled Irish invaders during the period of Roman occupation. Born early in the sixth century at Henfynyw, his mother was St. Non. According to tradition, David was first educated by Guistilianus. Later he is said to have become a disciple of St. Paulinus, himself a disciple of the great St. Germanus of Auxerre. Having chosen the life of monk, David eventually founded twelve monasteries, the most famous being that at Mynyw (Menevia) in the "vale of Rosina" at the very tip of the Dyfyd peninsula.

David's reputation for sanctity was widespread. Monks from Ireland, including the great St. Finnian of Clonnard, crossed the little sea to remain under his direction, often for years. But unlike other famous monasteries in Ireland and Britain, St. David's was famed not for its learning, but for its austerity and holiness. David and his monks often pulled the yoke in place of oxen. At times, they prayed standing in sea water up to their necks. Subsisting on a diet of bread, vegetables, and water, David and those of his companions able to endure such a vigorous form of life in the temperate climate of Wales were known as *Aquati* ("watermen"). His garb was similarly spare: animal skins in mild weather, with a few furs added in the often harsh winter months.

Such ascetical heroism was not undertaken for purposes of ostentation or misguided notions of reparation. Like their earlier contemporaries in the deserts of Egypt and Syria, from whom they had received their inspiration and form of life, the Celtic monks demonstrated their singleness of devotion in such ways. As often seems the case with saints, they found such extreme practices somehow necessary to overcome any possible distractions from long hours of prayer and meditation. Their powers of concentration were proportionately strengthened, in some cases to the heights of the masters of India and Tibet.

According to an account of his life written in 1095 by a monk named Rhigyfarch, David was elected bishop by popular acclaim at a synod held at Brefi during a crisis brought about by a reappearance of the Pelagian heresy. His monastery was declared the "metropolis" for Britain where his successors would also be regarded as archbishop. Far from being a royal prince of the Middle Ages, however, David was at most a tribal bishop, almost a Christian priest-king. His crozier a sapling, he went about his pastoral work carrying his bell, Bangu — "the dear loved one."

Over the centuries, the figure of this simple holy man came to fill a much grander role than he would have tolerated, but one calculated to establish the claims of the Welsh church against those of Canterbury and even of Rome. Thus, after his death, the monastic site at Menevia, St. David's, became a place of pilgrimage. A great cathedral was begun there in 1181, David's bones being placed in a special tomb where they still lie in peace amid the ruins of centuries of war, conquest, and calamity.

*The
Great
Invasion*

In the sixth and seventh centuries, Irish Christianity and its monastic tradition produced several generations of saints, scholars, and leaders. The spiritual strength of these men and women would fuel the reconversion of much of Europe, large areas of which were left pagan after the age of invasions. Among the great Celtic saints now mainly forgotten in the Romanized West were Brendan (484-583), Columba of Iona (521-597), Finnian of Ulster (495-579), Kieran (fl. 545), Cainnech (Kenneth) of Scotland (517-600), Kentigern (fl. 603), Finbarr (fl. 623), Cronan (fl. 626), Aidan of Lindisfarne (fl. 651), his successor Colman (676), and many outstanding women such as Ita (fl. 570) and the formidable Abbess Hilda of Whitby.

The patriarch of Irish monasticism was Enda of Aran (450?-535), a prince warrior of Oriel. When his fiancée died suddenly, he was persuaded by his sister Fanchea, a nun, to enter the priesthood. After training at Ninian's monastery at Candida Casa in Rosnat (southwestern Scotland), he obtained a grant of the Aran Islands from the King of Cashel. There he and his disciples lived in great austerity, disdaining even the use of fire. Among those he influenced were St. Brendan the Navigator and Finnian of Clonnard.

Seventh-century missionaries to France included Fiacre, Kilian, and Fursey. Another Kilian was martyred in Germany in 689. St. Gall established a world-famous monastery in Switzerland. Perhaps the greatest of all was Columban (543-615), whose establishments extended from Belgium to Switzerland and Italy, the most famous being the great monastery at Bobbio.

*Bride of Christ*

Double monasteries were often found in Celtic lands, the most famous being that of the co-patron of Ireland, St. Brigid of Kildare (ca. 450-523). Known as the "Mary of the Gael," she is one of the most beloved of saints. The daughter of a Leinster chieftain, and both beautiful and impetuous, she was named for the goddess of fire and educated by a druid. Her parents, it is believed, were baptized by St. Patrick himself. Spurning the husband selected by her father, she dedicated herself to Christ as a nun together with seven other young women.

As befit a chieftain's daughter and heir of the druids, Brigid was consecrated by two bishops, Saints Mel and Macaille. According to legend, Mel accidentally read over her the prayer for consecrating a bishop, to the astonishment of his colleague. In any event, Brigid would soon exercise episcopal powers, ruling the double monastery at Kildare with her great friend, the bishop St. Conleth, next to whom she was buried. Like her later namesake, St. Bridgit of Sweden, and St. Catherine of Siena centuries later, Brigid also counseled the mighty, organized convents, obtained freedom for captives, and won renown for her charity to the poor. A skilled poet, as befits one druid-taught, she became the patroness of that art.

So famous was Brigid for her learning and sanctity that under the diminutive of her name, Bride, she was honored in the place-names of churches and towns throughout Celtic nations as well as England, France, and Italy. Her office was said in Germany, Switzerland, and Italy. In Piacenza a beautiful and famous church was also built in her honor. So great was her fame, that in time, even an island off the coast of Japan and a peak in the Himalayan mountains received the name of Bride.

*A Passion for God*

Animating the spirituality of the Celts, particularly their monasticism, was a profound conviction of the living presence of God mediated through scripture, nature, sacrament, and the word of the Gospel preached. Their learning, art, and song were placed in wholehearted service of God and the Church. Nothing was done by halves.

Beyond producing many of the greatest treasures of the world's art, such as the Book of Kells, the Ardagh chalice, the Cong crozier and the earliest vernacular mythology in Europe, such enthusiasm overflowed into a love of men and women, children, the poor and outcasts, even animals, that swept across northern Europe during the seventh century like a wall of holy fire from Iceland to Italy and even beyond. For a century the Celtic invasion continued, until slowed by the devastating attacks of Viking raiders and halted by the land-hunger of newly Christianized kings who cast eager eyes towards the green isles of the Western Sea. A new age was beginning.

# NOTES

1. For a brief but valuable treatment, see Kallistos Ware, "The Origins of the Jesus Prayer: Diadochus, Gaza, Sinai," Jones et al., *The Study of Spirituality*, pp. 175-84.
2. See Irénée Hausherr, *Penthos: The Doctrine of Compunction in the Christian East* (Kalamazoo: Cistercian Publications).
3. The attribution to the first bishop of Athens was not pointless, since the author was probably a Christian Neoplatonist who had attended the Academy there. For a recent translation and commentary, see *Pseudo-Dionysius: The Complete Works*, trans. by Colm Luibheid and Paul Rorem (New York: Paulist Press, 1987). See also Andrew Louth, *Denys the Areopagite* (London and Wilton, CT: Geoffrey Chapman/Morehouse-Barlow, 1989), Andrew Louth, *The Origins of the Christian Mystical Tradition from Plato to Denys* (New York: Oxford University Press, 1981), pp. 159-78, and I. P. Sheldon-Williams, "The Greek Christian Platonist Tradition from the Cappadocians to Maximus and Eriugena," *The Cambridge History of Later Greek and Early Medieval Philosophy*, ed. A. H. Armstrong (Cambridge: The University Press, 1970), pp. 457-72.
4. For a succinct statement of the mystical esthetics of icon veneration, see Sheldon-Williams, art. cit., pp. 506-17, and Kallistos Ware, "The Spirituality of the Icon," *The Study of Spirituality*, pp. 195-98.
5. See Sheldon-Williams, art. cit., pp. 492-505, and Andrew Louth, "Maximus the Confessor," in *The Study of Spirituality*, pp. 190-94.
6. For an overview of the history of the Celtic churches and their missionary work, see John T. McNeill, *The Celtic Churches* (Chicago: The University of Chicago Press, 1974) and Kathleen Hughes and Ann Hamlin, *Celtic Monasticism* (New York: Seabury, 1981).
7. An excellent and perhaps the only treatment of St. David's life and work is that by E. G. Bowen, *Dewi Sant: Saint David* (Cardiff: University of Wales Press, 1983). See also G. H. Doble, *Lives of the Welsh Saints* (Cardiff: University of Wales Press, 1971), pp. 54-55 and passim.

# The Rebirth of Christendom

# 10

CLOVIS, THE BRILLIANT AND RUTHLESS KING of the Salian Franks and nominal Christian, succeeded in overthrowing and annexing the Visigothic kingdom of Toulouse in 507. He thus inaugurated the unification of France as well as the Merovingian dynasty (named for the legendary Salian chief, Merovech). The emperor, Anastasius, recognized him as honorary consul in 511, but Clovis died the same year. Clotilde, his widow, retired to the Abbey of St. Martin at Tours, where until her death some thirty years later, she continued her saintly activities.

For over fifty years, the nascent unity of Merovingian Gaul was disrupted by deadly power struggles among Clovis' sons and grandsons. Eventually, in 623, Pepin of Landen, mayor of the palace of Austrasia, forced the succession of Dagobert, the elder son of Clovis' son, Lothar II, thus paving the way for the usurpation of the throne by his own descendants, the Carolingians.

Pepin's illegitimate grandson, Charles Martel, became mayor of the Frankish palace in 715. An outstanding military leader from whom the great dynasty acquired its name, he successfully halted the Muslim invasion of Europe at the battle of Tours and Poitiers in 732. He also defeated and annexed the Kingdom of Burgundy three years later, finally uniting the Merovingian kingdoms under one rule.

Charles died in 741. He was succeeded as mayor by his son, Pepin the Short, who would depose the last Merovingian king, Childeric III, in 751. Pepin's son, Charles I, "the Great" or "Charlemagne" (742?-814), not only inherited the throne of the Franks in 768, but on Christmas Day in the year 800, had himself crowned new Emperor of the West in Rome by Pope Leo III.

With the birth of the "Holy Roman Empire," the Dark Ages came to an end, despite remaining years of struggle and terrorism — the first Viking raids on the Irish coasts had begun in 795. Practically all of Europe would soon fall prey to the rapine and slaughter of the Norsemen. Even Paris and Rome would be sacked. Political and eventually religious schism with the Eastern Empire may have been assured by Charlemagne's coronation. But his Carolingian "renaissance" also ushered in a century of dynamic growth in Europe, a prelude to the burgeoning of faith, scholarship, and the arts that would be called one day "the Middle Ages."

*The Carolingian Renaissance* Charlemagne remains one of the great figures of European history — military commander, statesman, educational reformer, and dedicated Christian prince. His vision of a new Roman empire was surprisingly international. Among his advisors, scholars, and the leaders he sought to reinvigorate the Church were Anglo-Saxons, Spaniards, Germans, Italians, and Celts from Ireland, Scotland, and Britain. And if the spirituality of the Carolingian epoch remained mainly monastic, change was already on the horizon with the development of the famous palace schools at Aachen and Laon. For there at least the rudiments of a classical education were provided for students from ranks of the laity as well as budding monks and clerics.

Two dazzling stars, Alcuin and John the Scot, an English monk and an Irish scholar, obscure a host of other luminaries such as Theodulf of Orléans, Hilduin, and Hincmar of Reims who populated the courts of Charlemagne and his descendants. Not without reason. Alcuin (735-804) was an outstanding teacher, scholar, and church leader. John Scottus was the most brilliant and daring Christian philosopher between Augustine and Thomas Aquinas. (The redundant Latin sobriquet *Eriugena* means "born in Eriu," i.e., Ireland, where the Scotti were an ancient and extensive tribe.)

*Alcuin: the Heritage of English Monasticism*
A native of Northumbrian Deira rather than the more Celtic Bernicia, Alcuin was nevertheless educated at York in the Celtic tradition as were Saints Cuthbert and Hilda. Like them and Bede, he held Irish scholars and missionaries in high regard, but also shared with Bede a low opinion of British Christianity in general. Alcuin's spiritual temperament was really Benedictine, and it was that monastic tradition which he favored both as master of the cathedral school in York and later as advisor and tutor of Charlemagne.

In almost every respect, Alcuin was a transition figure. He stands between the Celtic and English church traditions, between the Dark Ages and the Middle Ages, even between the Church and the Holy Roman Empire of succeeding generations. He is not easy to categorize. A chance meeting with Charlemagne in Parma in 781 led to an invitation for Alcuin to undertake organizing the palace school. In 796, after years of laboring to restore classical erudition to the new Empire, he was made Abbot of Tours and allowed to retire peacefully to the cloister he loved.

One of Alcuin's students also became an illustrious teacher and church leader — Rabanus Maurus (776-856), poet, educator, canonist, and theologian, later the Abbot of Fulda and Archbishop of Mainz, and reputed composer of the great hymn "Veni Sancte Spiritus." He, in turn, passed the torch of learning to Walafrid Strabo (808-849), a monk and later Abbot of Reichenau, also famed as a poet, theologian, and scholar.

John
Scottus
Eriugena

John of Ireland's influence on spirituality was more profound and lasting than Alcuin's, less because of his original works than his translations and interpretations of the writings of the great figures of the Alexandrian mystical tradition.[1]  It was largely through his efforts that the mystical Neoplatonism of the Eastern Church entered the Latin West.  Not surprisingly, those who paid the keenest attention were the mystics.

In 758, copies of the works of Dionysius the Areopagite were sent to Pepin the Short by Pope Paul I.  Other copies were brought West by Iconoclast refugees after the Second Council of Nicea in 787.  In 827, the Eastern Emperor Michael the Stammerer sent copies to Louis the Pious, Charlemagne's third son and ruling heir. Although he lacked his father's executive abilities, Louis had continued Charlemagne's efforts to further learning in the new Empire as well as to strengthen the organization and prestige of the Church.  Among other achievements, in 838 he employed Hilduin, Abbot of the Monastery of St. Denis, to translate the Dionysian corpus, with less than satisfactory results.

Over fifty international scholars had gravitated to the imperial court of Charlemagne and his heirs, among them about a dozen Irish monks and refugees.  Among them, John the Scot stood out for his brilliance and daring.  Whether or not he was a monk, his breadth of learning and skill at Greek were manifest, and in 860, Charles the Bald, Louis' son, commissioned him to attempt another translation of the Dionysian writings.

John's work was not only successful; it opened the floodgates of Neoplatonic Christian mysticism of the Eastern Church to the West. He next translated the commentaries of Maximus the Confessor and writings of Gregory of Nyssa.  He was literally absorbed by his work — one way or another, John of Ireland became a Neoplatonic Christian mystic.

His major work was the *Periphyseon* ("On the Division of Nature"), a monumental, five-volume scriptural, theological, and philosophical treatise on creation.  Structurally, it conforms to the dynamic Christian Neoplatonic vision of the emergence of the universe out of the creative mind of God and its return there transformed by conformity to the image of God in Christ. A surprisingly original work for the time, John's sources included Augustine, Ambrose, Marius Victorinus, and Boethius as well as Origen, Gregory of Nyssa, and Maximus the Confessor, as well as Pseudo-Dionysius.

Long and difficult, the *Periphyseon* eventually elicited charges of pantheism and other heresies against its author when read by less well-educated minds in subsequent centuries. But its importance lay less in its orthodoxy, which is now recognized to be generally solid, than in the fact that through it, Eastern Christian Neoplatonism successfully entered the West at the very dawning of the Middle Ages.

John the Scot's influence on later medieval theologians and spiritual writers was profound, not least because of his translation of the Areopagite, whose spurious apostolic authority was generally accepted in the West even after it was exposed by Peter Abelard in the twelfth century. But the Irishman's popularity with unorthodox writers such as Berengar of Tours, Gilbert of Poitiers, Almaric of Bène, and David of Dinant also brought his writings into disrepute with Church leaders. As much misunderstood as those of Origen had been and Eckhart's would be, his teachings were condemned at the Councils of Vercelli in 1050 and Rome in 1059, and finally in a Bull of Pope Honorius III in 1225.

For John, as for Dionysius, Gregory of Nyssa, and the major spiritual writers of the East as well as his own Celtic tradition, all creation is a theophany — a revelation of God under some sensible appearance, yet one also concealing the divine nature. Thus, he claims, through ordinary experience, we may know *that* God is, but not *what* God is. Our awareness of God as present to us in the depths of our own spirit is also a "dark" knowledge, an "unknowing." It is by entering this "cloud of unknowing" in faith and love that we experience God's presence in this life. And this, the ancient tradition teaches, is the heart and meaning of contemplative prayer.

*Britain:*
*The Parting*
*of the*
*Ways*

In 597, the year of Columcille's death on Iona, Augustine, the Italian missionary of Pope Gregory, arrived in Kent to undertake the conversion of the Anglo-Saxons. His success was limited, but the confluence of Celtic and English missions produced a Christian momentum that would eventually overcome all opposition, even, in time, that of the Viking Danes. But it also created turbulence, especially in the North, where the royal court of Northumbria was divided between the Celtic practices of King Oswy and the English customs of his Kentish Queen, Eanflaeda.

In 663 Oswy convoked a synod to resolve the conflict — superficially concerning disputes over the calculation of the date for Easter and the shape of the monastic tonsure. A deeper issue lay in the struggle for dominance between the two rival churches, whose spiritualities were in many respects as different as their language and customs.

In 601, St. Paulinus had been sent by Pope Gregory to Anglo-Saxon Britain (or England, as that part of the island was now called) to assist Augustine's mission. As bishop in York, he began work on the great cathedral there. But when Paulinus returned to Kent in 633 with Queen Ethelburga, King Oswald sent for Aidan, an Irish monk of Iona, to revive the missionary work Paulinus had begun. Made bishop in 635, he established his see at Lindisfarne, an island off the coast of Northumbria. There he also founded a school which included among its pupils twelve English boys who would in time become leaders of the English church. Among them were St. Chad, his brother St. Cedd, and St. Wilfrid, all future bishops.

Aidan and his successors, Saints Finan (d. 661) and Colman (d. 676) were Irish monks of Iona, and their custom was Celtic. Colman especially resisted the efforts of Queen Eanfleada and her Kentish followers to replace the Celtic practices favored by King Oswy with those of Rome. The English had a powerful champion, however, in Wilfrid, who had accepted the Roman tradition as a young man many years before at Canterbury.

In 653, Wilfrid had traveled to Rome with Benedict Biscop. Entering a Benedictine monastery, he remained in Lyons for three years. In 656, he was elected abbot of the monastery of Ripon in Northumbria, whose abbot, Eata, had returned to Melrose with St. Cuthbert and other Celtic monks when Roman observance was imposed by order of King Aldfrid. Wilfrid's presence at the Synod of Whitby in 664 must have been regarded as a dire omen by Colman, Hilda, and their supporters.

*The Synod of Whitby*

Saints opposed saints in the debate. Colman argued that Celtic practices were based on the ancient custom of the Apostle John. Wilfrid retorted, perhaps even more erroneously, that the Roman usage was that of St. Peter and appealed to the Council of Nicea. Oswy conceded, fearing to resist the keeper of the keys of heaven.

Although Oswy, Hilda, and many other adherents of the Celtic Church loyally adopted the Roman practices of the English Church, Colman resigned his see and with several of his monks left Lindisfarne for Iona and Ireland. To the dismay of native British Christians, who were engaged in a far more desperate struggle to preserve their lands and way of life, ecclesiastical ascendancy in Britain was thus secured for the English Church.

In Ireland itself, where the primacy of Rome had been neither doubted nor imposed, conversion to the new method of calculating Easter was accepted as a matter of course. But although the Irish Church would maintain its Celtic character and spirituality for many centuries more, the Synod of Whitby had raised a rock against which it, too, would someday flounder.

*Benedictine Evangelization and Agrarian Reform* The gradual replacement of Celtic monasticism in Britain by its Benedictine rival, with its vast spiritual network and strong ties to Roman obedience, was not an exceptional or isolated event. For over a century, Benedictine monasticism had been spreading slowly northward from Italy into the Gallic areas now identified with the Franks. Similarly, missionary monks such as the English bishop and martyr Boniface (680-754) made lasting spiritual and cultural inroads into densely pagan areas of Germany.

The reconquest of barbarian Europe by often newly and not too thoroughly Christianized kings was also followed by the establishment of monasteries, whose monks drained the marshes, cleared forested areas, and tilled the ancient fields. Christian Europe grew up around abbeys.

During the Carolingian renaissance, Benedictine monasticism entered a second spring as it was virtually refounded by saints such as Benedict of Aniane (750-821). A member of the court of both Pepin the Short and Charlemagne, Benedict became a monk in 773. Six years later, he founded a monastery on his property at Aniane. Soon it became the center of monastic reform, surpassed in time only by the great abbey of Cluny. Even at the great monasteries such as Bobbio, Benedict's Rule came to supercede that of the Celtic founders. The ancient Abbey of Luxeuil, founded by Columban in 590 and destroyed by the Moors in 732, was reestablished by Charlemagne under Benedictine rule. Many other Celtic monasteries were either refounded or converted, especially in England, where the Benedictine spring was in full bloom.

*Early English Spirituality* Under Benedictine tutelage, Anglo-Saxon Christianity produced a vigorous spirituality and a host of saints, who, if fewer than their Celtic rivals, were no less learned or renowned. Not unexpectedly, many of England's earliest saints were monks and nuns as well as missionary bishops. But a surprising number were also from various royal families, such as Bishop Aldhelm and

Kings Ethelbert of Kent, Oswald and Oswin of Northumbria, and Ethelbert of the East Angles — the latter three also martyrs. Women saints of royal families include the Abbesses Hilda and Etheldreda (or Audrey). Other notable women saints of the period were the Abbesses Werbergh and Ethelburga, who, like Hilda and Etheldreda, governed double monasteries.

St. Benedict Biscop (628-90), a friend and companion of St. Wilfrid, is considered the father of English monasticism. A Northumbrian by birth, Benedict was reared in the royal court at York. Accompanying Wilfrid to Rome in 666, he became a monk at Lérins. Three years later, however, he returned to England with St. Theodore of Tarsus, the Greek Archbishop of Canterbury. There, he became abbot of the monastery of Saints Peter and Paul.

In all, Benedict made five journeys to Rome, assuring the establishment of a truly Roman, Benedictine-guided church in northern England. He established many monasteries, including Wearmouth and Jarrow, and there introduced the use of the Roman chant known later as Gregorian. The most famous of his students came to him at the age of seven, an English boy the world would come to know and revere forever as Bede the Venerable, the earliest and greatest of English church historians and scholars.

One of the most charming stories of early English spirituality concerns St. Caedmon (d. 680). A simple herdsman at Hilda's Whitby Abbey, he would excuse himself after meals on feast days when the harp was passed among the community so that each could perform a song, for he was unable to play or sing. Bede, who recorded the account, suggests that he had a severe speech impediment. One night, hiding in the cattle barn out of shame, he dreamed that a voice called on him to sing.

"I cannot sing," the herdsman replied.
"Nevertheless, you must sing to me."
"What must I sing?"
"Sing of the beginning of things, of creation."

And Caedmon heard himself singing of God the Creator. When he awoke, he remembered the song and added several verses. When Hilda and the others learned of his vision, they asked Caedmon to compose another song based on a passage of scripture which they read to him. The following day, when his new song was performed to their satisfaction, he was invited to become a monk of the abbey. He remained there the rest of his life, composing songs and poems on themes of Christian history and hope — the father of Anglo-Saxon Christian poetry.

*Alfred: Greatness in England*

Like Charlemagne a generation before, but without the imperial trappings, Alfred, King of the West Saxons from 871 until his death in 899, not only successfully resisted the military conquest of his Christian homeland, in this instance by the Danes, but advanced both the cause of religious reform and scholarship. Gathering a band of international scholars to his court, he fostered translations from Latin works, some of which he even undertook himself. He founded several monasteries and planned the reorganization of dioceses. His hopes for monastic reform in England were perhaps premature, but not, ultimately, vain.

*Darkness in the East*

During the sixth and seventh centuries, as Europe struggled out of the carnage and waste of the barbarian invasions, the Eastern Empire and its Church still flourished. Led by his brilliant General Belisarius, the armies of Justinian (483-565, emperor from 527) were able to reclaim much of the territory of the Mediterranean basin that had been wrested away by Persians, Vandals, Goths, and Visigoths. Carthage was retaken in the summer of 533, Rome in 536, and Ravenna fell in 540.

Although orthodoxy prevailed in the empire as a whole, the Monophysite heresy remained strong throughout the East, with its own bishops, churches, and monasteries, spreading as far as Nubia and southern India. Efforts to end the schism by the Chalcedonian Emperor Maurice (582-602) were largely unavailing. Nestorian missionaries also spread eastward from Syria, reaching India and western China by the seventh century.

Following the murder of Maurice and his family by Phocas, the Eastern Empire fell under the rule of a succession of unworthy leaders. Persia remounted its war, nibbling away the eastern frontier. In 614, Jerusalem itself fell to the pagans. A truly new era began, however, with the advent of Muhammad (580-629) and in 634, the Jihad, the Holy War of Islam.

*The Rise of Islam*

From its original home in Arabian Medina, the Muslim tide swept inexorably over Egypt and North Africa, across the strait of Gibraltar, and by 711 had penetrated deeply into Spain and France. To the north and east, Arab armies pushed into Palestine, Persia, Syria, and what is now Turkey.

Constantinople was soon an island of Orthodox Christianity in a sea of hostile Islamic states. Only its strategic location saved the great city from conquest, for it could be provisioned by sea. There, and in parts of Greece and Armenia, "Byzantium" would endure for another eight hundred years. Pockets of Monophysite and Coptic Christianity would also survive in Egypt, Palestine, and Syria. Otherwise the vast empire of Constantine, Theodosius, and Justinian was now little more than a name and a memory of glory.

*The Image Breakers*

By the middle of the eighth century, as Benedictine monasticism entered its second springtime in Charlemagne's new Empire, the monastic spirituality of the Eastern church had already given way to a new, militant spirit that would not appear in the West until two centuries later with the Crusades.

The iconoclastic movement that shook the foundations of orthodox Eastern Christianity from about 725 to 843 had its roots in the apophatic or "negative" theology that stretched back through Dionysius to Gregory of Nyssa, Philo, and the ancient Hebrews' aversion to "graven images" alleged to represent God. The issues ran very deep and are in some respects perennial — the desire to know God, and the impossibility of doing so; the place of art in worship and spirituality; the lure of idolatry, mistaking the sign for the signified; and the threat of magic and superstition, using the sign to manipulate the signified. Perhaps, at bottom, the question is whether the world of matter is redeemed and therefore redemptive — or should "worship in spirit and truth" transcend all material embodiment? Is creation a sacrament of God's presence, a theophany?

Icons had long been an important element in Eastern liturgy and spirituality.[2] The movement against them became serious under Emperor Leo III, "the Isaurian" or Syrian — a capable, popular ruler and the first oriental emperor. Under his military leadership, Constantinople withstood a Muslim siege lasting thirteen months. Finally, in 718 he was able to destroy the Arab fleet, sparing Europe an invasion from the East fifteen years before Charles Martel halted the Islamic tide moving up from the south.

Leo III instituted many civil reforms, including a new code of law. He also attempted to initiate reforms in the religious sphere, including the suppression of icons, the now-extreme devotion to which he saw as a barrier to the conversion of Jews and Muslims. In this, he was opposed by the majority of Byzantine theologians, the monks, the Roman papacy, and most of the population. But he also had significant support, particularly from the military.

Germanus, the Patriarch of Constantinople, strongly protested when icons were ordered destroyed. He appealed to the pope, Gregory III, but was deposed by Leo in 730. From the relative safety of Syria, St. John of Damascus penned powerful defenses of the "way of images" in both theology and worship. Resisted most strenuously by the monks, Leo began a persecution of the "Iconodules," mainly in the monasteries.

Two Roman synods condemned Leo's policies in 731. The emperor responded by seizing the papal "patrimonies" in southern

Italy and Illyria. Having again defeated the Arabs in 740, Leo died the following year, leaving his war against icons for his son, Constantine V, to continue. The persecution intensified.

In 754, Constantine began the dissolution of resisting monasteries. Many monks accepted martyrdom rather than surrender their precious icons. After 775, when Constantine's son, Leo IV, succeeded to the throne, the persecution lessened. When Leo died five years later, his widow, the Empress Irene, defied the army and ended the conflict through the work of a General Council at Nicea in 787.

*The Second Assault*

Irene's restoration of icons was only temporary. She was dethroned in 802 by Nicephorus I. And in 814, the prohibition of icons and the persecution of iconodules were renewed when another imperial commander was elected by the army as Leo V. The patriarch Nicephorus was deposed, St. Theodore of Studios exiled for his defense of icons, and more monks sent to prison or put to death.

The second persecution raged for twenty-eight years. In 820, Leo was assassinated, ending the Syrian dynasty, but not its iconoclastic policies. Michael II, a Phrygian, and in 829 his son, Theophilus, continued and even increased the fury of the persecution. Only with Theophilus' death in 842 did the iconoclastic movement halt. In 843, Theodora, his widow and empress-regent for her son, Michael III ("the Drunkard"), supported the election of Methodius, an iconodule monk, as Patriarch of Constantinople, and on the Second Sunday of Lent in that year the first great Feast of Orthodoxy was held in honor of the restored icons.

A popular victory over imperial and academic purists, the defeat of iconoclasm increased devotion to the traditional images of Jesus, Mary, and the saints. On another level, however, the tension and confusion engendered by the long controversy greatly accelerated the approaching schism between the Eastern and Western churches. The growing power of the new "Holy Roman Empire" of the Franks caused the virtual amalgamation of ecclesiastical and imperial power in the East to be viewed with caution and finally alarm. Only a miracle could now prevent a final separation.

## NOTES

1. See John J. O'Meara, *Eriugena* (Oxford: Clarendon Press, 1988), an expansion of his earlier work by that title published by Mercier Press (Cork: 1969), John J. O'Meara and Ludwig Bieler, eds., *The Mind of Eriugena* (Dublin: Irish University Press, 1973), and I. P. Sheldon-Williams, "Johannes Scottus Eriugena," in *The Cambridge History of Later Greek and Early Medieval Philosophy*, ed. cit., pp. 518-33. For a brief overview of Scottus' teaching, see Edward Yarnold, "John Scotus Eriugena," *The Study of Christianity*, pp. 157-58.
2. See especially Kallistos Ware, "The Spirituality of the Icon," in Jones et al., *The Study of Spirituality*, pp. 195-98.

# Spiritual Reform and Military Conquest    11

HE END OF THE NINTH CENTURY found Europe poised between the Dark Ages and the exciting era that would represent the brilliant flowering of the seeds planted centuries before by Irish saints and scholars, missionaries such as Columban, Augustine, and Boniface, and the far-sighted Pope Gregory the Great. Led by Alfred the Great and Charlemagne, nations were emerging out of the welter of feuding, feudal principalities. Similarly inspired by Gregory and his successors, the Roman Church had extended itself from the edge of the Balkans to Iceland, overwhelming the last Aryan Visigoths and slowly assimilating the Celtic churches.

The spread of Islam had been thwarted in France. Constantinople was not only holding fast, but in 961 would retake Crete and four years later, Cyprus. The Scandinavian nations had been evangelized by St. Anskar (801-865), and the Viking scourge would soon be over. In the East, beginning in 863, Saints Cyril and Methodius had converted the Slavic nations. In 900, the Reconquest of Spain was begun under the King of Castile, Alfonso the Great. In 966, Poland embraced Western Catholicism, and by 988, Russia had accepted Byzantine Christianity. In 995, the Magyars were defeated decisively at Lechfeld, beginning the conversion of the Hungarian peoples.

*The Papacy: Hitting Bottom*    Yet at this critical moment, the institution which had guided the destiny of Europe as the sole source of moral and spiritual unity for the past five centuries found itself weary and weak, prey externally to the powerful political forces it had nurtured and vitiated from within by laxity and corruption.  On the very eve of Europe's emergence into the bright dawn of the Middle Ages, the papacy succumbed to the temptations of wealth, power, and luxury.  With the accession of Sergius III in 904 began the woeful period of papal history known as the Pornocracy.

Although vigorously opposed since the time of Gregory the Great, simony was rife.  Ecclesiastical preferments were for sale on every level, including abbacies, bishoprics, and the papal office itself, now the pawn of aristocratic families.  Blatant immorality scandalized even the jaded Romans as popes paraded their mistresses and catamites in public.  Marozia, Sergius' mistress, was also the mother of Pope John XI (931-36), the grandmother of Benedict VI (973), and the aunt of John XIII (965-72).

But even as the papacy reached the low point of its history, a strong and vital reform movement had already begun, one that would strengthen the ministry of priests, stabilize the form of medieval church administration, and enable the papacy to re-emerge as a truly potent and spiritual force for another three hundred years.  It started, as had so many reform movements in the history of the Church, as a flight from corruption and took the now familiar form of monastic foundations, traditionally the cradle of spiritual leadership.

*The Year 1000 and the End of the World*  The rebirth of monasticism and the mounting struggle for reform probably meant little to ordinary folk as the end of the tenth century approached. Europe's Christians were beginning to look back over the previous centuries with a tremor of dread anticipation.

Despite the calamities of economic ruin, social chaos, the barbarian invasions, and even ecclesiastical corruption, they had been *Christian* centuries. The Church had survived and, after the peril of the Dark Ages and the rot of the Pornocracy, was even beginning to flourish.

Thus the end of the first millennium brought with it memories of the apocalyptic vision of Rev. 20:3-15, with its frightening images of Armageddon, the final conflict, and the Last Judgment. Eschatological fervor found expression in preaching, art, and literature, even in the stone sculpture of the great cathedrals beginning to rise from the soil of renascent Christendom, their spires pointing heavenward as if in supplication from Augsburg, Worcester, Venice, Mainz, and Winchester.[1]

The year 1000 began ominously enough. Sporadic famine was followed by pestilence, an immense comet appeared from the west, bright enough to outshine the stars, and here and there a strange rain of stones formed large piles in the fields. Vesuvius erupted. There were also storms, earthquakes, and floods, perhaps no more than usual, but these, too, were recorded with particular interest. But then, except for the writing of *Beowulf*, the birth of Berengar of Tours, and the evangelization of Greenland, the year 1000 passed into history.

Christian Europe heaved a sigh of relief and exultation. The building of cathedrals escalated, as did ecclesiastical reform. But Christians had been alerted, and the dread knell continued to reverberate in the depths of European consciousness. The expectation of the End would linger, smoldering like an unwatched ember, ready to flare up again in due time.

*Cluny and the Cause of Reform*

In 910, long before the outbreak of millennial foreboding and in the very heyday of the papal pornocracy, the abbey of Cluny was founded by Duke William ("the Pious") of Aquitaine. Its first abbot was Berno of Baume. Under his successor, St. Odo (879-942), the abbey reached its first greatness.

Influenced by the Benedictine reforms of St. Benedict of Aniane, Cluny was soon associated with the cause of church reform in general and came to exercise spiritual sway throughout southern France and northern Italy. It is likely that Hildebrand (later the reforming Pope Gregory VII) was a monk at Cluny as a young man.

The Cluniac reform emphasized the spiritual life, worship, and especially the choral office. Its fifth abbot, St. Odilo (994-1048), organized a system or network of houses under Cluny's influence. By then, their number had grown from thirty-seven to sixty-five. Powerful abbots like Odilo, St. Hugh (1024-1109), and Peter the Venerable (1122-56) came from noble families well-connected in the courts of France, Germany, England, Scotland, and Italy. Within a century, more than 1000 abbeys and priories would orbit within its sphere, effectively dominating much of the European church in the eleventh and twelfth centuries.

*The Return of the Hermits*

Church reform acquired additional impetus from the revival of monasticism at the very gates of Rome. After a duel in which his father killed a man, the young nobleman Romuald of Ravenna (950-1027) retired to the Benedictine abbey of Sant'Apollinare, which had adopted the Cluniac reform. Elected abbot there in 998, he resigned after a year in order to seek a more perfect form of monastic life. Becoming a hermit, he established a cenobitic community at Campus Maldoli. The "desert of Camaldoli," as it came to be known, became the nucleus of the Camaldolese Order, which included among its earliest members St. John Gualbert (990-1073), who left Camaldoli to found a similar order of hermits at Vallombrosa, near Florence. Towards the end of his life, he would emerge from his "desert" to support the reforming popes Alexander II and Gregory VII, as did his energetic contemporary, St. Peter Damian.

*The Puritan: St. Peter Damian*

During the latter half of the eleventh century, Peter of Ravenna (1007-72) worked tirelessly and sometimes fanatically to eliminate simony, clerical marriage, and other abuses. Although forced by poverty to herd swine in his youth, he had eventually won recognition for his brilliance. His brother Damian sent him to Faenza and Parma for studies. In gratitude, Peter added his brother's name to his own.

Entering the Benedictine hermitage at Fonte Arvella, Peter soon won further renown for his extreme austerity. Elected prior, he preached widely and founded several new houses of strict observance. In 1057, he was made Cardinal Bishop of Ostia.

Often a difficult and unyielding critic, Peter Damian directed his efforts primarily against clerical abuses. At one point, however, he was gently reprimanded by the first great reforming pope of the Middle Ages. St. Leo IX (1002-54) preferred to act "more humanely" than Peter's excessive zeal compelled him to with regard to demoting priests guilty of sexual misconduct. And although Alexander II may have revoked Peter's cardinalate, and he was never formally canonized, in 1828 Pope Leo XII declared him a Doctor of the Church.

*Bec and the Norman Conquest*

Ironically, one of the most powerful monastic sources of church reform stemmed from the Viking invasions that had so grieved the church a century before. In the ninth and tenth centuries, Norwegian Vikings or "Norsemen" had not only ravaged the coastal areas and waterways of Europe from the Mediterranean to Ireland, they also settled in. Important colonies were established in Ireland,

England, and especially that region of northern France still called Normandy in their memory.

In each instance, the invaders were gradually assimilated, acquiring the language and customs of the people they subjected. In France, the Norsemen were Christianized within a generation. By 991, when Rolf the Ganger was made first Duke of Normandy by King Charles III, they had mastered the region. A century later, with the blessing of Pope Alexander II, the fourth in the ducal line, William II, invaded England. In 1066, the Middle Ages came to the island with a shock, as the five-hundred-year reign of the Anglo-Saxon monarchy came to a sudden end. But the Norman Conquest also initiated a lasting cultural and spiritual revolution.

Within four years, the Anglo-Saxon nobility was either dead or in flight. Bishops and abbots were also forced or eased out of office in favor of Franco-Norman loyalists, including some extraordinary figures such as Lanfranc and St. Anselm, both Archbishops of Canterbury. Through them, the vibrant scholarship and spirituality of the great Norman abbey of Bec entered and transformed the English church.

Bec had been founded inauspiciously enough in 1041. The next year, however, a young Italian nobleman entered, whose brilliance as a teacher and administrator soon raised it to preeminence. Lanfranc (1010-89) was prior from 1045 to 1063. Among his outstanding students were Anselm of Lucca (later Pope Alexander II) and another Italian from Aosta also named Anselm, who would later become the Archbishop of Canterbury and saint.

A confidant of William of Normandy ("the Conqueror"), Lanfranc was made Archbishop of Canterbury in 1070. Faithful to his patron, he gradually replaced the Anglo-Saxon bishops with Normans, thus bringing the English Church within the ambit of Continental Christianity and especially the reform movement now identified with Pope Gregory VII.

In most respects, Anselm (1033-1109) followed in the footsteps of his master, although excelling him as scholar, teacher, bishop, and saint. Anselm's influence on Christian spirituality was particularly great. As a monk and later abbot at Bec, he nurtured the faith of his brethren, especially in the case of those who had accompanied Lanfranc to England, by letters and written prayers.

After Lanfranc's death in 1093, Anselm was appointed Archbishop of Canterbury. He soon found himself embroiled in theological and ecumenical controversies with Greek Christians at the Council of Bari (1098), and with the struggle over lay investiture with Henry I in England. A profoundly committed believer, Anselm also attempted to demonstrate the cogency of "faith seeking understanding" by careful reasoning, preparing the way for the scholastic theology of Peter Lombard and Thomas Aquinas. In 1720, Pope Clement XI declared Anselm a Doctor of the Church.

*Reform from Within*

Beginning with St. Leo IX, a series of reforming popes attacked the abuses that had vitiated both the papacy and the clergy for almost a century. In 1059, Nicholas II set rules for the papal election itself that in large measure have been followed ever since, particularly with regard to the role of the college of cardinals. Thus, the papacy was removed from co-optation by the emperor, whose prerogative it had been to crown (and choose) the pope. But two centuries of strife between the empire and the papacy had also begun.

Clerical marriage presented a special challenge to the reform movement, not least because of the alienation of church property by inheritance. As an aspect of ministry, celibacy had been a widespread if not universal practice in both the Eastern and Western churches for centuries. It now acquired a new aura of respect in the wake of the sexual scandals of the tenth century and the manifest immorality of many of the clergy and monks.

Inspired partly by the powerful writings of Peter Damian, Pope Gregory VII, the former monk Hildebrand, inaugurated a campaign for universal celibacy that, despite strong resistance, would be imposed on the entire Western church by the Council of Rome in 1074. The demand for universal celibacy would be repeated with increasing success by later councils, culminating in the Second Lateran Council (1139), which invalidated the marriage of priests.

Among reform-minded popes, Gregory VII (1021-85) stands out as one of the greater figures of European history. He was born in Tuscany of impoverished parents. Although educated in a Benedictine monastery in Rome, young Hildebrand was probably not a monk when he was selected by Pope Gregory VI to be chaplain. Later, after the old pope's death, he seems to have retired to Cluny, where he was confirmed in his commitment to reform.

Brought back to Rome by St. Leo XI, Hildebrand's rise in church politics was meteoric, climaxing in his election as pope in 1073. The rest of his life was spent furthering the cause of church reform, including his famous duel of wills with the emperor, Henry IV, at Canossa in 1077. The issue was chiefly lay investiture — the practice by which kings and nobles appointed bishops in their realms and often controlled the local church through them.

Gregory's conflict with the emperor ended in ultimate victory for the Church despite Gregory's death in exile in 1085. (A similar struggle would end in the murder of the Archbishop of Canterbury, Thomas Becket, in 1170.) Among Gregory's other unrealized hopes was a reconciliation between the Eastern and Western churches and a crusade against the Turks. He was canonized in 1606.

*The White Monks*

Towards the end of the eleventh century, the reform movement of the early Middle Ages produced its final flower, two of the great monastic orders of the West — the Carthusians and the Cistercians. Since its founding in 1084 by St. Bruno of Cologne, the Carthusian Order has been regarded as the most austere in the Catholic Church, espousing a tradition of eremitical solitude, silence, abstinence, and contemplative retirement from the world that has changed little even since the Second Vatican Council.[2] Yet Carthusians such as Adam and Denis were paradoxically influential in the development of Western spirituality, and St. Hugh (1140-

1200), one of England's great saints, was a Carthusian monk before becoming Archbishop of Lincoln.

As a young nobleman, Bruno Hartenfaust (1032-1101) was educated in Cologne and later in Paris, Rheims, and Tours. In 1075, after becoming a canon of the metropolitan see in Cologne, he returned to Rheims as master of the cathedral school. Among his disciples were Odo of Châtillon (the future Pope Urban II), several other future bishops and abbots, and Hugh of Châteauneuf, the future bishop of Grenoble and saint-patron of the Carthusians.

For some time, Bruno found himself entangled in the bitter struggle between Pope Gregory VII and the emperor. Several times he abandoned the active ministry to seek monastic seclusion, but without satisfaction. Elected Archbishop of Rheims, he resigned and returned to his monastic pursuits. For a while, he joined St. Robert at Molesmes, but even there Bruno grew restless for greater seclusion and austerity.

Finally, in 1084, he departed with six friends for the rugged mountain district of the Dauphiné near Grenoble, where his former pupil Hugh was bishop. Inspired by a dream in which he saw seven stars descending into the remote valley of La Chartreuse, Hugh granted them the lands and guided the pilgrims there himself.

The companions constructed their first log-cabin hermitages around a small chapel. They were soon joined by two more hermits. But the dream was not to last. In the spring of 1090, Bruno was summoned to Rome by his former pupil, Odo, now Pope Urban II. Some of his companions followed Bruno to Rome. The others dispersed. But six months later, fired by Bruno's exhortations, they were back at La Chartreuse where, except for a period of exile from 1903 to 1940, the headquarters of the order has remained.

Bruno's counsel was so valued by Urban II that the pope refused him permission to return to France. He finally allowed the old man to retire into solitude, however, after Bruno rejected the offer of the archbishopric of Reggio. At La Torre, he established the second "Charterhouse" on lands donated by the Count of Calabria,

Robert Guiscard, whose Norman troops had once rescued Pope Gregory VII from imperial displeasure. There Bruno died on October 6, 1101.

The order soon spread to Spain, England, and the Netherlands, as well as France and Italy. Despite or perhaps because of the severity of Carthusian life, within a century there were thirty-three Charterhouses; by the time of the Reformation, some two hundred. Bruno left few writings, and even the Rules for the monks were informal. In one of his letters, however, he summarized the inspiration that had led him to reject success, prestige, and power to seek the presence of God in the mountain wilderness:

> What advantages and delights solitude and the silence of the hermitage bring to those who love it, they alone know who have had experience of it. It is there that generous souls can turn themselves inwardly as they will. They can dwell apart and attend uninterruptedly to the cultivation of the seeds of virtue and happily eat of the fruit of Paradise....

*Citeaux*

Entering the Benedictine Order at the age of fifteen, Robert of Molesmes (1027-1111) began a distinguished career as abbot and founder. Asked in 1075 by a number of hermits living in the forest of Colan to be their spiritual guide, Robert established a house of strict observance at Molesmes in Burgundy. The monastery flourished, grew wealthy, and relaxed its discipline. In 1098, twenty monks followed Robert to Citeaux, where they established another austerely primitive Benedictine abbey.

In 1100 Robert himself was entreated to return to Molesmes. There he was able to restore the original spirit of Benedictine austerity and devotion. The abbey at Citeaux grew even more famous, however, and the Cistercian Order became one of the most influential in the history of the Western church. A fountainhead of medieval spirituality, its most famous member, St. Bernard, would enter in 1112 with thirty other young Burgundians. Within a century, more than five hundred abbeys would have adopted the Cistercian observance. Their numbers and power, including those of nuns' abbeys, would continue to grow throughout the twelfth and thirteenth centuries.[3]

*The New Age*
Despite initial apocalyptic frenzy and the long struggle for reform, the spirituality of the eleventh and twelfth centuries was not particularly dour. A kind of exuberance permeated arts and letters as towns and cities grew, the weather improved, and prosperity prevailed. Monastic interpretations continued to dominate the sense of God's presence, especially because of the proliferation of monastery schools. Monks, above all, wrote.

But the expanding urban centers and new cathedrals began to produce a scholastic counter-force, one that would in due time overshadow the abbeys as great universities began to appear in Bologna, Padua, Paris, Oxford, and Cologne. The canons and professors who staffed these new centers of learning were often saintly as well as wise and studious, men such as Bruno, Norbert, Peter Lombard, and Dominic. Others, such as Berengar of Tours, Roscelin, and his student, Abelard, were daring and reckless.

The Middle Ages were growing restless intellectually, spiritually, and socially. Christian Europe had emerged from its cocoon and wanted to test its wings. It had also grown strong, and needed to test its muscle.

*Warriors of Christ: The Crusades*
By the end of the eleventh century, the Christian nations of Europe were capable of concerted action hitherto impossible, as they found greater cause for alliance than hostility. At a single stroke, Pope Urban II preempted the nascent military might of the Christian kingdoms for a colossal religious campaign to free the Holy Land and relieve the perennial pressure on Constantinople from the Turks.

The Islamic invasions that had seriously threatened Christian Europe had already been halted on three fronts — in southern France by Charles Martel and Charlemagne, in Spain, especially under the great national hero Rodrigo Dias, the Cid, and at Constantinople, which continued to hold firm under a series of brilliant emperors following the restoration of Orthodoxy. Moreover, the Arab masters of the Holy City had permitted and even encouraged access to Christian sites and on the whole had behaved well towards Christian pilgrims. But the danger of another European invasion remained real, and Italy itself was a prime target for pirate attacks and military colonization.

At first remarkably successful, the Crusades nevertheless proved disastrous in the long run. In 1099, by dint of a bloody conquest, Jerusalem was in Christian hands for the first time in five hundred years. Forced into renewed military efforts by this initial success, however, the Arab kingdoms from Egypt to Syria fought back bravely, wresting Jerusalem and many coastal areas from the Europeans in 1187. The Arab reconquest was inexorable. By 1400, all hope of freeing Palestine had vanished. Moreover, both Byzantium and Europe itself now faced a greater threat than before. Within sixty years, Constantinople would at last fall to the Turks, ending over a thousand years of Christian supremacy in the East.

The Crusades were not a total failure, however. As a series of virtually annual military expeditions, they welded European kingdoms into medieval Christendom. The war on Islam may have even been the inevitable consequence of the rising power and restless unity of the Christian nations. In any event, the Holy Roman Empire emerged during the struggle as an international force more powerful than Byzantium and often a match for the experienced armies of Islam. Great military orders such as the Templars and the Knights Hospitaller were founded as a kind of international police force of warrior monks.[4] Commerce, law, and industry were similarly galvanized by the immense effort.

But the social, spiritual, and material cost of the Holy War of Christendom far exceeded the abilities of popes, kings, and peoples to sustain.[5] For generations, the finest flower of European knighthood perished fruitlessly of plague, famine, or in battle. Further, much of the violent energy of their Christian armies was brutally diverted onto innocent victims — Jews, Eastern Christians, and Islamic women, children, and non-combatants. The military technology of the Crusades would be returned, moreover, with terrifying effect to Europe itself against pagan Slavs and heretics such as the Albigensians and Waldensians. Soon the armies of Christ would be attacking each other, and when war was not at hand, freebooting bands of unemployed mercenaries terrorized towns and villages, demanding provisions and tribute at the threat of slaughter.

Tragedies such as the sack of Constantinople (1204) and the Childrens' Crusade (1212) reveal the Crusades as a cultural and religious catastrophe, although a sadly invisible one to the majority of Christian historians until recent times. From a spiritual perspective, Pope Urban's great enterprise was a Frankenstein's monster that could be contained only by chance and cunning. And the dangerous legacy of the Crusades would survive for centuries as popes and Christian monarchs relied increasingly on military power and the use of war in order to promote the gospel of peace.

*Schism and New Seed*

The Crusades were not the only catastrophe of the eleventh century. Tensions between the Eastern and Western churches, acute since the Iconoclast controversies, erupted in formal schism in 1054, the year in which a portentous supernova appeared. The recriminations and mutual excommunications passed without great alarm. Leo IX had in fact died before his inflexible and insensitive legate, Humbert, excommunicated Michael Cerularius, the Patriarch of Constantinople, in the great basilica of Hagia Sophia.

The saintly Leo was succeeded after a year's vacancy in the Holy See by Victor II, a comparative non-entity. Michael Cerularius, a stubborn and ambitious man, was deposed and died in 1058. Many church leaders evidently expected the breach to heal more or less naturally, as several had in the past few centuries. It was not to be. East and West went increasingly separate ways.

Despite its capacity for disaster, the eleventh century was also distinguished by its zeal for reform, its heroic monastic founders, and its saints, including laymen such as Edward the Confessor (1002-1066), Eric of Sweden (d. 1022), and Vladimir of Kiev (d. 1015) — all kings. Once again, even popes were saints, such as Leo IX and Gregory VII, or saintly, as in the case of Urban II. In the East, St. Symeon the New Theologian reached the height of his powers as a spiritual writer. It was an era of burgeoning cities and expanding trade, of cathedrals, knighthood, and the beginnings of chivalry. Universities were growing, academic theology and philosophy had sprung to life.

The seeds of spirituality sown in the eleventh century were themselves the fruit of that earlier planting by missionaries, scholars, and monks from the edges of the world. These new seeds would in turn grow and come to flower in the twelfth and thirteenth centuries as the Middle Ages reached their peak and fulfillment, producing another, even more lavish harvest, one which continues to nourish the faith of Christians today and probably will forever.

## NOTES

1. See Richard Erdoes, *AD 1000: Living on the Brink of Apocalypse* (San Francisco: Harper and Row, 1988). The classic study of the eschatological fever of the late tenth century is art-historian Henri Focillon's *The Year 1000*, trans. by Fred D. Wieck (New York: Frederick Ungar Publishing Co., 1970).
2. For a brief history of the Carthusians, see Robin Bruce Lockhart, *Halfway to Heaven: The Hidden Life of the Sublime Carthusians* (New York: Vanguard Press, 1985). Other, more probing studies are Peter van der Meer de Walcheren, *The White Paradise*, preface by Jacques Maritain (New York: David McKay Co., Inc., 1952), and David Mathew and Gervase Mathew, O.P., *The Reformation and the Contemplative Life: A Study of the Conflict between the Carthusians and the State* (London: Sheed and Ward, 1934.)

3. See Jean Leclerq, *Bernard of Clairvaux and the Cistercian Spirit*, trans. by Claire Lavoie (Kalamazoo: Cistercian Publications, 1976).
4. For a brief account of the military orders, see Terence Wise, *The Knights of Christ: Religious/Military Orders of Knighthood 1118-1565* (Osprey Men-at-Arms series 155. London: Osprey Publishing Co., 1984).
5. The standard and still unsurpassed account of the crusade movement is Steven Runciman's great work, *A History of the Crusades* (3 vols., Cambridge University Press, 1962-66). For an estimate of the final debacle, see also Barbara Tuchman, *A Distant Mirror: The Calamitous Fourteenth Century* (New York: Knopf, 1978).

# The Medieval Explosion 12

STABILIZED BY THE CONVERSION of both the barbarian invaders and the pagan tribes of the North, and the retrenchment of the Islamic tide in the southwest and east, Europe fully entered into the Golden Age of Christendom in the twelfth century. With political and religious stability came prosperity and even relative peace. Towns and cities burgeoned, trade enriched the rising merchant class, and guilds of artisans sprang up. Nurtured by palace and cathedral schools, intellectual ferment was giving rise to novel ideas and new structures: the universities, with their vital, flexible scholasticism.

The bond that unified this unwieldy, sometimes explosive amalgamation of tribes, nations, kingdoms, and classes, was a common faith in the favor and mercy of God dispensed through the Catholic Church. Even here, however, new and startling developments were already beginning to unsettle the foundations.

The spirituality of the period was dominated by the Cistercian ideal, especially as developed by the first great mystical doctor, theologian, poet, reformer, and controversialist, St. Bernard of Clairvaux, one of the most powerful and interesting figures of the Middle Ages. Other important developments in the twelfth century included the shift in the position of women in both civil and ecclesiastical society, the consolidation of authority in the hands of the pope and emperor by means of the "two swords" of temporal and religious power, and the appearance of influential heretical and schismatic groups in southern Europe.

*Bernard of Clairvaux: Last of the Fathers* At the age of twenty-two, Bernard (1090-1153) arrived at the gate of Citeaux in the company of thirty other young nobles of Burgundy.[1] Only three years later, the abbot, St. Stephen Harding, sent him to establish a new house at Clairvaux, partly to relieve the crowded conditions at the Cistercian motherhouse. Within a few years, Clairvaux had become as famous as Citeaux and Bernard was recognized as one of the most influential religious leaders of his time.

Appointed secretary to the Synod of Troyes, he secured approval of the rule of the Knights Templar, which he most likely composed himself. Bernard's subsequent support of Pope Innocent II secured the papacy against the claims of the antipope, Anacletus. Innocent responded naturally enough by favoring the Cistercians in general, and Clairvaux in particular. In 1145, when a former student of Bernard's was elected pope as Eugenius III, the pontiff made his teacher both advisor and confidant. Among other tasks, Bernard was called upon to preach the Second Crusade, during which he sped from place to place to prevent massacres of Jews, which the Crusaders willingly assumed was part of their religious duty to perpetrate.

Bernard was called "the Great Reactionary" even by his admirers because of his implacable enmity towards those he regarded as unorthodox, such as Peter Abelard, Arnold of Brescia, Henry of Lausanne, and Gilbert of Poitiers. But in regard to supporting the authenticity of the visions of St. Hildegard, his friendship with saints such as Aelred of Rievaulx, William of St. Thierry and Malachy of Ireland, and in his lyrical, non-dogmatic approach to teaching, he more nearly resembled the ancient patriarchs of the desert than the schoolmen who would dominate the next century.

Not without reason, he was also known as "the Last of the Fathers."

The core of Bernard's spirituality was a truly mystical love of God, particularly an ardent love of the human Christ as "the Bridegroom of the soul." At once the source and the antithesis of the romanticism of courtly love that pervaded European culture in the twelfth and thirteenth centuries, Bernard employed (and reinterpreted) the language of erotic love to express the deepest mysteries of mystical union. Among his 332 sermons, he composed eighty-six on the Canticle of Canticles alone. Thus, the ancient biblical theme of "bridal mysticism" became the dominant motif of Western spirituality, influencing writers and mystics from Eckhart to John of the Cross and providing a model for the nuptial symbolism of the consecration of nuns.

*The Cistercian Kingdom of Love*

Bernard's contribution to medieval spirituality lay as much in the clarity as in the fervor with which he described the union of the soul with God. But as both saint and Doctor of the Church, the influence of his personality was greater than that of his learning.

And although his temperament and writings overshadow those of most of his contemporaries, Bernard was not the only Cistercian whose influence shaped the course of medieval spirituality. Among those whose lives he touched and in turn guided hundreds of others were William of St. Thierry and Aelred of Rievaulx.

Born in Liège, William entered the Benedictine monastery at Rheims. In 1119, he was elected abbot of St. Thierry. He had already come to know Bernard, who resisted the older man's desire to join the Cistercians at Clairvaux. In 1135, however, William resigned as abbot and entered the Cistercian house at Signy. A prolific writer, William is perhaps best remembered for the "Golden Epistle" that he addressed to the Carthusian monks at Mont-Dieu. Like Bernard, he was also a controversialist, and wrote against both William of Conches and Peter Abelard. He composed two commentaries on the Canticle of Canticles and left unfinished a biography of Bernard.[2]

"God
is
Friendship"

Far to the north, Cistercian influence came to England in 1132 with the foundation of Rievaulx Abbey in the Yorkshire dells. A year later, the young son of a Saxon priest of Hexham stopped for a visit while on a mission for King David of Scotland to the Archbishop of York, the patron of the abbey. On his return, young Ethelred (whose name had been shortened to its Norman form, Aelred), petitioned to enter as a monk.[3]

Under excellent abbots, not least of whom was Aelred himself, Rievaulx grew to house over six hundred monks. Other foundations were made, but Rievaulx remained the heart of the Cistercian movement in several respects. Chief among them was, perhaps, Aelred's example and writings. His beautiful book *On Spiritual Friendship* remains the principal work on the subject during the Middle Ages. Authentic spiritual friendship, he wrote, "is sought, not with an eye on any worldly expediency, or for some ulterior motive, but simply on account of its own natural worth and the inclination of the human heart, so that its profit and its reward is nothing other than itself."

So beloved was Aelred that after his death, he was declared a saint, not by distant Rome (which had not as yet formalized canonization procedures), but by the monks and people to whom he had devoted a lifetime of loving care.

The Matter
of
Women

In the relatively stable if not exactly peaceful era ushered in by the Carolingian Empire, it became possible for the first time in centuries to establish monastic enclosures for women outside the Italian peninsula or the relative safety of Britain and Ireland. In the ninth and tenth centuries, several large houses were founded by royal decree, particularly in Germany.

Here the high-born widows and daughters of the aristocracy could retire into seclusion for political or religious purposes. Such women were "canonesses" rather than nuns, however, for they did not make vows of poverty although they did profess chastity and obedience to the rule. Thus, many of them, especially abbesses, exercised extensive influence over their domains.

One of the most interesting of these royal or at least noble ladies was the Saxon canoness Hrotsvit (or Roswitha) of Gandersheim (c. 940-1002), a well-educated, powerful writer who composed the first Christian dramas among other works, including legends of the saints, epics, and poetry.[4] Her explicit task, she tells us, was to glorify Christian womanhood in contrast to the developing view of women as weak, wanton, and a certain danger to the virtue and therefore the salvation of men.

An early feminist theologian, Hrotsvit was principally concerned to correct the negative judgment on women found in both pagan and Christian authors. Thus, she chose the comedies of Terence as models for her own plays. How successful she was in reversing Christian misogyny in her own time can only be conjectured, for her writings were lost for over five hundred years. But she may well have influenced another German writer, the formidable Benedictine abbess Hildegard of Bingen, who flourished in the twelfth century.

*Twelfth Century Women*

As the stabilizing influences of the early Middle Ages solidified into the characteristic structures of medieval Christendom, the situation of women in both secular society and the Church steadily grew more visible and more important. Few modern figures can compare to Eleanor of Aquitaine (1122-1204), wife to King Louis VII of France and Henry II of England and monarch in her own right. Incensed at Henry's infidelities, Eleanor set up a separate court at Poitiers in 1170. There, the cult of courtly love prevailed in a setting of unparalleled artistic creativity. She supported her sons in a fruitless rebellion, suffered imprisonment for it, but lived to see two of them, Richard and John, themselves become kings.[5]

In the twelfth century, women writers achieved recognition for the first time in secular letters. Among them were Marie de France and two Provençal poets, the Countess of Dia and Castelloza.[6] Religious women were also coming into prominence. Early in the century, new abbeys following the Rule of St. Benedict or St. Augustine were founded for women by St. Robert of Arbrissel in France, and in England by St. Gilbert of Sempringham. Older foundations still flourished. One of them would become the home of a nun whose power may have exceeded even that of the redoubtable Queen of the Aquitaine.

*The Sibyl of the Rhine*   Hildegard was born at Bingen in Hesse at the very end of the eleventh century. A visionary from the age of three, she was reared from her eighth year in the Benedictine convent there by the Abbess, Jutta, who was also her tutor. In 1136, she succeeded her mentor as abbess. Two years later, guided by an interior voice, she began committing her visions to writing.

Most of her revelations were strikingly apocalyptic in tone as suited her role as reformer and prophet. For her counsel was sought by bishops, priests, monks, nuns, and a variety of lay persons of both sexes, including princes and the Emperor Frederick Barbarossa himself. Her replies to over three hundred letters are extant, and she left a major book, the *Scivias*, containing her visions and revelations. In addition, she wrote scriptural commentaries and composed hymns for the liturgical office. She also demonstrated an extraordinary interest in scientific observation.[7]

Guided by St. Bernard, his former teacher, Pope Eugenius III warily approved Hildegard's visions in 1147. In an age in which ecstatic experience was popular and hysterical religiosity would soon become a major problem for civil and ecclesiastical authorities alike, Hildegard insisted that her "visions" were not physical or even psychological experiences. Rather, they flowed from contemplative union with God in the depths of her soul. In this life, she wrote, God is present to us in all things, and is revealed in scripture and contemplation. Even here, however, we experience God's presence "darkly," through "the windows of faith." Clear vision awaits the full light of glory.

Although sickly all her life, Hildegard lived to be over eighty, dying in 1178. Great in her own time, her influence would extend through the centuries, finding its first resonance in the major women mystics and saints of the next century, Mechthild of Magdeburg, Mechthild of Hackeborn, and Gertrude the Great.

Ecstatic revelations figured prominently in the life and mission of another German nun of the time, St. Elizabeth of Schönau, who also manifested the extraordinary physical and spiritual sufferings that would become associated with mystical spirituality in the coming centuries. Like Hildegard, Elizabeth committed her visions to writing, and corresponded extensively with abbots, bishops, and lay persons of both sexes. For all its mystical sublimity, however, her spirituality, also like that of Hildegard and her successors of the next century, remained centered on the liturgical celebration of the divine presence in scripture and sacramental worship.

### The Cistercian Abbesses

One of the most surprising developments of women's rise to prominence in the twelfth century occurred within the framework of the dominant monastic order of its time, one peculiarly hostile to the influence of the fairer sex. (For all his tenderness towards male friends, St. Bernard in particular opposed any association with women, all of whom he saw as a threat to chastity.) Nonetheless, the success of the Cistercian ideal attracted a large number of bright, well-educated women. Soon, to the surprise and dismay of the monks, convents of women professing to be Cistercian began to appear throughout Europe. Eventually, "Cistercian" abbesses began to exercise their not inconsiderable influence on the order as a whole and in the larger Church as well.[8]

At first, unlike the Norbertines, Gilbertines, and other monastic orders which undertook the care of nuns and canonesses, and even despite the contrary example of St. Robert of Molesmes, the early Cistercians firmly refused to have anything to do with women, religious or otherwise. Later in the century, when great numbers of women flocked to their care, the other orders came to regret their initial openness. Despite even papal efforts to protect the rights of their women members, these groups began to expel the nuns. One Premonstratensian abbot, Conrad of Marchtal, stated with what was becoming typical medieval excess that since "the wickedness of women is greater than all the other wickedness of the world, and that there is no anger like that of women" (among other vices), by unanimous vote he and his community henceforth "will avoid them like poisonous animals."

But the Cistercians gradually relaxed their exclusiveness. By the end of the twelfth century, Cistercian nunneries were proliferating everywhere. In many areas, their number exceeded that of houses of monks. By the end of the next century, the six hundred houses of women nearly matched the total number of male communities.

Earlier, however, the nuns had spontaneously adopted the Cistercian rule and observances without permission or approval. Only in 1187 does a nunnery finally claim to have been Cistercian from the outset, that of Las Huelgas in Spain, which enjoyed the favor of King Alfonso VIII of Castille. There, to the scandal of Pope Innocent III, the abbesses assumed the power and privilege of abbots, even hearing confessions and blessing novices, duties reserved to priests.

Reaction in the order came too late. By 1220, and again in 1228, statutes were enacted in general chapters to prevent the further incorporation of convents into the order. Control seems to have been the major worry, a problem inherited from the earlier part of the twelfth century, when Cistercian nuns neither asked for nor received official approbation. The abbesses now were powerful, often being of royal or at least noble families, and like the canonesses of a previous era, able to resist male domination. In any event, the effort to resist the influx of women into the Cistercian order proved in the long run to be futile.

*Vita Activa, Vita Contemplativa*  Although preeminent, the Cistercians did not completely dominate the spirituality of the twelfth century. Among the clergy or "canons" attached to cathedrals, the eleventh-century movement towards adopting the "regular" life of study, work, and prayer according to one of the great monastic rules of the past reached its culmination in the rise of the Premontratensian Order founded by St. Norbert and at the Abbey of St. Victor founded by William of Champeaux.

The ensuing rivalry between the spirituality of the canons and that of the monks produced an influential body of literature centered on the relation between apostolic work and prayerful seclusion. Reconciling action and contemplation would become the preoccupation of spiritual writers throughout the medieval period and afterwards, occupying the genius of Richard of St. Victor, Bonaventure, Thomas Aquinas, Ignatius of Loyola, and, in our own time, Thomas Merton among many others.

The one clear principle that all orthodox writers have espoused is that in Christian spirituality as a whole there can be no radical separation of God-centered prayer and loving service, especially to the poor, sick, and suffering. The Spirit of God is found no less present in answering the needs of the hungry, the destitute, and the oppressed than in public worship or the silent attentiveness of the heart (see Matt. 25:31ff.). It is in denying one or other that the danger of one-sidedness lies, and with that, the loss of the sense of God's presence overall. Working out the relative *balance* between the active and contemplative dimensions of Christian spirituality thus became a matter of the particular character of different traditions and the temperamental variations among different people.

|            | The canons regular of Premontré (Norbertines) were |
| :--- | :--- |

*The*
*Canons*
*of*
*Premontré*

The canons regular of Premontré (Norbertines) were founded in 1119 by St. Norbert Gennep of Cologne as a monastic order which engaged in preaching and other forms of pastoral ministry as an aspect of its mainly contemplative spirituality. As the order spread to France and England, and even by 1136 to Palestine, however, preaching assumed greater prominence.

Also characteristic of the early Premonstratensians was their openness to admitting women as members of the order. Although this attitude would shift in later years, Norbert himself founded one of the few double monasteries of the Middle Ages.

*The*
*Victorines*

The hermitage of St. Victor at the gates of Paris achieved prominence when in 1108, William of Champeaux (1070-1122) moved there with several of his disciples following his humiliation in the famous dispute with his former student, Peter Abelard, at the cathedral school of Notre Dame. Adopting the Rule of St. Augustine, William and his followers became canons regular, although William himself was made Bishop of Chalons in 1113. But the school he established survived and flourished under his successors, attaining its greatest fame because of its two most famous and saintly teachers, Hugh and Richard.

Hugh of St. Victor (c. 1180-1142) succeeded William as Master. A theologian, philosopher, and scripture scholar, he left 39 treatises, 171 "sentences" (theological opinions), 23 letters and 10 sermons. His major works were the extended biblical allegory *Noah's Ark, The Soul's Three Ways of Seeing, On the Nature of Love*, and his *Didascalion*.[9] But above all, Hugh was a master of the spiritual life, looking back towards the integral approach of the monastic and patristic tradition for his model rather than to the academic method developing in the universities. Although Christocentric and sacramental, Hugh's spirituality was deeply influenced by the writings of the Pseudo-Dionysius and Augustine, a Christian Neoplatonic emphasis which would be passed on to his disciples.

One of them, a Scot (or Irishman) named Richard, would become the greatest mystical theologian of his time.

Entering the Abbey of St. Victor about ten years after Hugh's death, Richard was strongly influenced by the old master. Like him, the young canon wrote extensive biblical allegories, continuing a tradition stretching back to Philo. Although he composed philosophical and scriptural commentaries as well, his most influential work comprised the extended treatises on contemplation, *Benjamin Minor* and *Benjamin Major* (also known as *The Twelve Patriarchs* and *The Mystical Ark*).[10]

Richard's own life was a mixture of action and contemplation, as he became prior of St. Victor in 1162. His later years were vexed by the ineptitude of a spendthrift abbot, who was finally removed from office in 1171, only two years before Richard's death. Nevertheless, Richard's approach to contemplation ("the free, more penetrating gaze of the mind, suspended with wonder in regard to manifestations of Wisdom") would influence the writings of Bonaventure, Thomas Aquinas, the author of *The Cloud of Unknowing*, the Rhineland mystics, and, through Bernadino of Laredo, Teresa of Avila and John of the Cross.

**Apocalypse Revisited**

Toward the end of the twelfth century, the apocalyptic writings of a former Cistercian abbot, Joachim of Fiore (1132-1202), excited great attention in southern Europe. His personal sanctity was never questioned, but some of his more extreme writings were condemned well after his death by the Fourth Lateran Council (1215).[11]

Joachim and his followers (of whom there would be many in the next two centuries) viewed the whole of human history as a Trinitarian epic, in which the Old Testament period was under the aegis of the Father, the New Testament period under the Son, but a "new age" beginning sometime around 1260 would be the era of the Holy Spirit prior to the end of the world. In the coming last age, he predicted, humankind would enter its spiritual maturity, introduced by the appearance of new religious orders. This prophecy would be applied with great latitude in the thirteenth century to a host of unorthodox cults and sects as well as the new mendicant orders, particularly the Franciscans and Dominicans.

For centuries (and today as well), such apocalyptic visions have fueled the expectations of people weary of "ordinary" religion and longing for a reawakening of enthusiasm. The "new age" is always one in which men and women will worship "in spirit and truth," unhindered by official regulations and institutional restraints, sharing their possessions freely, and able to express love without taint of jealousy, rejection, or reprisal. Such "true believers" impatiently await an era of peace, freedom, truth, and justice — the Promised Land, the Kingdom of Heaven, the City of God, the millennial ideal of a wholly spiritual church.

As tends to happen in such instances, the hordes of disaffected serfs and opportunistic scoundrels as well as high-minded spiritual seekers who seized fervently upon Abbot Joachim's utopian prognostications soon attempted to hurry things along by social uprisings. The exigencies of living in a real and very imperfect world (as well as the stern arm of the Inquisition) eventually brought the visionaries back to earth, sometimes violently. The legacy of apocalyptic spirituality tends to remain tragic.

*Heresy, Schism, and Reaction*
Even in the twelfth century, the high idealism of the times that energized Cistercian spirituality ignited a host of cults or at least fed the flames of enthusiasm among a variety of religious and lay communities. Gospel preaching became the order of the day. Long before the incendiary pronouncements of Joachim of Fiore, the advent of an "order of preachers" was foretold by Richard of St. Victor, Anselm of Laon, and Martin of Laon. An apostolic class that would rival or even replace the monastic and episcopal orders, the preachers would be characterized by the voluntary poverty and common life that had graced the primitive Church.

Soon, groups of lay and religious enthusiasts were vying for audiences and spreading their version of the true Gospel. *Bogomils* had migrated from Bulgaria into western Europe by the end of the eleventh century, rejecting church structures, sacraments, and the Old Testament. The radical moral and metaphysical dualism that pervaded their preaching derived from Manichaean contacts as far back as the eighth century. Imported into Europe, it strongly influenced the *Cathars* (the "pure ones") and *Albigensians* of northern Italy and southern France (the Albi), widespread and powerful lay movements which sought reform and greater participation in religious life.

Separating themselves from the "official" Church, the radical sects soon developed distinctive titles, sacraments, and practices, most of them directly opposed to those of the Roman Church. But the generosity, concern, and heroic asceticism of the "perfect" among their membership, who provided spiritual and sometimes political leadership to disaffected peasants and the new urban classes, quickly attracted great numbers of adherents to their cause.

Typical, perhaps, of the impact of the new spirit among otherwise orthodox Christians was the case of Arnold of Brescia, a student of Peter Abelard. Early in the twelfth century, he began to preach the necessity of evangelical poverty, attacking the wealth and aristocratic stratification of the Church as contrary to the Gospel of Christ. Ultimately, Arnold's supporters rose in revolt, seizing Rome itself and driving the pope into exile. After a series of reverses and successes, Arnold's communards were defeated by troops loyal to Pope Hadrian IV. Arnold himself was captured and strangled, his body burned and the ashes cast into the Tiber. Henceforth, civil and ecclesiastical reaction to the appearance of sectarian preachers advocating poverty, reform, and personal freedom tended to be swift and final.

More heterodox groups clamoring for reform included the *Humiliati*, who appeared in northern Italy between 1160 and 1170; the *Waldensians*, followers of Waldo (or Valdes) of Lyon (c. 1150-1215); a union of the two groups known after 1184 as "the Poor Lombards"; the *Luciferians*, *Patarini*, and *Almaricans*. The latter were followers of Almaric of Bène (d. 1207), a philosopher who taught at Paris and whose mystical but pantheistic doctrines would be condemned there in 1210 and again at the Fourth Lateran Council in 1215.

Not all groups affected by the evangelical spirit were inclined toward heresy or schism. Among the outstanding proponents of apostolic life was Lambert le Bègue (d. 1177), a priest of Liège who preached against the worldliness and immorality of both clergy and laity alike. Lambert himself achieved little lasting success. But about this time, lay men and women seeking the simplicity of the *vita apostolica* began to establish themselves in communities segregated by gender but without rule or ecclesiastical approval. Described eventually as "Beguines" and "Beghards," probably because they were suspected of being heretical Albigensians, they supported their life of prayer, good works, and service to the poor and sick by begging or, more typically, craft work such as weaving or making lace.[12]

The most famous communities of women were known as "Beguinages," some of which still exist today in Belgium. Although the Beguines eventually ran afoul of ecclesiastical suspicion and the fear of women, the Beghards managed to escape condemnation or absorption into other orders. Their most notable spiritual descendants are the Alexian Brothers, a non-clerical religious order who continue to administer hospitals, homes for the aged, persons with AIDS, and other poor people in many parts of the world.

## NOTES

1. For an account of Bernard and the origins of the Cistercian reform, see Jean LeClerq, O.S.B., *Bernard of Clairvaux and the Cistercian Spirit*, trans. by Claire Lavoie (Kalamazoo, MI: Cistercian Publications, 1976).
2. On William of Thierry, see the collection of essays *William, Abbot of Saint Thierry*, trans. by Jerry Carfantan (Kalamazoo, MI: Cistercian Publications, 1988). For a selection of William's writings, see the following works available from Cistercian Publications: *On Contemplating God, Prayer, Meditations; The Nature and Dignity of Love; The Golden Epistle; The Enigma of Faith; Exposition on the Epistle to the Romans;* and *The Mirror of Faith*.

3. See Aelred Squire, *Aelred of Rievaulx: A Study* (London: S.P.C.K., 1973). Also see *For Crist Luve: Prayers of Saint Aelred Abbot of Rievaulx*, ed. by D. Anselm Hoste, trans. by Sr. Rose de Lima (The Hague: Martinus Nijhoff, 1965). The following works are available from Cistercian Publications, Kalamazoo, MI: Vol I: *Treatises, The Pastoral Prayer*; Vol. II: *Spiritual Friendship*; and *Dialogue on the Soul*.

4. On Hrotsvit, see Katharina M. Wilson, "The Saxon Canoness: Hrotsvit of Gandersheim," in *Medieval Women Writers*, pp. 30-63.

5. See Desmond Seward, *Eleanor of Aquitaine: The Mother Queen* (New York: Dorset Press, 1978).

6. See the essays by Joan M. Ferrante and Peter Dronke in *Medieval Women Writers*, ed. by Katharina Wilson, pp. 64-89 and 131-52.

7. On Hildegard, see Sabina Flanagan, *Hildegard of Bingen: A Visionary Life* (London and New York: Routledge, 1989), and "The German Visionary: Hildegard of Bingen," by Kent Kraft in *Medieval Women Writers*, ed. by Katharina Wilson, pp. 109-30. Recent editions of Hildegard's works include the *Book of Divine Works, with Letters and Songs*, ed. by Matthew Fox (Santa Fe: Bear and Co., 1987) and *Scivias*, trans. by Bruce Hozeski (Santa Fe: Bear and Co., 1986).

8. On the Cistercian abbesses, see Richard Southern, *Western Society and the Church in the Middle Ages* (New York: Penguin, 1970), pp. 309-18, and Sally Thompson, "The Problem of the Cistercian Nuns in the Twelfth and Early Thirteenth Centuries," *Medieval Women*, Derek Baker, ed. (Oxford: Basil Blackwell, 1978), pp. 227-52.

9. See *Hugh of St. Victor, Selected Spiritual Writings*, trans. by a Religious of C.S.M.V. (London: Faber and Faber, 1962).

10. See Richard of St. Victor, *The Twelve Patriarchs, The Mystical Ark, Book Three of the Trinity*, trans. by Grover A. Zinn (New York: Paulist Press, 1979), and Clare Kirchberger, ed. and trans., *Richard of St. Victor: Selected Writings on Contemplation* (London: Faber and Faber, 1957).

11. See Bernard McGinn, trans., *Apocalyptic Spirituality: Treatises and Letters of Lactantius, Adso of Montier-en-Der, Joachim of Fiore, the Franciscan Spirituals, Savonarola* (New York: Paulist Press, 1979). For a brief account of Joachism and subsequent millennial beliefs, see E. R. Chamberlain, *Antichrist and the Millennium*, New York: Saturday Review Press/E.P. Dutton, 1975. Cf. also Norman Cohn, *The Pursuit of the Millennium* (New York: Oxford University Press, 1970).

12. See Ernest W. McDonnell, *The Beguines and the Beghards in Medieval Culture* (New Brunswick, NJ: Rutgers University Press, 1954).

# The Golden Age    13

 ESPITE THE FREQUENT LAMENTS of the mystics and saints of the high Middle Ages at the perceived laxity of the times, Christian spirituality was more often intense, pervasive, and varied. Above all, it manifested a new characteristic, at least one not seen in the West since the age of Augustine. It was increasingly urban.

Favorable conditions in the eleventh and twelfth centuries had resulted in a sudden growth in population, especially in the cities, which were often congested and explosively volatile. Among the very poor, matters worsened. But a rising middle class had the money and leisure for education. New ideas were everywhere in the air. Theological speculation and consequent disputes were rife. Religious groups of all kinds were burgeoning, some orthodox, others heretical to one degree or another, all claiming to have recovered the authentic apostolic life of the early Church. Many also claimed, therefore, to be the only legitimate continuation of that Church, to the detriment of all other claimants, including the Church of Rome.

The great majority of Christians were probably not affected by theological controversy or sectarian rivalries, however. Spirituality for them tended to focus on a variety of practices, both new and old — devotion to the Eucharist, to the humanity of Christ, to Mary and other saints, the veneration of relics, pilgrimages to well-known tombs, shrines, caves, wells, and pools, as well as to Rome and the Holy Land, and participation in a welter of feast days, fairs, fasts, and other liturgical celebrations.

Despite the external and even superstitious element in such forms of popular piety, interiority was not alien to high medieval spirituality. The influence of the Dionysian writings as well as the tradition of Augustine and Benedict had maintained the ancient contemplative spirit of Christian prayer. The love-mysticism of St. Bernard had transformed it into a deep and divine Romance. The thirteenth century may have been a period of theological unrest and extraordinary development, a violent epoch marked by continuing crusades and wars of religion. But it was also an age of remarkable faith, the spiritual peak of the medieval range.

As there was new life, however, there was also a kind of slow death. The great spiritual and religious revolutions of the twelfth century that vitalized continental Europe also witnessed the end of a major Christian era in the north. Elsewhere, the High Middle Ages were in full flower, but for Ireland and Wales, the Dark Ages were just beginning as first their nation and then their church were engulfed in Norman England's expanding sphere of influence. Even here, the ubiquitous hand of the Cistercian reform was not lacking.

*The Decline and Fall of the Celtic Church*

Beginning in 795, recurrent and devastating Viking attacks on the monasteries of Ireland and Wales, as well as the rest of Europe, had already brought the golden age of Celtic spirituality to a bloody end. With it passed much of the vitality of the Celtic churches.[1]

Plundering attacks were not new when the dragon ships first appeared. Pagan Irish, Pictish, and Saxon pirates had attacked Celtic monasteries for centuries. But the Scandinavian onslaught was not merely a matter of booty, rapine, and slaughter. Pressed by rising population at home, Danes and Norwegians now established colonies and settled farmers in Ireland, England, and France.

Sometimes the Irish and Christian English were able to contain and even repel the invaders. Using military force and strategy, the Danes were temporarily halted in England by Alfred the Great in 878 and again in 895, and the Norwegians were defeated in Ireland by Brian Boru at Clontarf in 1014. Both Christian realms remained prey to Viking raids, however, whose prime targets were still the art treasures and wealth of the monasteries, especially in Ireland.

Although the island tribes were united for a time under a High King, the incessant feuding and rivalries of petty kings and chieftains undermined even this potential source of strength. By the time the Norsemen had been Christianized and assimilated, the mere march of time had seriously weakened the Celtic churches. Pressured first by Christian Anglo-Saxons and then by their Anglo-Norman supplanters, abbots in Wales and Ireland gradually acceded to the assimilation of their tradition by the thriving Benedictine observance with its strong Roman connections. The imperious Norman bishops from Bec, Lanfranc and Anselm, strove to have the Celtic church as a whole submit to Canterbury, in large measure succeeding in Wales and almost so in Ireland.

For some time, Irish bishops had looked to Rome and even Canterbury for support in reforming the church. Guided by papal legates, synods at Rathbreasil in 1110 and Kells in 1152 brought Irish customs into still closer conformity, while avoiding complete submission to Canterbury. But as more episcopal sees were created, the power of the ancient monasteries and the hegemony of their abbots and abbesses was increasingly curtailed and with it the characteristic "shape" of the old spirituality.

The alleged "donation" of Ireland to Henry II of England in 1155 by Pope Hadrian IV (Nicholas Breakspear, the only English pope), and the Norman invasion fourteen years later further eroded the ability of Ireland and its native church to withstand transformation. In 1172, Henry convoked another synod of bishops at Cashel. Here the Roman form of baptism and tithing among other usages were imposed on the Irish church, in effect ending the long history of the Celtic church.

The most perspicacious of Irish church leaders had long since recognized that a major change had occurred and the days of their distinctive form of Christianity were rapidly passing. St. Malachy, for a while archbishop of Armagh (1134-37), was the foremost Irish bishop of his time and, like other Romanizing church leaders, looked to the continent for spiritual leadership. On a trip to Rome in 1139 following the resignation of his see, he visited Clairvaux, where he became friends with St. Bernard. He also succeeded in bringing four monks back to Ireland and established the first Cistercian house at Mellifont in 1142. On a return trip to Clairvaux in 1148, he suddenly fell ill and died in Bernard's arms. His biography was composed there by the great Cistercian saint and doctor himself.

Another sainted churchman of the period was Laurence O'Toole, who spent much of his youth as a hostage during the power struggles among Irish chieftains prior to the Norman invasion. For a while abbot of Glendalough, Laurence was made archbishop of the new see of Dublin in 1162, and represented Irish interests at the court of Henry II. He attended the Third Lateran Council in 1179 and in that year was made papal legate. He died, however, en route back to Ireland.

With O'Toole passed much that was distinctive of ancient Celtic Christianity. The Irish church would survive, as would the nation, but only in the shadow of its powerful neighbor to the East which would attempt with some success during the next three centuries to suppress every vestige of language, custom, and art there as well as in the Celtic realms of Wales, Scotland, Cornwall, and Man.

Popular forms of spirituality survived, however, as monastic practices disappeared. Former missionary migrations to the continent were now echoed by pilgrimages to remote places of holy memory, such as St. Patrick's Purgatory on Lough Derg in Donegal, or St. Kevin's Bed at Glendalough. For centuries to come, persistent visionary elements and tales of the miraculous such as the "Voyage of St. Brendan" preserved the sense, if not the substance, of the ancient church.

If the brilliance of Celtic spirituality was reduced to a dull glimmer by the Viking and Norman onslaughts, the impact of that spirituality on Europe remained bright. In 1089, a Russian mission was undertaken by the Irish monks of the monastery of St. James in Regensburg, the center of the nine surviving Celtic monasteries (Schottenklosters) in Germany. Their monastery in Kiev continued at least until 1242. Other great Columban monasteries such as Bobbio became Benedictine or Cistercian, but the love of scripture study, theology, and philosophy as well as art, poetry, and music remained alive in the West. The love of nature as image and abode of the Creator also survived, flaring up especially in the Franciscan order, much as the love of learning soared to new heights with the coming of the Dominicans.

*Vicar of Christ*

At the end of the twelfth century, the welter of new religious movements, some of them heretical, and the need to distinguish among them, plus the growing tension between the Holy Roman Emperor and the popes concerning territorial sovereignty and the appointment of bishops, together with the challenge of Islam, required to the mind of the new young pope that a major council be summoned. The pope was Innocent III, Lotario di Segni (1160-1216), elected in 1198. The convocation of bishops that met during November, 1215, is known as the Fourth Lateran Council.

This twelfth Ecumenical Council (representatives of the Eastern Church were present) was the turning point of the Middle Ages. Its motivating force was one of the great leaders of the West, a man of great vision, enormous ambition, and true genius. Under Innocent, the medieval church asserted itself as the dominant power in Europe, and he presided over that power as Vicar of Christ — a papal title heard first during his pontificate.

Despite its brevity, the Council addressed many of the major problems of the time in both civil and religious society — trial by ordeal, the challenge of the Albigensians and Waldensians, the proliferation of cults and sects, the administration of the sacraments, and the founding of new religious orders, the council's prohibition of which was to have serious implications for a Spanish canon on his way to Rome for just that purpose.

Fortunately, if not a saint himself, Innocent recognized sanctity when he saw it. And what he saw before his death at the age of fifty-six changed the shape of Christian history forever.

*The Coming of the Friars* Dominic Guzman (1170-1221) was born of a knightly family in Caleruega, Spain.[2] As a young man, he entered the Canons Regular of St. Augustine at Ozma and devoted himself to study and contemplation, a personal characteristic which would one day mark the Order he would found. As sub-prior of the cathedral chapter, he was selected in 1206 to accompany the bishop, Diego de Azevedo, on a mission of state to Scandinavia. Passing through southern France, they encountered the Cistercian legates of Innocent III, who were preaching with little success against the Albigensians.

On their return from Denmark, Diego and Dominic joined the preaching mission, adopting the voluntary poverty that distinguished the highest-ranking members of the heretical movement, which had grown extensive and powerful in the Midi because of the collusion of many of the local nobility. Their mission, which had been sponsored by Bishop Fulk of Toulouse, was only partially successful. Then, late in 1207, Diego died on a return trip to Spain to recruit more preachers. Before his departure, however, Diego established a convent at Prouille for women who had left the Albigensians – an event of much greater significance than at first evident.

Dominic was left in charge, and he slowly drew a band of followers around himself as the nucleus of a community of friars and nuns. The center he selected was the strategic city of Toulouse. In 1215 Fulk recognized the small band of preachers that

Dominic had assembled there as a preaching order. The following year, Dominic traveled to Rome to seek papal approval.

But Innocent III, who had approved the original preaching mission, had died. To avoid the prohibition of the Fourth Lateran Council, Dominic was advised by the new pope, Honorius III, to adopt an existing rule for his order. Returning to Toulouse, Dominic conferred with his friends and selected with them the familiar Rule of St. Augustine, which admirably fit the objectives of the new preaching friars.

Approved by Honorius later that year, the Order of Friars Preachers began its work in Italy and France, espousing evangelical poverty as a sign of their mission. Dominic's love of study was reaffirmed by substituting it for manual labor as the "work" of the brethren. Error could only be overcome by truth, and it was Truth, therefore, that became the motto of the order.

Dominic's emphasis on study was furthered by sending the young recruits to the major universities for their studies in scripture and theology — notably Paris and Oxford. St. Albert the Great, St. Thomas Aquinas, and Meister Eckhart all studied at the priory in Paris and Cologne, and a Dominican soon came to occupy the position of official theologian to the pope — the Master of the Sacred Palace.

Dominic's last years were spent in ceaseless journeys in Italy, Spain, and France, preaching and founding priories. Exhausted by his labors, and cheated of his desire to work among the nomads of eastern Europe, he fell ill and died in Bologna in 1221. In 1234 he was canonized by his chief supporter in Rome, Cardinal Ugolino, now Pope Gregory IX.

The contemplative and mystical dimension of Dominican spirituality was enhanced among the early friars by the example and teaching of Albert of Lauingen, known in his own lifetime as "the Great" for his astonishing mental powers and sheer physical stamina.[3] A natural scientist, philosopher, theologian, and saint, Albert in 1248 established the great House of Studies at Cologne, around which the university grew up. There he attempted to synthesize the major strands of Neoplatonic, Jewish, and Islamic philosophy and theology with Christian belief and the new Aristotelian thought introduced to the West by the Arabs.

Opposed both within the Order and by traditionalist theologians in Paris and Oxford, neither Albert nor his disciples fully succeeded. The theological and philosophical synthesis was carried out largely by his most brilliant student, Thomas Aquinas (1224-1274), while his scientific interests, which were far-ranging and progressive, were continued by Dietrich of Freiburg and Ulrich of Strassburg. The mystical element of Albert's teaching found its main support in the teachings of Meister Eckhart and his disciples of the fourteenth century, Henry Suso and John Tauler.

Despite the fragmentation of Albert's project, it would be a mistake to conclude that Thomas was not a mystic or Eckhart a philosopher and theologian. Nevertheless, the great synthesis was never achieved. In 1277, many of Thomas' teachings were condemned at the Universities of Paris and Oxford. In 1329, fifteen propositions taken from Eckhart's sermons and scriptural commentaries were condemned by a papal bull. Albert himself narrowly escaped censure. Eventually both he and his greatest student were canonized and declared Doctors of the Church. Eckhart, however, would not fare so well.

**Dominican Women**

From its beginning, women constituted an important part of the Dominican Order.[4] Dominic himself founded three convents before his death, and a fourth was approved a year later. Soon, dozens of monasteries for cloistered Dominican nuns and lay sisters had attracted hundreds of women, including many Beguines, who were eager as well as able to share in the Order's apostolate of preaching and teaching. They would also in time perpetuate the great mystical tradition which originated in the Neoplatonic revival of Albert the Great and was promoted by Meister Eckhart.

Younger than Dominic, Francis Bernadone (1182-1226) succeeded in establishing his Order of Friars Minor earlier than his Spanish friend, and thus avoided the restrictions of the Fourth Lateran Council.[5] But other, even more trying difficulties lay ahead of him, many of his worst trials arising from within his Order itself.

The son of a prosperous cloth merchant, Francis followed his father's profession until twenty. A romantic, carefree young man, Francis dreamed of knighthood and gallant adventures. The attraction of chivalry and courtly love never abandoned him, but was transformed into the most Christ-like spirituality of his age.

A civil war between Perugia and Assisi gave Francis the opportunity to win his spurs, but also resulted in several months of captivity as a prisoner of war. Beset by a serious illness on his return, Francis turned his thoughts to God, and especially to the service of the poor. He made a pilgrimage to Rome and on impulse exchanged clothing with a beggar one day. Having spent a day begging alms, Francis' commitment to radical poverty was deepened even more.

Back in Assisi, Francis was disowned by his father and, stripping himself in public before the bishop, the youth renounced his patrimony and undertook a life of mendicant service in strict fulfillment of Jesus' words in the tenth chapter of St. Matthew's gospel. At first, Francis sought to serve lepers, for whom he retained a special devotion all his life. He also sought to rebuild the old church of San Damiano in response to a vision. After three years, his first disciples joined him. Soon, there was a community of twelve and, in 1209, Francis journeyed to Rome to seek approval of his 'primitive rule' from Pope Innocent III.

Having been befriended by Cardinal Ugolino, Francis obtained access to the pope and secured verbal assent to his plans. He returned to Assisi, and the numbers of his followers increased. In 1214, Like bishop Diego and Dominic, Francis set out on a preaching mission through southern France and Spain, and was turned back from crossing into Africa only by illness. Again in 1219, he preached in eastern Europe and eventually reached Egypt.

In 1221, overwhelmed by the immensity of his growing family, Francis relinquished leadership to Elias of Cortona, who represented those who wished to mitigate the severity of the primitive rule. By then, there were more than 3000 members. Disillusioned, Francis sought spiritual refuge on Mt. La Verna in the Apennines. There, in 1224, after much suffering and nearly blind, he received during an ecstatic trance the wounds of Christ's crucifixion in his hands and feet – the first known instance of the Stigmata. Two years later, surrounded by his brothers, he died in the chapel of the Portiuncula. Less than two years afterwards, he was canonized by his old friend Ugolino, who had become Pope Gregory IX in 1227.

Francis' spirituality was generous, ardent, and tender.[6] He was fully absorbed by his love for Christ, whose compassion and poverty he wished to emulate as closely as possible. To many, Francis *was* another Christ. He was able to find God present wherever he looked – among the poor and suffering, in prayer and contemplation, in nature – perhaps especially in nature. His "Canticle of the Sun" is one of the greatest expressions of creation mysticism even written. Yet Francis also knew the darkness of desolation and sense of God's absence, and his nature mysticism counterpointed a deep and abiding passion for social justice.

*Clare: Sister Moon*

Unlike St. Dominic, Francis did not begin his order with a foundation for women, although it is told that when he began to rebuild the old church of San Damiano, he said "Here there will be a convent of holy virgins of Christ." And women were not long in becoming members of Francis' community of disciples. About the year 1210, a young noblewoman, Chiara (Clare) of Assisi (1193-1253), was attracted by Francis' preaching and example, and, after several secret meetings, succeeded in overcoming her parents' opposition to her desire to enter religious life as a nun. Despite their efforts to bear away her and her sister Agnes by force, in 1212, Clare became the leader of the small community at San Damiano. In 1216, although only twenty-two, she became abbess.

The same year, Jacques de Vitry, on his way to Acre as bishop, noted at Perugia the existence of both Little Brothers and Sisters of the Poor – the early Franciscans. At San Damiano, however, it was not clear that the new foundation was to be distinctively Franciscan. In 1219, Cardinal Ugolino, protector of both the Franciscan and Dominican orders, placed the whole group of women's houses under the Rule of St. Benedict. Only in 1253, two days before Clare's death, was her own Rule approved by the pope.[7]

Clare is one of the most appealing saints of the period. Much younger than Francis, she was one of his dearest friends. How many times he visited San Damiano on his travels is not known. But it is certain that he was nursed back to health there at least once, and there he composed his great "Canticle of the Sun."

*Anthony: The Teacher*

Another outstanding member of the early Franciscans famed for his preaching and miracles was Anthony of Padua (1195-1231), the special patron of the poor. Named Ferdinand by his well-born parents in Lisbon, he was drawn first to the Augustinian Canons. A desire for martyrdom led him to the Friars Minor when the remains of several Franciscan missionaries were returned from Morocco in 1220. He received the habit in the chapel of St. Anthony at Olivares, changing his own name.

After the General Chapter of 1221, Anthony was made the first lector of theology with Francis' approval and was charged with the instruction of new members. Active in preaching and reform in France and Italy, he was relieved of administrative duties in 1230 in order to devote himself more fully to preaching in the region of Padua. He died there a year later. Canonized within a year, he was declared a Doctor of the Church by Pope Pius XII in 1946.

*Bonaventure: The Seraphic Doctor*

Francis' Order of Little Brothers and Sisters continued to grow. But the inevitable differences among so many thousands of members that troubled the community even before his death were fated to develop into fractures after his passing. The major conflict arose between the "Spirituals," who maintained the ideal of the most radical poverty, and the "Conventuals," who were able to compromise with the demands of a dynamic society without abandoning Francis' essential vision. Their intermittent but increasingly bitter quarrels were abated, if only for a time, by the accession of one of the most astonishing saints of the Middle Ages as Minister General of the Order.

John of Fidanza (1217-74), the son of a noble Italian family, was cured of a serious illness as a child when his mother prayed to St. Francis. In 1243, he joined the Order in Paris, where he had already entered the university, and received the name Bonaventure.

Having trained under the English Franciscan, Alexander of Hales (1175-1245), Bonaventure's remarkable career as a scholar found him occupying a chair of theology at Paris at the same time as his younger contemporary and friend, the Dominican Thomas Aquinas. In 1257, however, his election as Minister General gave him the opportunity to pacify the feuding branches of his Order. He also began to compose his great spiritual masterpieces, *The Soul's Journey into God*, *the Tree of Life*, and his *Life of St. Francis*, which became the official biography of the founder.[8] In 1273, Bonaventure was made cardinal, and, having been called to the Council of Lyons in 1274, he died while it was still in session, only a few months after the death of his Dominican colleague. Canonized in 1482, he was declared a Doctor of the Church in 1588.

Bonaventure's major spiritual work, *The Soul's Journey into God*, continues and develops Francis' mystical sense of God's presence in creation. Bonaventure saw the entire universe both as a mirror that reflected God and as a ladder of ascent by which we pass over into God. The powers of the human soul, similarly, both image God and also lead to union with God. His spirituality was, moreover, intensely Christ-centered, for Jesus was ultimately not only the ladder, but the door, the goal as well as the way.

**The Flowers of St. Francis** Francis had not intended his friars to be scholars, yet Bonaventure — teacher, cardinal, and Doctor of the Church — was one of the greatest of Franciscan saints. His contemporary in England, Roger Bacon, was one of the greatest scientists of the period, and Duns Scotus (1266-1306) one of the greatest theologians of the Middle Ages. Nor did Francis establish the order as a clerical foundation, and he himself accepted ordination as a deacon only late in life. And while many of his greatest followers were in fact priests, lay members of the Order soon distinguished themselves as saints, mystics, and (also) scholars.[9]

Blessed Angela of Foligno (1248-1309) represents the impact of the Franciscan ideal on ordinary lay persons in the thirteenth century. After the death of her husband, Angela became a Franciscan tertiary or lay sister and lived as a hermit near the church of the Friars Minor at Foligno for the rest of her life. The record of her mystical revelations, *The Book of Divine Consolation*, is one of the treasures of medieval Italian literature.[10]

Although a woman of penetrating intellect, Angela's intense and lyrical love of God overshines her other gifts. Riveted on Christ, her contemplative gaze rarely wavers. But it was she who brought together two of the major strands of medieval imagination into a wonderful unity in her representation of her holy father, Francis, surrounded by his "Knights of the Round Table."

Ramon Lull (1233-1315) was born in Majorca and trained as a knight under James I of Aragon. A vision of the crucified Christ led him to dedicate himself to the service of God, particularly to convert the Muslim nations to Christianity. Also a Franciscan tertiary, Lull was advised by St. Raymond of Peñafort, a Dominican, to devote himself to the study of Arabic and Christian thought. As well as a philosopher, theologian, missionary, and linguist, Lull was also a mystic, and his major spiritual writings, *The Art of*

*Contemplation* and *The Book of the Lover and the Beloved* are filled with characteristic Franciscan love-mysticism, but also foreshadow the teachings of the great Carmelite mystics of the sixteenth century.[11] According to later accounts, Lull was martyred in North Africa.

Above all else, the thirteenth century was the epoch of the Mendicant Friars. Although the Franciscans and Dominicans were the most famous and most successful of the mendicant orders, they were only two of many orders of friars that flourished in the thirteenth century. The Carmelites, Augustinian Hermits, Servites, Trinitarians, Mercedarians, and Crosiers were also mendicant friars.[12] Their contribution to the Church was enormous, as was that of a still-amazing confederation of women, both lay and religious, who, as we shall see, continued the medieval revolution well into the next century.

## NOTES

1. See John T. McNeill, *The Celtic Churches* (Chicago: The University of Chicago Press, 1974).

2. For a brief account of Dominic Guzman's life and times, see Guy Bedouelle, O.P, *Saint Dominic: The Grace of the Word*, trans by Sr. Mary Thomas Noble, O.P (San Francisco: Ignatius Press, 1987). For a brief history of the Order of Preachers, see William A. Hinnebusch, O.P., *The Dominicans: A Short History* (Staten Island, NY: Alba House, 1975; Dublin: Dominican Publications, 1985). See also Simon Tugwell, O.P., "The Spirituality of the Dominicans," in Jill Raitt, ed., in collaboration with Bernard McGinn and John Meyendorff, *Christian Spirituality: High Middle Ages and Reformation* (New York: Crossroad, 1987), pp. 15-31.

3. For a brief introduction to the life and spirituality of St. Albert the Great, see Sr. Mary Albert, O.P., *Albert the Great* (River Forest, IL: *Spirituality Today Supplement*, Autumn, 1987). Also see Simon Tugwell, O.P., ed. and trans., *Albert [the Great] and Thomas [Aquinas], Selected Writings*, (New York: Paulist Press, 1988).

4. See Simon Tugwell, O.P. trans. and ed., *Early Dominicans: Selected Writings*, New York: Paulist Press, 1982, and Richard Woods, O.P., *Eckhart's Way* (Wilmington, DE and London: Michael Glazier/Darton, Longman and Todd, 1986), passim.

5. For a now-classic account of Francis' life, see G. K. Chesterton, *St. Francis of Assisi* (Garden City, NY: Doubleday Image Books, 1957 [1924]). See also Julien Green, *God's Fool: The Life and Times of Francis of Assisi*, trans. by Peter Heinegg (San Francisco: Harper and Row, 1985). For a complete edition of Francis' writings, the earliest Lives, and legends, see Marion A. Habig, ed., *St. Francis of Assisi: Writings and Early Biographies, An English Omnibus of the Sources for the Life of St. Francis* (Chicago: Franciscan Herald Press, 1973).

6. The nucleus of Francis' spirituality can be found in his few written works, including pre-eminently the Rule and his "Canticle of the Sun," all of which are found in the "Omnibus of Sources" ed by Marian A. Habig, pp. 1-176. They are also published together with the writings of Clare of Assisi in Regis Armstrong, O.F.M. Cap., and Ignatius C. Brady, O.F.M., trans. and ed., *Francis and Clare: The Complete Works* (New York: Paulist Press, 1982). Much of the authentic spirit of the early Franciscans is caught in the imaginative tales of *The Little Flowers of St. Francis of Assisi*, which is available in many modern editions. See especially the "Omnibus of Sources" ed. by Marian A. Habig, pp. 1267-1530.

7. See Armstrong and Brady, *Francis and Clare: The Complete Works*, ed. cit., and Regis Armstrong, O.F.M. Cap., trans. and ed., *Clare of Assisi: Early Documents* (New York: Paulist Press, 1988).

8. See Ewert Cousins, trans. and ed., *Bonaventure: The Soul's Journey into God, The Tree of Life, The Life of St. Francis* (New York: Paulist Press, 1978).

9. See J. A. Wayne Hellmann, "The Spirituality of the Franciscans," in Raitt, *Christian Spirituality*, ed. cit., pp. 31-50.

10. Angela of Foligno, *The Book of Divine Consolation*, trans. by Mary G. Steegman (New York: Cooper Square Press, 1966).

11. See Ramon Lull, *The Art of Contemplation*, trans. by E. Allison Peers (London: S.P.C.K., 1925) and *The Book of the Lover and the Beloved*, ed. by Kenneth Leech, trans. by E. Allison Peers (New York: Paulist Press, 1978).

12. See Keith J. Egan, "The Spirituality of the Carmelites," in Raitt, *Christian Spirituality*, ed. cit., pp. 50-62, and Adolar Zumkeller, "The Spirituality of the Augustinians," ibid., pp. 63-74.

# The Mystical Revolution 14

URING THE HIGH MIDDLE AGES, the sense of God was an almost palpable presence, especially in the lives of the outstanding saints of the period such as Francis, Bonaventure, and Thomas Aquinas. But if the spirituality of the era was characterized by its urban setting and the coming of the friars, it was no less influenced by the first great awakening of religious women as a spiritual force in Christianity, whose sense of God was no less keen or their response less ardent.

Spiritually, the fourteenth century would be dominated in Europe by Dominican and Franciscan friars, notably Meister Eckhart, Henry Suso, and John Tauler. St. Gregory Palamas towers above spiritual writers in the East — and even many in the West, where his mystical doctrine was most seriously challenged. But the amazing mystical revolution that characterizes the century was from first to last the burden, task, and glory of Christian women such as Mechthild of Magdeburg, Catherine of Siena, Bridgit of Sweden, and the lay movement known as the Beguines.[1]

*Women of God*

The lives of a number of saintly women in the Low Countries of the early thirteenth century were written by Bishop Jacques de Vitry of Liège and Thomas of Chantimpré, an Augustinian Canon who later entered the Dominicans and became the biographer of St. Albert the Great. The lives of other women are known from similar sources. But the bishop knew these women directly, having aided and guided them, and not infrequently defended them against civil and ecclesiastical adversaries. For contrary to custom and even some popular feeling, these Beguines, while profoundly religious, were neither nuns nor recluses, choosing to live in the world according to a simple gospel spirituality.

The most famous of the early Beguines was St. Marie of Oignies (c. 1177-1213). Married at fourteen, she persuaded her young husband not only to live with her in sexual abstinence, but even to join her in tending lepers. Eventually, she established herself at the priory of St. Nicholas at Oignies, where she became the leader of a sizable network of like-minded women.

The visionary poet Hadewijch of Antwerp is today perhaps the best known of the Beguines, although little information about her life can be discovered from her poems, letters, and prose works, which are some of the first works in the Dutch vernacular.[2] The theme of ecstatic love found in the writings of St. Bernard permeate her works and through them, *Brautmystik* — the "bridal mysticism" of loving union with God — became a major element in Beguine spirituality.

As for many of her contemporaries, for Juliana of Cornillon (d. 1258) the sense of the presence of God was centered on the humanity of Jesus and the Eucharist. She especially promoted the feast of Corpus Christi, which, from a local devotion in Liège in 1242, was extended to the whole Church by Pope Urban IV in 1264 and became one of the most popular feasts of the Middle Ages.

Other outstanding women of the Low Countries were Beatrice of Nazareth and especially the amazing Christina of St. Trond (1150-1224), who claimed to have returned from purgatory after reviving at her own funeral. Ivetta of Huy (1157-1228), a friend of Marie of Oignies, was married at the early age of thirteen. Widowed at eighteen with two sons, five years later she left them in the care of her father and opened a hostel for pilgrims, then a leper colony.

Margaret of Ypres (1216-37) was an early Dominican tertiary. Lutgard of Aywieres (c. 1182-1246) became a Benedictine at twelve.

At twenty-four, on her election as abbess, she left for the Cistercian priory at Aywieres where she spent the rest of her life in humility and obscurity. She, too, knew and visited Ivetta of Huy.

The spirituality of these remarkable women embodied many of the essential elements of medieval religion in its most intense expression — it was primarily a lay movement rather than clerical or monastic; it was feminine; it encompassed a life of mystical contemplation focused on the divine humanity of Christ; it embraced a life of voluntary poverty, humility, and chastity; and it found characteristic expression in the service of the poor, sick, and suffering.

Many Beguines begged on the street, even in defiance of ecclesiastical prohibitions against mendicancy. Others supported themselves by handiwork, particularly weaving, spinning (from which comes the epithet "spinsters"), and sewing, and gave any surplus income to the poor. When their daily duties were finished, they joined in common prayer, scripture study, and what today we would call theological reflection. In many respects, the Beguines and similar associations of holy women in the thirteenth century created the first "base communities" in the new urban environment. Their influence on the mendicant orders coming into existence at that time was both powerful and reciprocal.

*The German Mothers*

One of the most impressive thirteenth-century mystics was for most of her life a lay woman, whether or not she is to be considered a Beguine — Mechthild of Magdeburg (c. 1210-82).[3] She was strongly influenced by Dominican spirituality, as she testifies in the preface to her remarkable book *The Flowing Light of the Godhead*. Towards the end of her life, ill and growing blind, she entered the Cistercian abbey at Helfta, where she may have taken vows. There she finished her great book of prophecies, poetry, visions, parables, and letters, one often so critical of the spiritual laxity she perceived in the world around her that threats were made to burn it.

The convent at Helfta had been relocated from Rodersdorf in 1258 by its abbess, St. Gertrude of Hackeborn (1232-1292), one of the three outstanding nuns there when Mechthild entered. Dedicated to promoting the contemplative life, Gertrude had made the Abbey a recognized center of mystical spirituality, attracting to it saints such as her sister, St. Mechthild of Hackeborn (1241-1299) and St. Gertrude the Great (1256-1302), both poets and scholars.[4]

The influence of Mechthild of Magdeburg on this coterie of holy women was at least as profound as its effect on her. Perhaps the first mystic to have received a vision of the heart of Christ as the focus of divine love and human compassion, Mechthild's devotion to the Sacred Heart became especially characteristic of the Helfta nuns.

*Ecclesiastical Reaction* At the beginning of the fourteenth century, the trials and tragedies that for the next two hundred years would befall Christendom, its mystics not least of all, were ominously presaged by the execution of Marguerite Porete, a French Beguine whose teachings were twice condemned, once by the bishop of Cambrai and again by twenty-one regent masters of the University of Paris.[5] Delivered to the provost of Paris for sentencing, she was publicly burned at the stake on 1 June 1310, along with a relapsed Jew, in what was apparently the first such execution in Paris.

The trials and death of Marguerite Porete as a heretic illustrate the controversy over mystical spiritualities which had arisen in Europe with the quest for the *vita apostolica* and the awakening of theological speculation. Although evidently well-born and theologically educated, Porete was pantheistic in her expression and inclined toward quietism. That is, she believed that the being of all things was that of God, and that in the final stages of spiritual development, the purified and illuminated soul passively abstained from all activity.

Two of Marguerite's teachings seemed especially ominous to the commissions that examined her: the annihilation of the soul in

God, and salvation by faith without works. In *The Mirror of Simple Souls*, the book for which she was burned (and which, the authorities believed, perished with her), she epitomized the offending doctrine in a single sentence: "Of [the peace of charity in annihilated life], says Love, we wish to speak, asking that one find a soul who saves herself by faith without works, who is alone in love, who does nothing for God, who leaves God nothing to do, who can be taught nothing, from whom nothing can be taken, to whom nothing can be given, who has no will."[6]

At another time, a God-intoxicated laywoman like Marguerite might have been reprimanded and given penance for her theological unwariness. But times had changed. Institutionally, the Church was both powerful and under attack politically, theologically, and spiritually. Dissent would not be tolerated for long.

Shortly after Porete's execution, the Council of Vienne (1311-12) took drastic steps to stem the tide of popular enthusiasm, aiming stringent condemnations at the Beguines in particular. Six of the bishops who had condemned Porete in Paris also attended the council, and it is not an accident of history that henceforth the terms "Beguine" and "heretic" would be synonymous. Nor is it an unrelated coincidence that not long afterward, the shadow of the Inquisition fell over the path of the greatest preacher and mystic of the century, several of whose teachings resembled those of Porete, especially the nothingness of the soul compared to God, and the priority of faith over works.

**Master of Mystics**
Eckhart of Hochheim was born about 1260 in a Thuringian village in northeastern Germany near the town of Erfurt.[7] When he joined the Dominican Order about 1275, he would have been called Friar Eckhart. But after he completed his advanced studies at the University of Paris in 1302, he would be known henceforth and forever as "Meister" (Master) Eckhart — the only medieval figure bearing that title who is still known by it today.

As a student friar, Eckhart went to Cologne in 1280 for his initial studies. There he seems to have met the aged "Bishop Albrecht" — St. Albert the Great, who died in the autumn of the same year. Eckhart was definitely schooled by Albert's disciples, themselves now professors, and although Thomas Aquinas had been dead for some six years, young Eckhart became an ardent if selective Thomist. In 1293, he was sent to Paris for doctoral studies. Even so, he was also elected to a number of important positions in the Dominican Order, and obtained his magistral hat only nine years later.

After a year as Regent Master, Eckhart, now forty-three, was elected provincial of Saxony and placed in charge of the nuns of the region. At this time, large numbers of Beguines had already entered Dominican convents, and both Dominican and Franciscan friars had also been charged with responsibility for the spiritual direction of many Beguine houses which were not formally related to either order. Whole convents of other religious orders had also changed their affiliation to the Dominicans, and several new foundations were made.

What attracted large numbers of devout, well-educated women to the Dominicans in the late thirteenth and early fourteenth centuries was, it appears, the emphasis placed on study in the order as well as the mystical character of its spirituality at this time. This characteristic is traceable in great measure to the influence of Albert the Great, who had himself been a scientist, theologian, philosopher, and mystic.

The encounter between the dynamic preacher and the God-centered women produced one of the most spectacular upsurges of mystical spirituality in the history of the West. The Quaker historian Rufus Jones aptly named it "the flowering of mysticism." Eckhart, of course, was not the only Dominican, nor the only preacher influential in the formation of the mystical revolution of the fourteenth century. But he was undeniably the greatest.[8]

His sermons were memorized by the nuns and committed to writing. Although seized by the Inquisition as evidence, over one hundred of the Meister's authentic sermons have survived to the present. Several volumes of his Latin writings, mainly theological works and scriptural commentaries have also been discovered as well as four German treatises on the spiritual life.

After several years of preaching and teaching in Strassburg and its environs, Eckhart was recalled to Cologne in 1322 to follow in the footsteps of Albert the Great once again as Regent Master. Three years later, however, at the age of sixty-six, he was accused of preaching heresy by the Franciscan bishop of Cologne, the formidable Henry of Virneburg.

Although Eckhart defended himself strenuously, claiming that the charges were lodged out of jealousy, the verdict went against him. Supported by his brethren, Eckhart appealed to the pope, and after several months of preparation, walked over 500 miles to Avignon to plead his case. The process dragged on for more than a year. Sometime before the final judgment, the old friar died, having first retracted anything that could be proved heretical in his teachings while still denying that either his intention or actual words were in fact contrary to the faith.

Although the papal bull published in 1329 condemned as heretical fifteen propositions taken from Eckhart's works, modern scholarship and the opinion of mystics and spiritual leaders the world over have testified to their orthodoxy, as well as to their depth and brilliance. Eckhart continues to influence God-seekers today and will, no doubt, forever.

*The Birth of God*

The central teaching of Eckhart's spirituality concerns the birth of the Word of God in the souls of the just. Built upon a thorough knowledge of scripture, the ancient spiritual theology of Alexandria, the teachings of the Cappadocian Fathers, and the Dionysian writings translated by Eriugena, Eckhart infused both Thomistic and Jewish elements into his great mystical synthesis.

For Eckhart, God was uniquely present in the deepest abyss of the human soul, waiting only to break forth into joyful consciousness and prevented only by our inattentiveness, greed, and indifference to justice and love. Radically apophatic, Eckhart asserted that nothing could describe either God or the soul. Rather, their absolute simplicity and mutual longing were the condition for a realization of union which transcended all categories of understanding. Becoming one with God by ridding the mind of all images and the heart of all attachments was the true and only work to which the human spirit was called.

Not even condemnation could dispel the force of Eckhart's teaching, which was preserved by the Dominican friars and sisters throughout the Rhineland. (Nearly six hundred excerpts from Eckhart's commentary on John's Gospel copied by the friars at Erfurt were discovered as late as 1960.) Two of Eckhart's students, Blessed Henry Suso and John Tauler, preached extensively and wrote, cautiously perpetuating their master's authentic spirituality. Within a generation, it had even reached England, where it would deeply influence the author of *the Cloud of Unknowing*.[9]

A Germanic mystical movement known as "the Friends of God" developed under the preachers' influence, extending from Switzerland to the Netherlands, where the shrewd Jan van Ruysbroeck carefully distinguished between "true" and "false" or heretical Friends of God. For heterodox preachers and writers had availed themselves of Eckhart's reputation even before his death, publishing their antinomian tracts under his name, a fact that may have weighed heavily against Eckhart in his trials.

Another anonymous disciple, perhaps a member of the Teutonic Knights, interpreted Eckhart's doctrine in the *Theologia Germanica*, a book so highly valued by Luther that he published versions of it in 1516 and 1518.[10] The Reformer was also profoundly affected by some of Eckhart's sermons which were attributed at the time to Tauler. Typically for Rhineland Dominican spirituality at the time, they opposed humble and radical faith to ascetical works as the way to union with God.

Although Eckhart's teaching had been opposed by William of Ockham and other Spirituals, by the turn of the century, even Franciscan mysticism had taken on an Eckhartian flavor. In the following century, his mystical doctrine found an attentive student in the brilliant Neoplatonist, Cardinal Nicholas of Cusa. In time, Eckhart's mysticism would come to impress some of the deepest minds of Europe, America, and Asia, especially Zen Buddhists.

*The Singer of Songs*     Although the spirituality of the fourteenth century was largely dominated by Dominicans in the vast territories of the Rhineland, Franciscan influence remained extensive there and elsewhere. Not even the tragic schism between Conventuals and Spirituals could diminish the authentic spirit of the Poor Man of Assisi, especially in the cities among lay men and women such as Angela of Foligno and the reckless poet, Jacopone da Todi (1230-1306).

A light-hearted young lawyer, Jacopone was suddenly jolted into new depth and seriousness when his beloved wife was killed in an accident. For some time, he wandered with the Spiritual Franciscans, becoming a lay member of the Order in 1278. Granted permission by Pope Celestine V in 1294 to live with his community in the strict simplicity of the early Order, Jacopone found himself burdened by its reversal in 1298 by Boniface VIII. Among other Spirituals, he was imprisoned until 1303. He died three years later.

Even in prison, Jacopone's lyricism did not desert him. But in addition to poems and hymns, including the immortal *Stabat Mater*, he penned satirical attacks on Boniface, an error of judgment which ultimately prevented his canonization, since the old pope died a virtual martyr from mistreatment at the hands of William de Nogaret and the French troops of King Philip IV in 1303.

In the late Middle Ages, lay members of the great mendicant orders achieved heights of sanctity often lacking among the clerical friars. Few, if any, can compare with a frail young Italian girl who attempted — and very nearly succeeded — to heal the greatest breach in the Western Church before the Reformation.

**Catherine the Greater**

Like Pietro Bernadone, the father of Francis of Assisi, Giacomo Benincasa was a dyer. He had a large family, the youngest of twenty-four children being a radiant girl named Catherine. (Giovanna, her twin, died shortly after birth.) A visionary from the age of six, Catherine pledged herself to be Christ's bride at the age of seven. At fifteen, refusing to marry despite her mother's distraught entreaties, she cut off her glorious hair at the advice of her cousin, a Dominican friar.[11]

No amount of drudgery imposed on her by her grief-stricken mother could shake Catherine's resolution. By the age of eighteen, she had overcome all resistance and joined a group of *Mantellata* — laywomen, most of them elderly widows, associated with the Dominican Order.

Catherine now undertook a life of seclusion, asceticism, and prayer as a hermit in her father's house. After three years, however, she underwent a mystical transformation. She emerged from seclusion determined to serve the poor and wretched of Christ. But her ministry quickly took her beyond the lepers, plague victims, poor, sick, and homeless citizens of Siena. Until her death at the age of thirty-three, Catherine addressed her considerable energies to peace-making among warring Italian cities and even the restoration of the papacy to Rome.

Since 1305, the papal court had resided at Avignon, where weak French popes were controlled with little difficulty by strong French kings such as Philip IV, whose troops had murdered Boniface VIII, and who had effectively destroyed the Order of Knights Templar, the most powerful military order in the Church, in the vain hope of despoiling their treasury.

From the Holy City, saints such as Bridgit of Sweden (1303-73), a widow, mother of a large family, visionary, and prophet, had exhorted and begged the pope to return to the seat of Peter. But Rome was not only languishing, it was decayed, depopulated, crumbling, filled with unhealthy mists from the Tiber's swamps as well as unruly mobs of poor and desperate citizens. Avignon was sunny, warm, beautiful, and, above all, safely French.

In 1376, at the age of twenty-nine, Catherine and her followers journeyed to Avignon to plead with Pope Gregory XI on behalf of the city of Florence, which had taken up arms against the papal forces and was under interdict. She took advantage of the occasion to persuade the pope to return to Rome and end the "Babylonian captivity" of the Church imposed by the French kings. Against his better judgment, the pleas of his family, the horror of the French cardinals, the will of the king, and the advice of his councilors, Gregory did as Catherine (and others) had bade.

After a terrible journey, the pope solemnly entered the City in 1377. Unhappy in Rome, however, and largely unsuccessful in subduing the rebellious papal states, Gregory was planning to return to Avignon when he died the following year. The Roman populace demanded an Italian pope. Terrified of the mob, the cardinals elected the Archbishop of Bari as Urban VI, the first non-French pope in sixty years. But Urban was also impulsive, violent, and mentally unstable. So aggravating was his reign that after four months of mounting terror, the French cardinals fled Rome, nullified Urban's election on the basis of duress, and elected Robert of Geneva as Clement VI. At least as brutal as Urban, the antipope was not mad, however, and established his pontificate at Avignon.

Not even war could overcome the breach; the Great Western Schism had begun — a wound in the Body of Christ that would not be healed until the Council of Constance in 1417. Catherine of Siena, who had returned to her birthplace a year after Gregory's entry into Rome, became an ardent supporter of Urban VI despite his excesses, for she — more clearly than most — was able to perceive the difference between the office and the man. Regardless of Urban's manifest failings, he *was* the legitimate pope. As such he was the successor of Peter and therefore, for her anyway, "Christ on earth."

In Siena, Catherine had just completed her masterwork, *the Dialogue*.[12] Returning to Rome, Catherine wrote, preached, and worked tirelessly for two years to pacify and unify the Body of Christ — pushing herself beyond the limits of even her formidable stamina. At last she fell seriously ill, and could neither eat nor drink. For the last two months of her life, she lay paralyzed, then, on 29 April 1380, died in the arms of her disciples calling on the mercy of the Blood of Jesus. One of the most gifted and extraordinary Christian women of any era, Catherine was canonized in 1461 and declared a Doctor of the Church in 1970.

*The Beginning of the End*

In 1347, the year of Catherine's birth, trading ships returning from the East along trade routes opened by the Crusades had brought back with them more than spices, silks, and treasure. Rats infected with plague-carrying fleas had boarded in some distant city, and now disembarked at various ports along the Mediterranean coast. Soon, the bubonic plague that may have already killed as much as half the population of Asia was spreading northwards along European trade routes.[13]

The depths of suffering and despair experienced in Europe between 1347 and the end of the century were as great or greater than any since the barbarian attacks of the early fifth century. But in the latter days as in the former, the heights of holiness achieved by ordinary men and women conscious of the divine bond of presence were still greater. Many died nursing the sick, others suffered in defense of the poor, the oppressed, the defenseless.

In Cologne and other German cities, the "Cellites," Beghards who followed the spiritual teaching of Eckhart, attended the dying and buried the dead with outstanding dedication. Like their Meister, they freely and even gladly took upon themselves the weight of suffering as well as glory promised to those who would be the friends of God. Not surprisingly, when persecuted in later years by the Inquisition for their adherence to Eckhart, the Cellites received protection from civil magistrates, bishops, and even the pope. They were eventually recognized as the Alexian Brothers, one of the Church's great nursing orders.

The century that began with the burning of Marguerite Porete ended with a third to half the population dead of plague, as well as an intermittent war between England and France that would last for a century and leave both nations bloodied, depleted, and poor by the time a relative peace was finally achieved. The Church itself was also divided between as many as three rival popes at one time. Confusion and disorder were rampant. It was an age born to woe, perhaps one made endurable only by the remarkable flowering of mysticism that would continue to invigorate the spirituality of the coming troubled centuries.

## NOTES

1. See especially Caroline Walker Bynum, "Religious Women in the Middle Ages," in Raitt, *Christian Spirituality*, ed. cit., pp. 121-39.
2. See *Hadewijch: The Complete Works*, trans. by Mother Columba Hart (New York: Paulist Press, 1980) and Ria Vanderauwera, "The Brabant Mystic: Hadewijch," in Katharina Wilson, *Medieval Women Writers*, pp. 186-203.
3. See Mechtild of Magdeburg, *Revelations, The Flowing Light of the Godhead*, trans. by Lucy Menzies (London, 1953). See also John Howard, "The German Mystic: Mechthild of Magdeburg," in Katharina Wilson, *Medieval Women Writers*, pp. 153-85.
4. See Gertrud the Great of Helfta, *Spiritual Exercises*, trans. and ed. by Gertrud Jaron Lewis and Jack Lewis (Kalamazoo: Cistercian Publications, 1989), St. Gertrude the Great, *The Life and Revelations* (Westminster, MD: Christian Classics, 1986), and Theresa A. Halligan, *The Booke of Gostlye Grace of Mechtild of Hackeborn* (Toronto: Pontifical Institute of Medieval Studies, 1979).
5. See Gwendolyn Bryant, "The French Heretic Beguine: Marguerite Porete," in Katharina Wilson, *Medieval Women Writers*, pp. 204-26.
6. See Marguerite Porete, *Speculum Simplicium Animarum*, ed. by Romana Guarnieri (Turnholti: Brepols, 1986 [Corpus Christianorum, v. 69]).
7. On the Rhineland mystics, see Alois Maria Haas, "Schools of Late Medieval Mysticism," in Raitt, *Christian Spirituality*, ed. cit., pp. 140-75, and Oliver Davies, *God Within: The Mystical Tradition of Northern Europe* (London: Darton, Longman and Todd, 1988 and New York: Paulist Press, 1988). For a general introduction to Eckhart's life and teaching see Richard Woods, O.P., *Eckhart's Way*, op. cit. For a study of his language and doctrine, see Frank Tobin, *Eckhart, Language and Thought* (Scranton: University of Pennsylvania Press, 1987). The best translation of Eckhart's German *Sermons and Treatises* is the three-volume set by M. O'C. Walshe (Longmead, Shaftesbury, Dorset: Element Books, 1987). Selected German and Latin works can also be found in the two volume edition, *The Essential Sermons, Commentaries, Treatises and Defense*, edited by Bernard McGinn and Edmund Colledge, and *Meister Eckhart: Teacher and Preacher*, ed. by Bernard McGinn and Frank Tobin (New York: Paulist Press, 1985 and 1987).
8. See Rufus Jones, "Meister Eckhart: The Peak of the Range," *The Flowering of Mysticism in the Fourteenth Century* (New York: Hafner Publishing Co., 1971 [1939]), pp. 61-85.

9. English translations of Suso's works are found in *The Exemplar, with Two German Sermons*, trans. and ed. by Frank Tobin (New York: Paulist Press, 1989); *The Little Book of Eternal Wisdom and the Little Book of Truth*, trans. by James M. Clark (New York: Harper and Row, 1953); and *The Exemplar: Life and Writings of the Blessed Henry Suso, O.P.*, ed. by Nicholas Heller, trans. by Ann Edwards, O.P., Dubuque, IA: Priory Press, 1962. A collection of Tauler's *Sermons* has been translated by Maria Shrady (New York: Paulist Press, 1987). See also *Spiritual Conferences*, trans. and ed. by Eric Colledge and Sr. Mary Jane, O.P. (St. Louis: B. Herder, 1961). On the influence of Rhineland mysticism on the Cloud author, see Dom David Knowles, O.S.B., *The English Mystical Tradition* (New York: Harper and Bros., 1961), pp. 38, 71, 76-77, 95-96.

10. See *Theologia Germanica*, trans. by Susanna Winkworth, London: Macmillan, 1901 and especially *The Theologia Germanica of Martin Luther*, trans. by Bengt Hoffman, New York: Paulist Press, 1980. Cf. Oliver Davies, "Ruysbroeck, á Kempis and the *Theologia Deutsch*," in Jones, et al., *The Study of Spirituality*, pp. 321-24.

11. For a general overview of Catherine's life and teachings, see Mary Ann Fatula, *Catherine of Siena's Way* (Wilmington, DE: Michael Glazier, 1987). *The Prayers of Catherine of Siena* have been translated by Suzanne Noffke, O.P., (New York: Paulist Press, 1983). The first volume of Dr. Noffke's translation of *The Letters of Catherine of Siena* was recently published in the Medieval and Renaissance Texts and Studies series by the State University of New York Press (Binghamton, NY, 1989).

12. Catherine of Siena, *The Dialogue*, ed. and trans., Suzanne Noffke, O.P. (New York: Paulist Press, 1980).

13. For a general account of the great plague, see Philip Ziegler, *The Black Death* (New York: Harper Torchbooks, 1971).

# The Autumn of
# Christendom $15$

D ESPITE THE EXECUTION of Marguerite Porete and the condemnation of certain of Eckhart's teachings, the mystical revolution of the fourteenth century continued to flourish in the Netherlands, especially under the influence of Jan van Ruysbroeck, and suddenly in England. The spiritual skies were darkening, however, and the even more turbulent atmosphere of the fifteenth century would engender a reaction against both the intellectual mysticism and the corporate spirituality that had characterized the former era.

*Flemish Mysticism*

At the northern reaches of the Rhine, the great spiritual outflowing associated with Eckhart was channeled in less dangerous directions by the brilliant Jan van Ruysbroeck (1293-1381) and his followers at their haven called Groenendael, "the Green Valley."[1] The spirituality of the brethren at Groenendael, who took the habit of Canons Regular of St. Augustine, would greatly influence the *devotio moderna* in the fifteenth century. But it would also become less open and more other-worldly as the fourteenth century descended into the gloom of the Great Western Schism and recurrent episodes of plague and violence.

Ruysbroeck, who remained prior until his death, was not so greatly disillusioned as were his followers. His works, principally *the Spiritual Espousals, the Kingdom of the Lovers of God,* and *the Seven Steps of the Ladder of Spiritual Love,* remain classics of western spirituality.[2] Ruysbroeck was beatified in 1908.

One of Ruysbroeck's disciples, Geert (or Gerard) Groote (1340-84), was converted from a life of indolence in 1374 and retired to a monastery. Advised by the Flemish master to undertake a more active ministry, he became a celebrated preacher in Utrecht. Criticized, then suspended for his attacks on clerical abuses, Groote died before his appeal was heard. The community he had gathered at Deventer continued to develop, however, and adopted the name of the Brethren of the Common Life.

Originally a lay community without vows, some members of the group later became Augustinian canons. Famed for their teaching, the Brethren founded free schools throughout the Netherlands and Germany. Much of their time was spent in copying manuscripts and eventually in printing. Some of their illustrious members were Florenz Radwijns, Gabriel Biel, and Adrian Dedel (later Pope Hadrian VI). Thomas à Kempis, Nicholas of Cusa, Desiderius Erasmus, and Martin Luther were among their students.

The
English
Mystics

There had been saints and mystics in the British Isles for a thousand years before the flowering of mysticism in the fourteenth century. The five great figures of that period are known as *the* English mystics, however, and for much the same reason that Meister Eckhart, Catherine of Siena, and Jan van Ruysbroeck lay claim to similar titles in their respective nations.[3]

Like the continental mystics, the English also wrote in the vernacular at the moment in which the language was finding its first and possibly finest literary expression. It was the age of Chaucer, Langland, and Malory, and the writings of Richard Rolle, Walter Hilton, the author of *the Cloud of Unknowing,* Julian of Norwich, and, at the end of the century, even the lovable, somewhat dotty Margery Kempe show much of the same vitality, richness, and originality as well as spiritual depth and (with the exception of the latter) good common sense.

*Fire and Love*

Richard Rolle, the earliest of the fourteenth century English mystics, greatly resembled Francis of Assisi in many aspects of his life and teaching.[4] Turning to the contemplative life in his late teens, apparently after suffering rejection in an affair of the heart, Richard decided upon the life of a hermit, eventually coming to live near Hampole. The nuns there regarded him a saint; after his death (sometime after 1347, probably tending victims of the Black Death), they composed an office commemorating his memory.

In his poems and especially his prose works, some of which were the earliest vernacular writings in Middle English, Rolle developed his themes of God's interior presence, which manifested itself by the effects of "heat, sweetness, and song." These mystical, indeed bodily experiences of sudden inner warmth, an overwhelming sense of gentle joy, and the sound of celestial music (sometimes associated with angel choirs), became the goal and sign of spiritual seeking for many of those influenced by Rolle's writings, especially the *Fire of Love* and the *Amending of Life*. Refuting some of the cruder physicalism of such enthusiasts occupied the attention of two of the greatest writers of the period immediately following — the anonymous author of the *Cloud of Unknowing* and a half-dozen shorter masterpieces of Dionysian mysticism, and the Augustinian canon, Walter Hilton.

*The Cloud and the Ladder*

According to a contemporary writer, Dionysian spirituality "ran across England like a deer" when the works of the Pseudo-Areopagite were introduced then translated into the vernacular — the *Cloud* author's free version of the *Mystical Theology* being one of the most important.[5] Evidently a priest, a hermit, and probably Dominican-trained if not a friar himself, the anonymous master of the spiritual life was in any event deeply influenced by Rhineland mysticism.[6] Written perhaps in the mid-1370s, the *Cloud of Unknowing* and its attendant works are the only English spiritual writings of the period that show this influence. Many passages in the *Cloud* were most likely paraphrased or freely translated from Eckhart's sermons.

Concerned with contemplation and union with God, the *Cloud* author, like Eckhart, presupposes the ordinary commitments and observances of Christian religion. His works were written for disciples well along in the spiritual life rather than for beginners. He is chiefly preoccupied with ridding consciousness of all attempts to conceptualize God, and with removing the obstacles to contemplative union posed by self-concern. In passages of quaint humor, he disparages spiritual seekers who attempt to force mystical awareness into the often illusory forms of physical phenomena.

Like the *Cloud* author, Walter Hilton wrote primarily for those already engaged in the contemplative life, particularly nuns. His scope is much broader, however, if his insights and style are less daring. He is a solid rather than an exciting writer. Nevertheless, in his masterwork, the *Scale of Perfection* (which he modeled in some respects on the work of St. John Climicus), he proposes the reformation of spiritual life "in faith and feeling" — a holistic and radical transformation of the human image into the Image of Christ.[7]

In his little masterpiece, *On the Song of Angels*, Hilton, also like the *Cloud* author, distinguishes helpfully between true and illusory physical phenomena. He thus provides, by the way, a telling witness to the authentic experience of the celestial music reported by Rolle and in later centuries found in the lives of mystics both East and West.

*Dame Julian: Anonymous Anchorite*

Like the *Cloud* author, the mystical writer greatly beloved as "Julian of Norwich" has evaded every attempt to uncover her identity. The name was attributed to her from the parish church in Norwich where she was walled into a cell to spend the rest of her life in prayer and contemplation.[8]

"Dame" Julian's spiritual odyssey began on 8 May 1373. Gravely ill with an unspecified disease, possibly the plague, she received fifteen visions during an ecstasy that lasted about five hours. On regaining consciousness, she found herself cured, to the alarm of some of those in attendance who thought she had died. The following day, she received another vision which amplified and clarified the meaning of the others.

As she never tires of repeating in her amazing manuscript, *Showings of Divine Love*, the meaning is simply Love. God as pure Love is the origin, the goal, the way, the means, and the motive of everything that is. Although focussed on the passion and death of Christ, her revelations encompass an astounding range of topics and express an unquenchable optimism in God's power to bring good out of evil. "All shall be well," she reiterates. "All shall be well, and all manner of thing shall be well."

Although a recluse, Julian was well educated theologically and spiritually, possibly having been a Benedictine novice before her illness and ecstatic revelations. She also gave spiritual advice, as we know from the reference to her in the precious single manuscript of a very different, lovable, but undoubtedly unusual lay mystic of the turn of the fifteenth century who consulted her.

*Margery Kempe: Would-Be Saint*

Margery Burnham (c. 1373-1433), was the daughter of the Mayor of Lynn, Norfolk, the wife of John Kempe, a merchant of the town, and the mother of fourteen children.[9] After the difficult birth of her last child, she experienced a mystical revelation in which she was promised to become Christ's bride, thus obligating her to a life of continual sexual abstinence. After some time, she convinced her husband of the correctness of her vision, and they joined a pilgrimage to Canterbury, the first of many for Margery. In 1413 the couple exchanged vows of chastity before the bishop of Lincoln.

Accused of being a Lollard (a follower of John Wycliffe's radical teachings) because of her denunciations of clerical immorality and general vice, Margery Kempe narrowly escaped censure and even imprisonment on several occasions. Her long (and often harrowing) pilgrimages to Rome, Jerusalem, Compostella, Norway, and Danzig between 1413 and 1433 thus served a tactical as well as spiritual purpose.

In her wonderful journal, published only in 1935 as *The Book of Margery Kempe*,[10] the "apprentice saint" described in the form of memoirs dictated at the end of her life the misadventures that befell her during these pilgrimages. It is easy to dismiss her as a mere hysteric, and thus well to remember that Margery was perhaps the first laywomen ever to attempt the composition of such a work in any language.

Further, she lived and "wrote" at a moment in spiritual history in which the rich network of support and advice that had nurtured Mechthild of Magdeburg and Catherine of Siena was now shattered. The chief source of inspiration was now one's own inner experience, which in Margery's case and that of many others of the time often took the form of ecstatic raptures and public displays of religious emotion. The "modern devotion" had begun.

Other literary works of mystical significance were composed during the fourteenth century, such as the anonymous poems "The Pearl," "Cleanness," and "Patience," and the romantic allegory *Sir Gawain and the Green Knight*, which blends Arthurian and Celtic themes.[11] Sometime after the middle of the century, William Langland, an otherwise unknown minor cleric of Shropshire, penned one of the treasures of early English literature. His long, satirical poem, *Piers Plowman*, testifies to the depth of spirituality among ordinary people as well as its lack among many of the clergy of the time.[12]

*The Fall of the East*    The climax of Christian mystical spirituality in the fourteenth century was not limited to Europe. The declining years of the Byzantine Empire also witnessed the last great development of classical Eastern spirituality, that long tradition stretching back to Philo's Alexandria.   Paradoxically, because of its controversial character, what was a major breakthrough in mystical theology also became a factor in the growing rift between Constantinople and Rome.

Tensions between East and West, not least in spirituality, had a long history before the "Great Schism."   In 917, the Bulgarian church had separated from both Rome and Constantinople.   The mutual excommunications of 1054 themselves attracted only minor attention from Eastern or Western writers of the time, acquiring a definitive character only in hindsight.   And although tensions mounted critically during the first three crusades, military cooperation was still possible.   Several attempts at theological reunion very nearly succeeded, moreover, the most noteworthy being the Council of Lyons in 1274, which St. Bonaventure attended, and the Council of Florence in 1439.

In both instances, formal reconciliation was effected by official delegates of the popes, emperors, and at least several Eastern patriarchs.  But the reunion was strongly repudiated by the Eastern clergy, monks, nuns, and lay people, not in small measure because of the lasting and terrible memory of the Western sack of Constantinople in 1204, the imposition of a Latin imperium over the East for fifty years, and the attempt by Innocent III and his successors forcibly to "Romanize" the Byzantine Church.

*The March of Folly*    The spirit of Crusade that had arisen from a sincere desire to reclaim the lands of Christ from their Muslim conquerors had plunged to its nadir in 1203. Led by the rival princes Boniface of Montserrat and Baudoin of Flanders, the armies of the Fourth Crusade were diverted from Palestine and Egypt by the blind Doge of

Venice, Enrico Dandalo, because of his city's intense commercial rivalry with Constantinople.

The siege and capture of the imperial capital, and the three days of looting that followed, left thousands of Greek Christians dead and wounded, including vast numbers of women, children, and the aged. It was the only achievement of the Crusade, which served mainly to satisfy the Doge's need for revenge, Baudoin's lust for power, and the Western monarchs' greed for the riches and relics of centuries. In the popular mind, it also rendered permanent the schism between East and West.

The violent Baudoin was elected Latin Emperor of the East in 1204. Killed in a disastrous battle with rebellious Greeks and their Bulgar allies barely a year later, Baudoin was succeeded by his comparatively chivalrous brother, Henry of Flanders. In 1262, Constantinople was reclaimed by the Greeks, and the usurper Michael Paleologus proclaimed Emperor. But its wealth, relics, and art treasures were largely flown, its spirit crushed, and its population demoralized as well as surrounded (as always) by hostile Muslim states. The Great City would never recover its former power and glory. It would endure as a Christian city only two hundred years longer, falling at last to the Turks in 1453. Nevertheless, during the interim, Byzantium was able to achieve a modest renaissance in art and literature, and even more so in spirituality.

**The Hesychast Controversy**

Despite the decline of Byzantium as a political power and theological capital, during the fourteenth century, the spiritual tradition known as *hesychasm* reached a peak of development among the monks of Mt. Athos, and particularly as articulated defensively by one of the most remarkable figures of the period, St. Gregory Palamas.

*Hesychia*, "calm" or "quietude," had long been considered the contemplative ideal in the desert spirituality of the East. A state of bodily, mental, and spiritual tranquillity achieved by "placing the mind in the heart," controlling breathing, and focussing attention, hesychasm resembled both Hindu and Buddhist practices in some respects. What is most remarkable about its emergence in a spiritual and intellectual climate pervaded by Platonic and Neo-platonic teachings is the integral role it gave the body in achieving closeness to God. It was this aspect, among others, that excited the violent opposition of the Italian Greek philosopher, Barlaam of Calabria.

*Athos: God's Holy Mountain* Mt. Athos is a rocky peninsula that thrusts off the Macedonian coast into the Aegean Sea between Greece and Bulgaria. Founded in the late tenth century, the community of monasteries clustered about the mountainside has remained the center of Byzantine monastic orthodoxy and spirituality for 900 years. Fundamental to its practice was the repetition of the "Jesus Prayer," based on Mt 9:27 (cf. Mark 10:47): "Lord Jesus Christ, Son of God, have mercy on me, a sinner," together with breathing and centering exercises.

Developed at the monastery of St. Catherine on Mt. Sinai, these practices had been taught for centuries by orthodox spiritual guides such as St. Diadochus of Photike in the fifth century and St. John Climicus in the eighth, who advocated "attaching the name of Jesus to one's breath." But in the heated, exciting atmosphere of late Byzantium, they suddenly became the focus of opposition and debate.

*Gregory Palamas: Champion of Orthodoxy* Born into a noble Greek family in 1296, Gregory Palamas decided upon a monastic life at the age of twenty and entered the Great Lavra of St. Athanasius on Mt. Athos.[13] There he was trained in the hesychast tradition as refined and developed by Saint Symeon the New Theologian (949-1022) and other spiritual leaders.

Driven from Mt. Athos by Turkish raids in 1325, Gregory and several companions found refuge in Thessalonika, where his commitment to the Jesus prayer and hesychasm was deepened. Ordained in 1326, Gregory returned to Mt. Athos in 1331, where he began to publish his teachings on spirituality.

Shortly afterwards, spurred by the attacks of Barlaam, Gregory undertook his famous *Triads for the Defense of the Holy Hesychasts* — three sets of three volumes of explanation and theological counter-attack. The debate continued for several years, both in writing and personal confrontation. Finally, two councils held at Constantinople in 1341 upheld the "Palamite" theology against Barlaam, who returned to Italy.

The polarity between Gregory Palamas and the monks of Mt. Athos on one side and Barlaam and certain imperial theologians on the other was soon amalgamated to the political struggle. The hesychasts became identified with the nationalistic, anti-Western faction, while the "Essentialists" ranged themselves with the proponents of union with Rome. The vindication of the Athonite position thus heightened tensions with the West, while it endorsed the holistic methods of prayer practiced by the hesychasts and the daring theological speculations of Gregory Palamas.

The central issue between Gregory and Barlaam concerned whether human beings can directly experience the immediate presence of God — the major and most ancient claim of all true mystics. If God's existence was simply identical with his essence, as Barlaam insisted (similarly to Thomas Aquinas and the dominant theology of the West), such experience would be possible only by means of created intermediaries (such as angels or actual graces). But in the latter case, direct participation in God's own life, an element of biblical as well as theological belief, was ruled out, and true union with God was rendered impossible. Given the claims of the mystics, the only alternative explanations seemed to be either illusion or pantheism — the confusion of the creature with the creator. Barlaam accused the hesychasts of both.

Gregory replied with his famous distinction between the essence and the operations ('uncreated energies') of God — God's direct and immediate presence and action in the world. More dynamic than the Western notion of 'uncreated grace,' the 'energies' of God permitted true mystical experience, in fact, required it for full spiritual development.

Although vindicated by successive councils, Gregory Palamas was not finished with controversy, whether political or theological. Attacked again by Barlaam's partisans, Gregory Akindynos and Nicephoras Gregoras, the doctrine of Gregory Palamas was upheld by further councils in 1347 and 1351. Abbot for a time, Gregory was also elected Archbishop of Thessalonika. Captured by Turks in 1354, he spent a year in prison before being ransomed by Christian Serbs. He died in Thessalonika in November, 1359, and was canonized by the Synod of Constantinople in 1368.

*The Experience of God*

With its emphasis on the bodily effects of the experience of God's presence, the mystical spirituality of Gregory Palamas more resembled that of Richard Rolle than Meister Eckhart, although both continued the Neoplatonic tradition of Origen, Evagrius of Pontus, and Dionysius. In Eckhart's view, matter, time, and bodily nature are obstacles to spiritual growth which must be transcended. Gregory, following in the line of Gregory of Nyssa, the Pseudo-Macarius, St. Maximus the Confessor, and his own master, Philotheus Kokkinus, was more holistic in his teaching. For him the experience of God transformed the body, likewise overcoming the limitations of temporality and 'multiplicity.'

Thus, in Palamite theology, enlightenment was not merely mental illumination or insight, but a participation in the divine Light itself, the glory that the disciples witnessed on Mt. Tabor when Jesus was transfigured. Such "Taboric Light," described by St. Symeon the New Theologian and other writers, manifested itself physically, but was of a wholly supernatural origin.[14] In time, experiencing it even became a criterion of authentic spiritual progress in hesychast mysticism.

Gregory and his followers also employed the ancient term *theosis* ("deification") to express the total human sanctification that was the goal of the life of prayer. For Gregory and the Athonite tradition as a whole, both the process and its effects were produced by grace rather than by unaided human nature. Barlaam objected that hesychasm in effect denied the utter unknowability of God with its claims of "unknowing" or "spiritual" knowledge, and because of its bodily practices promoted the illusion of "seeing" the essence of God with eyes of flesh — the error of the Messalians (or Bogomils, as they were called in the West).

Like Thomas Aquinas, however, and unlike Augustine, Gregory taught that grace perfected nature rather than opposing it. That is, the total human reality of the person was healed, ennobled, and eventually transformed by God's activity of forgiveness, reconciliation, and sanctification which were accomplished through the Incarnation of the Word. Thus the deeper issue behind the debate was the status of revelation and therefore of biblical faith as a source and criterion of theology and spirituality. Although a radical thinker and a devout believer, Barlaam was a rationalist at heart, while Gregory was a true mystic.

During the hesychast controversies, the Athonite position was strongly supported by other spiritual writers, notable among them Nicholas Cabasilas (c. 1322-71), a layman and the last great Byzantine mystic. Although more reserved than Gregory Palamas, Nicholas was a strong adherent of the doctrine of Taboric Light, and wrote several books on sacramental mysticism, including *the Life in Christ*.

The West was deprived of the major benefits of both hesychasm and Palamite theology by the collapse of efforts to achieve reunion at the Council of Florence and by the fall of Constantinople to the Ottoman Turks in 1543, which brought the Eastern Empire to an end. The great spiritual tradition survived in both Greek and Russian orthodoxy, however, becoming the basis of most subsequent mystical spirituality. Hesychasm thus contributed substantially to the very survival of Christianity during the long, difficult centuries of Turkish domination in the Balkans and Eastern Europe.

*New Rome*

During the long decades of ecumenical negotiation before the fall of Constantinople, Russian delegates such as Isidore of Kiev had often supported reunion between East and West. With the triumph of the Turks, however, and with the memory of Latin atrocities indelibly etched in their own consciousness (Russia was saved from forced conversion by the Teutonic Knights in 1242 only through the efforts of St. Alexander Nevsky, the prince of Kiev), Moscow was soon hailed in the East as the New Rome. In monasteries there and scattered along the frontiers of the Greek peninsula, the ancient theology and its spirituality would survive for centuries more.

*Action versus Contemplation*

As Dionysian mysticism had flourished in fourteenth century spirituality, so action, especially political activity, dominated most Western spirituality during the fifteenth. The remainder was characterized by a more moderate mysticism than the Rhenish radicalism of Eckhart and Ruysbroeck, and the emergence of what became known in later ages as *devotio moderna*. This "modern devotion" was rooted in the heart rather than the head, extolled feeling over thought, and tended to view the world negatively as a whole.[15]

A central motif was the necessity of imitating Christ, especially in his suffering. Not by chance, the most popular work of devotion to emerge from this period, and one of the most successful ever written, was *the Imitation of Christ*, attributed to Thomas à Kempis (1380-1471), an Augustinian canon of Agnietenberg.[16]

Thomas Hemerken was born at Kempen, Germany, about 1380 and was educated in Deventer under the Brethren of the Common Life. He received the habit of a Canon Regular in 1406, and remained virtually enclosed for the rest of his life. Although a popular spiritual director and writer, his vision of the world was sometimes as bleak as his devotion to the humanity of Christ and the sacraments, especially the Eucharist, was intense: "The greatest Saints shunned the company of men when they could, and chose rather to live unto God in secret. As often as I have been among men, one said, I have returned less a man."

In addition to his other-worldliness, an anti-intellectual strain wanders throughout Thomas Hemerken's works, clearly revealing the wide gulf that now existed between the high mysticism of the fourteenth-century Rhineland and the emerging pietism of the fifteenth: "I would rather feel compunction than know how to define it."

*The Lay Spirit*
The new spirituality was "evangelical" in terms of the modern use of the word — individualistic, humanistic, but uncompromisingly other-worldly. In many respects it was thus well-suited to the emerging sentiment in public affairs and even the radical theology of the period.

During the struggles between the pope and emperor in the fourteenth century, the notion had appeared in the writings of Marsiglio of Padua and his Spiritual Franciscan allies that the state should be independent of Church control in the temporal order. In the fifteenth century, this view became widespread. The Church itself also began to be seen more as the whole body of Christian believers rather than a hierarchical pyramid run from the top.

The dismaying spectacle of two, three, and, at one time, four popes all claiming to be the valid successor of St. Peter also greatly strengthened the "lay spirit" of the age, which found one expression in "Conciliarism" — the position that a general Council had authority over the whole Church, including the papacy. In fact, several popes were deposed by the Councils of Pisa (1409), Constance (1414-18), and Basle (1431). Despite the effort to interpret the Church more holistically, however, the rise of individualism in society as well as in the Church itself doomed such idealism to increasing failure as the rift between East and West multiplied itself alarmingly in the fragmentation of Catholic Christendom.

# NOTES

1. See Oliver Davies, *God Within: The Mystical Tradition of Northern Europe* (London: Darton, Longman and Todd, 1988 and New York: Paulist Press, 1988), pp. 118-56, and "Ruysbroeck, à Kempis and the *Theologia Deutsch*," in Jones et al., *The Study of Spirituality*, ed. cit., pp. 321-24.
2. English versions include John Ruysbroeck, *The Spiritual Espousals and Other Works*, ed. and trans. by James A. Wiseman, O.S.B. (New York: Paulist Press, 1985); Jan van Ruysbroeck, *The Seven Steps of the Ladder of Spiritual Love*, trans. by F. Sherwood Taylor (Westminster: Dacre Press, 1943).
3. On the English mystics, see David Knowles, O.S.B., *The English Mystical Tradition* (New York: Harper and Brothers, 1961), Geraldine Hodgson, *English Mystics* (London: A. R. Mowbray, 1922), Charles Davis, ed., *English Spiritual Writers* (New York: Sheed and Ward, 1961), Clifton Wolters, "The English Mystics," in Jones et al., *The Study of Spirituality*, ed. cit., pp. 328-37, and Bernard McGinn, "The English Mystics," in Raitt, *Christian Spirituality*, ed. cit., pp. 194-207.
4. For a selection of Rolle's vernacular works, see Rosamund S. Allen, ed. and trans., *Richard Rolle: The English Writings* (New York: Paulist Press, 1988). *The Fire of Love*, trans. by Clifton Wolters, is available from Penguin Books (Baltimore: 1972). Also see *Some Minor Works of Richard Rolle*, trans. and ed. by Geraldine Hodgson (London: John M. Watkins, 1923).
5. Various reliable translations of the *Cloud* are available, including those by William Johnston, S.J., (Garden City, NY: Doubleday Image); Justin McCann, O.S.B., (Westminster, MD: The Newman Press, 1952); Ira Progoff, (New York: Dell Publishing Co., 1957); James Walsh (New York: Paulist Press); and Clifton Wolters (London: Penguin Books, 1961). The six minor works, including "The Epistle of Privy Counsel," can be found in James A. Walsh, ed. and trans., *The Pursuit of Wisdom and Other Works by the Author of the Cloud of Unknowing* (New York: Paulist Press, 1988), and Edmund G. Gardner, ed., *The Cell of Self-Knowledge: Seven Early English Mystical Treatises Printed by Henry Pepwell in 1521* (New York: Cooper Square Publishers, Inc., 1966). On the spirituality of the *Cloud* author, cf. also Richard Woods, O.P., *Mystical Prayer* (Credence Cassettes, National Catholic Reporter, Kansas City, MO).
6. Regarding the the influence of Eckhart and the Rhineland mystics on the *Cloud* author and other English mystics, see Dom David Knowles, *the English Mystical Tradition* (New York: Harper, 1961), pp. 36-38, 74-77, 95-96. For the author as a (former) Dominican, see esp. p. 71. As there were Dominican hermits in fourteenth century England, there is no compelling reason to assume that the author was an ex-Dominican, however, simply because he was a solitary.
7. See Walter Hilton, *The Scale of Perfection* (London: Burns, Oates and Washbourne, Ltd., 1927, a modern version of Wynkyn de Worde edition of 1494); *The Stairway of Perfection*, M.L. del Mastro (Garden City, NY: Doubleday Image), and Walter *The Scale of Perfection*, trans. by Leo Sherley-Price, (London and Baltimore: Penguin), and an abridgment of the same by Dom Illtyd Trethowan, St. Meinrad, IN: Abbey Press, 1975; *The Goad of Love*, trans. by Clare Kirchberger, London: Faber and Faber, 1952. "On the Song of Angels" can be found in Gardner, ed., *The Cell of Self-Knowledge*, pp. 61-73.

8. Edmund Colledge, O.S.A., and James Walsh, S.J., eds. and trans., *Julian of Norwich: Showings* (New York: Paulist Press, 1978). An earlier translation by James Walsh, *The Revelations of Divine Love of Julian of Norwich*, was published by Anthony Clarke Books (Wheathamstead, Hrts., 1973). See also *Julian of Norwich: Revelations of Divine Love*, trans. and ed., by Clifton Wolters (Baltimore: Penguin Books, 1966). In terms of closeness to the grace and beauty of Julian's original language, the best translation is still that of Grace Warrack, *Revelations of Divine Love* (London: Methuen and Co., 1901). For a commentary on Julian's experiences and teaching, see Robert Thouless, *The Lady Julian: A Psychological Study* (London: S.P.C.K., 1924).

9. For the life and times of Margery Kempe, see Louise Collis, *The Apprentice Saint* (London: Michael Joseph, 1964), Clarissa Atkinson, *Mystic and Pilgrim: The Book and the World of Margery Kempe* (Ithaca and London: Cornell University Press, 1983), and Martin Thorton, *Margery Kempe: An Example in the English Pastoral Tradition* (London: S.P.C.K., 1960).

10. *The Book of Margery Kempe*, ed. and trans. by W. Butler-Bowden (New York: Devin-Adair Co., 1944). For a modern version, see B. A. Windeatt, trans., *The Book of Margery Kempe* (London and New York: Penguin, 1985).

11. See *Pearl, Cleanness, Patience, and Sir Gawain and the Green Knight* (London and New York: J. M. Dent and Co, and E. P. Dutton and Co., 1962).

12. William Langland, *Piers the Ploughman*, trans. by J. F. Goodridge (Baltimore: Penguin Books, 1966).

13. See Gregory Palamas, *The Triads*, ed. by John Meyendorff and trans. by Nicholas Gendle (New York: Paulist Press, 1983) and Georg Mantzaridis, "Spiritual Life in Palamism," in Raitt, *Christian Spirituality*, ed. cit., pp. 208-22.

14. See Symeon the New Theologian, *The Discourses*, trans. by C. J. DeCatanzaro, New York: Paulist Press, 1980.

15. See John van Engen, ed. and trans., *Devotio Moderna: Basic Writings* (New York: Paulist Press, 1988), and Otto Gründler, "Devotio Moderna," in Raitt, *Christian Spirituality*, ed. cit., pp. 176-93.

16. For editions see Thomas à Kempis, *Imitation of Christ*, trans. by Ronald Knox and Michael Oakley (New York: Sheed and Ward, 1959), and also that by Harold C. Gardiner, S.J., (Garden City, NY: Doubleday Image).

# Dismemberment and Rebirth 16

URING THE FIFTEENTH CENTURY, diverse spiritualities became increasingly identified with emerging nation-states rather than schools such as the apophatic or kataphatic traditions, Franciscan, Dominican, Carmelite, etc. Thus, we hear of Spanish and Italian mystics, or English, Flemish, and Russian spiritualities, among others.

Such ways of Christian life were coming to be differentiated from one another not only by language, but also the historical and psychological factors that formed the context of life for dominant figures such as Erasmus and Martin Luther, than by clear strands of tradition. In an age of humanism, originality and personality mattered more than adherence to classical views of the spiritual life.

The historical factors influencing the shape of fifteenth and sixteenth-century spiritualities were themselves complex events that developed out of a confluence of temperament and opportunity. Among them were the Black Death, which continued to ravage large sections of Europe in recurrent waves; the witchcraft persecution that occurred in large measure as a reaction; the Great Western Schism, which eroded confidence in the papacy and led to conciliarism; the corruption, greed, and venality of many clergy; the Hundred Years War between England and France and similar conflicts among other nations and princes; the advance of Islam; and the replacement by superstition and devotion of biblically-based, traditional forms of religious life.

Fifteenth-century spirituality also tended to place personal experience over institutional authority with regard to questions of conscience. When buttressed by uncommon courage, prophetic zeal, and uncompromising integrity, such a personalistic attitude toward religion could produce amazing results. It could also lead to tragedy. The spiritual history of the fifteenth century in fact begins and ends with the execution of visionary and prophetic reformers.

*The Death of Hus*

A Bohemian priest, John Hus (1369-1415) had obtained a Master's gown at Prague University in 1396. Elected dean of the philosophical faculty and then rector of the university in 1402, he was well known for his preaching ability. Influenced by the political ideals of the developing lay spirit, especially those emanating from John Wycliffe and his Lollard followers in England, Hus' sermons and writings promoted personal faith and gospel poverty. His attacks on wealth and the corrupt morals of the clergy soon earned him the adulation of the people but the enmity of most of the hierarchy and nobility as well.

Caught up in the intrigues of the struggle for papal supremacy at the height of the Great Western Schism, Hus was excommunicated by Pope John XXIII, himself soon to be deposed by the Council of Constance and imprisoned. Before that, however, Hus appealed his case to the Council and, having been granted safe conduct by the Emperor Sigismund, traveled to Constance in 1414. There, however, he was imprisoned, condemned, and, despite Sigismund's efforts to save him, burned at the stake in 1415.

Like his later counterparts Savonarola and Thomas More, John Hus died as an advocate of reform and in defense of the sanctity of conscience. Proclaimed a martyr by the University of Prague and soon a national hero of the Czech people, his ideals of reform and independence survived him. Not even military expeditions could shake the loyalty of his followers in the centuries to come.

*The Maid of Orleans* Born in Domrémy in the Champagne in 1412, Jehanne (the name by which she always referred to herself) was only thirteen when she experienced her first revelations — voices accompanied by glorious radiance.[1] Gradually, the young shepherdess came to recognize among them St. Michael the Archangel, St. Catherine, and St. Margaret.

Joan believed that her voices commanded her to liberate France from the English, who had seized large portions of it during the Hundred Years War. After considerable and understandable resistance from the military authorities, she was able through her prophetic gifts to convince them of the divine character of her mission. She was presented at court and in the same way persuaded the Dauphin, Charles VII, to commission her to raise the siege at Orléans.

Joan succeeded in the campaign, and stood beside Charles when he was crowned at Rheims in 1429, thus returning hope to France as a nation. She attempted the following year to expel the English completely. Taken prisoner by Burgundian troops in May, she was sold to the English by the Duke of Burgundy. A year later, she was tried for witchcraft and heresy. She was tricked into admitting that her voices were false and diabolical, thus saving her life, but Joan soon recanted her confession. She was then condemned as a relapsed heretic and executed at Rouens on 23 May 1431.

In 1456, her trial was reopened by papal order and Joan was declared innocent of all charges. Because of her heroic charity and the purity of her life and witness, she was canonized on 9 May 1920 by Pope Benedict XV and, in 1922, was recognized with St. Denis as the Co-Patron of France.

Joan of Arc wrote nothing in her nineteen years on earth, had no spiritual doctrine, and her followers were mainly soldiers and the poor. She was a country maid who put her trust not in the might of the crown or the power of the Church, but in her voices and the Spirit of God she knew in the depths of her own experience. As a consequence, her accomplishments and spiritual influence as a woman, a saint, and a liberator, remain lasting and profound.

**The Witchcraft Mania** The execution of Joan of Arc as a witch as well as a heretic ominously anticipated the outbreak of a persecution later in the fifteenth century that would gravely affect not only Europe, but also the New World. Spiritually as well as mentally and physically oppressed by the horrors of the fourteenth century, Christendom as a whole had grown more defensive and less optimistic by the end of that century. As conditions worsened in the following decades, the quest for an explanation — or a scapegoat — became a veritable obsession.

At first, Jews were accused of instigating plague and other disasters, but they were too frequently victims themselves of the calamities of the fourteenth and fifteenth centuries to be easily dismissed — or dispatched — as perpetrators. The answer had to lie elsewhere. Inexorably, the fear and animosity of Europe turned toward the only possible source of such vast and endless troubles — the devil himself. Even the art of the period reflects an unhealthy preoccupation with death and hell, as seen in the paintings of Hieronymus Bosch, Pieter Breughel, Albrecht Dürer, and the anonymous scenes of the *Danse Macabre*. But if Satan was immune from reprisal, his servants were not. Witches and sorcerers were, after all, the likely agents of the horrendous mischief the devil had visited on the age. Finding and suitably punishing such malefactors thus became the business of the day.[2]

At first denounced as superstitious, the belief in witchcraft soon became a preoccupation even of church leaders. In 1484, Pope Innocent VIII unleashed the fury of the Church against suspected witches with the publication of his bull, *Summis desiderantes*, which authorized torture and execution on a vast scale.

In effect, the Inquisition was transformed into a witch-hunting agency. Authorized "handbooks" for witch-hunters such as the infamous *Malleus Mallificarum* ("The Hammer of Witches") were widely distributed. Published in 1487 by two Dominicans, Henry Kramer and James Sprenger, this manual went through twenty-nine editions until suppressed in 1669.[3] The official guide to investigations and interrogations, it is a masterpiece of paranoid fantasy, pathological in its fear and hatred of women.

Where witches could not be found, they could be made. Over the next three centuries, millions of innocent persons, most of them women, were forced by torture to confess to beliefs and practices they had hardly heard of. Hundreds of thousands were executed on the flimsiest of charges. Not even the tumultuous efforts at Reformation and Counter-reformation in the sixteenth century could stem the tide. If anything, they increased the carnage, as from northern Italy to Scotland Protestants and Catholics used the fearful accusation of witchcraft to ruin and destroy each other. By the end of the fury in the late seventeenth century, witchcraft trials had in fact degenerated into a little more than a weapon of sectarian violence and political assassination.

**The Movement towards Reform**

If great darkness lay over Europe in the fifteenth century, there were also moments of intense light. Its spirituality was volatile and highly variegated, even in terms of the active life. Contrasting strongly with visionary reformers such as Jan Hus and world-weary monks like Thomas á Kempis were Jean Gerson, the chancellor of the University of Paris, and Cardinal Nicholas of Cusa, both of whom enjoyed high regard within the Church during their lifetimes.

A major spiritual writer of the early fifteenth century, Jean Charlier de Gerson exemplifies the shift in spiritual currents leading towards the Renaissance and Protestant Reformation. Reacting even more strongly than Ruysbroeck and his followers against the speculations of the Rhineland mystics, for Gerson, contemplation was a form of ecstatic love, guided more by the will than the intellect.

Born in 1363, Gerson entered the priesthood and studied under the illustrious Pierre d'Ailly.[4] After becoming a doctor of theology in 1394, he succeeded d'Ailly as chancellor of the University of Paris. Internal reform of the Church became his life-long goal. A preacher and theologian of note, he labored to heal the Great Western Schism and participated in the Council of Constance which condemned Hus and deposed John XXIII. The contemporary and subsequent influence of his spiritual writings was enormous, especially *On the Manner of Conducting Oneself in a Time of Schism*, *The Mountain of Contemplation*, and *On Mystical Theology*.

But it is perhaps with Gerson that the divorce begins between doctrine and mysticism. Although a mystic himself, he severed mystical theology from speculative or doctrinal theology on the basis of the difference between the "objects" of the two theological approaches. The mystic seeks union with God perceived as ultimate Goodness, while the dogmatic theologian pursues intellectual knowledge of God as Truth. This cleavage between practice and theory would survive and widen with unfortunate consequences until the twentieth century.

Gerson also sharply separated action and contemplation, denying that all Christians are called to contemplative union with God. Many, he believed, are capable only of active life in the world, achieving salvation by faith and virtuous works apart from any conscious experience of God's presence. As a result, contemplation came to be considered the prerogative of an elite, even aristocratic class who could afford to gain entrance to monasteries and convents or undertake the spiritual life under private direction in their palatial homes.

Gerson himself was a true contemplative, but one far removed from the lure of quietistic withdrawal from worldly concerns. His contributions include the strong emphasis on the necessity of spiritual direction and the need for discernment of spirits. Always active in promoting ecclesiastical reform, towards the end of his life Gerson continued to advance the work of education, especially of poor children, even after he had retired to the Celestine monastery in Lyons where he died in 1429.

*Nicholas of Cusa: The Wise Fool*

Although not commonly recognized as a mystic or spiritual writer, Cardinal Nicholas of Cusa (1400-64) was one of the most influential theologians of the fifteenth century as well as an exemplary church leader in a time of turmoil. A thinker in the Neoplatonic tradition, he was particularly indebted to Dionysius the Areopagite and Meister Eckhart, annotated copies of whose works were found in his library. Nicholas was also influenced by the writings of Augustine and Bonaventure.

The son of a boatman, Nicholas was born at Cues on the Moselle. He was first educated by the Brethren of the Common Life at Deventer, where his spirituality developed under the influence of the *devotio moderna*. At sixteen, he entered the University of Heidelberg, transferred to Padua the following year, and received a doctorate in canon law at the University of Cologne in 1423. Ordained in 1430, Nicholas rose rapidly in church administration by dint of his brilliance, diplomatic skills, and irenic temperament. He was an advocate of reform as well as reconciliation with both the Hussites and Greek Orthodox Christians, participating actively in the Councils of Basle (1433) and several local synods.

In 1437, Pope Eugenius IV sent Nicholas as envoy to Constantinople in one of the last efforts to achieve reunion. In recognition of his service in effecting a reconciliation between Rome and the Holy Roman Emperor in 1448, he was created Cardinal by Nicholas V. Appointed Bishop of Brixen and papal legate for the Germanies in 1450, Nicholas' reforming zeal earned him the lasting enmity of the powerful Duke Sigismund. Eventually, overt warfare forced him to seek asylum in Rome, where he spent his remaining years as Camerarius of the Sacred College of Cardinals attempting to bring reform into Rome itself.

*Coincidentia Oppositorum*    As a mathematician in the Neoplatonic tradition, Nicholas of Cusa anticipated many of the insights of Nicholas Copernicus. In his mystical writings, he similarly espoused the apophatic tradition of the East, especially in *On Learned Ignorance* (1440) and *The Vision of God* (1453).[5] Perhaps as a result of the influence of Meister Eckhart, he had to defend himself in his *Apologia for Learned Ignorance* against charges of pantheism brought by Johann Wenck, a Heidelberg professor.

Not surprisingly, Nicholas' teaching affirmed the incomprehensibility of God, the possibility of union with God through love and right moral conduct, and the universal impetus towards the reconciliation of all oppositions in the unifying nature of God itself.

Despite his superior intellectual gifts, Nicholas of Cusa was more active than contemplative in his own spirituality. Yet on the very eve of the Protestant Reformation, he powerfully reaffirmed the deep mystical vision of the Church, the ancient heritage of Alexandrian Christianity shared by both East and West. Moreover, had his program of ecclesiastical reform found acceptance rather than opposition, his abiding faith — a truly mystical confidence in the unifying power of God's presence in history — might well have enabled the Church to overcome the growing schism with the East and the coming disaster in the West.

*The Rebirth of Humanism*    The New Devotion that had its origins in the fourteenth century Rhineland found expression in the Christian humanism of the Italian Renaissance that began with the work of Dante Alighieri of Florence (1265-1321), poet without peer, philosopher, and political theorist. Its prime mover, however, was the son of an exiled Florentine family, Francesco Petrarca (Petrarch, 1304-74), linguist, moralist, theologian, spiritual leader, and above all, poet.

The rebirth of art and scholarship in the fifteenth century takes its name from the rediscovery of the classical heritage of Rome, although largely as romanticized by the humanists of the period. Repelled by the sterility of late scholasticism, Renaissance writers and artists redirected attention away from logic and natural law to the realm of the properly human and particularly the body, which they celebrated in poetry, painting, literature, and even music.

Medicine and the sciences of anatomy and physiology also flourished, as did architecture and engineering. Nowhere is this more evident than in the works of Michelangelo (1475-1564) and especially Leonardo da Vinci (1452-1519). The art of politics was refined and embellished by writers such as Niccolò Machiavelli. Spiritually, too, the activist, service-oriented emphasis of the *devotio moderna* overshadowed more contemplative interests.[6]

As a result, the mystical sense of God's immanence retreated, even as the awareness of God Incarnate in human form was increasingly celebrated. Focus was on the human. The transcendence of God became absolute, completely removed from the scope of human knowledge, accessible only through loving if blind desire.

Lorenzo Valla (1406-57), the most creative and profound thinker of the early Renaissance, proposed a holistic approach to human experience, embracing paradox and logical contradiction, a reflection of the same "learned ignorance" that moved Nicholas of Cusa. Although a Christian humanist, Valla emphasized the complete dependence of humankind on God for salvation, which comes through faith in the redeeming acts of Christ. Itself a grace received from God, such faith finds expression in works. The conservative, Augustinian element in Renaissance spirituality was thus subtly redirected toward building up the City of Man — the Christian republic of political freedom, expressive and heroic art, elegance in literature, and progress in science.

Other Renaissance figures of importance to the history of Christian spirituality include Phillip Paracelsus in Switzerland, Giovanni Pico della Mirandola in Italy, John Colet and Thomas More in England, and above all, Desiderius Erasmus of Rotterdam — reformer, theologian, patristic scholar, and linguist.[7] Outstanding among the predominantly male figures of the period is Christine of Pisa (1364-1430), poet, classicist, and writer.[8] As the humanism of their contemporaries moved ever closer to secularism, these Christian scholars, writers, and diplomats worked — and in some cases died — defending the priority of the City of God.

*Catherine of Genoa: The Nurse*
Although for the most part the late fifteenth century was not mystical in its spirituality, mystics of a very high order continued the tradition of the earlier period, but often without benefit of adequate direction or guidance. Among the greatest was Catherine of Genoa (1449-1510).[9]

Married against her will at the age of sixteen, she shared a life of comfort and enjoyment with her husband, the violent and dissolute Giuliano Adorno. Unexpectedly converted some years later, she began to mature spiritually, eventually bringing even her husband to a new commitment to Christ in the service of the poor. Both became actively involved in caring for the sick and in other works of mercy.

Towards the end of her life, Catherine experienced great trials and sufferings, some of which may have been psychological in origin. A visionary throughout much of her life, she described many of them to her spiritual director and circle of friends. Edited and highly colored by the religious attitudes of the time, these were published as her *Treatise on Purgatory*. Because of her influence on nursing care, in 1944 Catherine was proclaimed patroness of Italian hospitals.

*Savonarola: The Meddlesome Friar*
The hub of the Italian Renaissance, fifteenth-century Florence was also the center of a powerful reform movement associated with the Dominican order, which for some time had been attempting to regain the spirit of strict observance. Blessed John Dominici, St. Vincent Ferrer, and other Observant friars of the period achieved success and even sanctity, but none has ever captured the attention that has focused on Girolamo Savonarola.[10]

The son of the court physician of Borso d'Este, Savonarola was born in 1452 in Ferrara, where he received an education suited for a future physician. Following an unsuccessful marriage proposal to the beautiful girl next door, however, Jerome turned his back on the allurements of the world and joined the Dominicans at Bologna in 1474. (By all standards, Savonarola was remarkably ugly as well as devout and headstrong.)

At Bologna, the young Dominican met one of the great scholars and most engaging personalities of the Italian Renaissance, Giovanni Pico della Mirandola, then only a teenager. They remained friends until Pico's death in 1494 at the age of thirty-one, when on his deathbed he requested that Savonarola clothe him in the Dominican habit.

Sent back to Ferrara after ordination, Savonarola was not at first a successful preacher, although already noted for his austerity and zeal. In 1482, he was transferred to the great priory of St. Mark in Florence. Two years later, he received the gift of prophecy and began an apocalyptic preaching career that would thrust him into prominence, power, and ultimate calamity.

Predicting political and natural calamities for Italy, he attacked clerical abuses and civil immorality. As a result, the people thronged his sermons. In 1491, he was elected prior of St. Mark's. Fearless and honest, he neglected to pay the expected courtesy visit to the ruler of Florence, Lorenzo de Medici ("the Magnificent"), whose antagonism toward the friar began to blow hot.

Lorenzo died in 1492, however, calling for Savonarola to attend him: "I know of no honest friar, save this one." But in the same year, Rodrigo Borgia, a Spaniard, bribed and bullied his way to the papal throne as Alexander VI. A brilliant, energetic, and thoroughly dissolute man, he twisted the papacy to his own ends, especially promoting the interests of his six children, primarily Cesare and Lucrezia, whom he installed in the palace next to St. Peter's.

In a vision, Savonarola saw a huge black cross rising out of Rome and overshadowing the world. Schooled in the biblical prophets, he was led to call it "the cross of the wrath of God." Although Savonarola did not attack the pope directly, it was soon clear that Alexander would have to deal with the friar if only for political reasons. Florence was too valuable a prize to leave to the

Medici or their rivals. Savonarola, meanwhile, preached widely, incurring the wrath of the nobility, who on more than one occasion tried to have him assassinated.

In 1494, Savonarola stopped in mid-sermon to announce that his predictions were coming true; he had seen thousands of French troops pouring into Italy. Following the flight of Piero de Medici, Florence submitted to the invaders. Savonarola was chosen to meet with Charles VIII and succeeded in winning favorable terms for the city, over which he now exercised virtual dominance.

Under French occupation, there was at last a chance for reform. While his influence endured, Fra Girolamo was able to close the brothels, stop usury, and reform clerical morals — especially the selling of offices. He organized children into clubs which scoured the city for "vanities" and worldly art which were gathered and publicly burned. He also bought the entire Medici library, pledging the priory itself as credit, so as to prevent its deportation to France.

So great was his reputation for honesty that many treasures of the city were brought to St. Mark's for safe-keeping even by Savonarola's enemies. Charities were created to assist the poor and sick. St. Mark's became the center of a flourishing art and craft movement. Oriental languages were also studied there. Aspirants to the Dominican order crowded the novitiate.

*The Changing Tides of Favor*  Despite the fact that Florence was enjoying remarkable prosperity under the democratic leadership of Savonarola's followers, it was not difficult for the pope's agents and the friar's own enemies to stir up trouble by reminding the citizens of Savonarola's acceptance of French rule. After Charles VIII returned to France in 1495, the tide of popular favor slowly withdrew from the reforming friar, whose puritanism was becoming tedious to the pleasure-loving Florentines.

He had also made lasting and bitter enemies, especially among the entrenched political factions called the "Die-hards" and the *Compagnacci* or "Gangsters." In 1497, Savonarola's enemies gained control of the Signary and immediately sought to curtail his preaching, even by blowing up the pulpit if necessary. During his Lenten sermon, a riot broke out and an attempt was made on his life. He was hurried to safety at St. Mark's, where he finished the sermon.

Savonarola's enemies soon enlisted the pope in their cause. Summoned to Rome, Jerome pleaded illness and danger to excuse himself from falling into Borgia hands. In May, Alexander VI circulated a highly irregular Bull of Excommunication. It was widely ignored, and Savonarola defended himself in an appeal. The pope retaliated by ordering the Signary to arrest the friar. Again ignored, the pontiff threatened to place Florence under interdict in 1498. Finally, the Signary ordered all sermons to stop.

In March, Savonarola wrote the crowned heads of Europe, calling on them to convoke a general council in order to depose the pope, a conciliarist move that has not endeared him to proponents of papal supremacy. He was supported, however, by the wily Cardinal Julius Della Rovere (later Pope Julius II), a bitter enemy of the Borgias.

On 7 April, Savonarola was accused of witchcraft and heresy by the Franciscans and challenged to an ordeal by fire. He accepted, but the whole affair ended in fiasco, with both sides claiming victory. That night, Palm Sunday, a riot broke out, and a mob attacked St. Mark's, threatening to burn it down. Savonarola agreed to surrender under a writ of safe conduct, and he and Fra Domenico were bound and led to prison.

After eleven days of torture, including being racked daily and having live coals placed to his feet, Savonarola was judged in the Tribunal by his mortal enemy, Doffo Spini, the vicious leader of the Compagnacci. Verbal confessions were obtained, then rejected for a written admission (which Savonarola later retracted) that the friar's preaching emanated from personal motivation rather than divine inspiration. Although falsified by the notary, the confession demoralized his followers, excepting the faithful Domenico.

Unsatisfied, the pope ordered another trial. After twenty-four days of solitary confinement, during which he wrote his commentary on Psalm 51, the *Miserere*, Savonarola was tortured again for four days in the presence of a papal commission which included the Master of the Dominicans. A foregone conclusion, sentence of death was read on 22 May. On 25 May, Jerome Savonarola was led with two disciples, Friars Domenico and Sylvestro, to the public square, where they were stripped of their habits, hanged, then burned.

Savonarola's enemies celebrated his death riotously. Gangs of boys were paid to stone the half-burned bodies. Even at St. Mark's, it was forbidden to mention his name. But for the next two hundred years, flowers would be placed at the site of execution every night on the anniversary of the friar's death. Many Florentines regarded him as a saint and martyr. Among those he guided was Michelangelo's mother, and the great artist himself said that he would never forget the sound of that great, harrowing voice. In the next century, St. Catherine de Ricci claimed that she was cured of a serious illness through his intercession. His canonization was promoted by St. Philip Neri, the son of one of Savonarola's followers, and later, by Pope Benedict XIV.

In addition to his poems and sermons, fifteen of which were later placed on the Index of Forbidden Books, Savonarola's chief writings, and the best statement of his spirituality, are his *Compendium of Revelations* (1495), *The Triumph of the Cross* (1497), and *The Simplicity of the Christian Life*. It is said that after his farewell sermon at St. Mark's, he was asked what reward he would have. "Martyrdom," he replied. "I am content to endure it. I pray for it each day, O Lord, for love of this city."

With Savonarola's death, the last chance for internal reform may have slipped into history. The papacy had sunk to depths redolent of the scandals of the tenth century. Disillusionment, disgust, and resentment percolated throughout Europe. The effort towards reform of Gerson, Nicholas of Cusa, and saints such as the Franciscans Bernardino of Siena and Juan Capistrano, and Dominicans such as Vincent Ferrer and Antoninus of Florence, only illuminated the depravity and wantonness found at every corner. Much as he

had predicted, the flames that devoured Savonarola would soon
engulf the Church as well.

## NOTES

1. Still excellent despite their age are studies of Joan's life by Victoria Sackville-West, *Saint Joan of Arc* (Garden City, NY: Doubleday, Doran, and Co., 1936), Mary Purcell, *The Halo on the Sword* (Westminster, MD: Newman Press, 1952), and Lucien Fabre, *Joan of Arc*, trans. by Gerard Hopkins (New York: McGraw-Hill, 1954).

2. See Norman Cohn, *Europe's Inner Demons: An Enquiry Inspired by the Great Witch-hunt* (New York: Basic Books, 1975), and William E. Monter, *European Witchcraft* (New York: Wiley, 1969).

3. See Montague Summers ed. and trans., *The Malleus Maleficarum of Heinrich Kramer and James Sprenger* (New York: Dover, 1971).

4. See D. Catherine Brown, *Pastor and Laity in the Theology of Jean Gerson* (Cambridge University Press, 1987), and James L. Connolly, *Jean Gerson: Reformer and Mystic* (Dubuque, IA: Brown, 1962 [1928]).

5. See Nicholas Cusanus, *On Learned Ignorance*, trans. by Germanus Heron, O.F.M. (London: Routledge and Kegan Paul, 1954); Nicholas of Cusa, *The Vision of God*, trans. by Emma Gurney Salter (London and New York: J. M. Dent and E. P. Dutton, 1928). See also Jasper Hopkins, trans. and ed., *Nicholas of Cusa's Debate with John Wenck: A Translation and an Appraisal of De Ignota Litteratura and Apologia Doctae Ignorantiae* (Minneapolis: A. J. Banning, 1981) and Jasper Hopkins, trans. and ed., *Nicholas of Cusa's Dialectical Mysticism: Text, Translation and Interpretative Study of De Visione Dei* (Minneapolis: A. J. Banning, 1985).

6. See William J. Bouwsma, "The Spirituality of Renaissance Humanism," in Raitt, *Christian Spirituality*, ed. cit., pp. 236-51.

7. See Roland Bainton, *Erasmus of Christendom* (New York: Charles Scribners and Sons, 1969) and Johan Huizinga, *Erasmus and the Age of Reformation*, Princeton, NJ: Princeton University Press, 1984.

8. See Charity Cannon Willard, "The Franco-Italian Professional Writer: Christine de Pisan," in Katharina M. Wilson, *Medieval Women Writers*, pp. 333-63.

9. See Catherine of Genoa, *Purgation and Purgatory, The Spiritual Dialogue*, trans. by Serge Hughes (New York: Paulist Press, 1979). The classic study of the spirituality of Catherine and her circle is the two-volume masterpiece of religious psychology by Baron Friedrich von Hügel, *The Mystical Element of Religion as Studied in St. Catherine of Genoa and Her Friends* (London: J. M. Dent and Sons and James Clarke and Co., 2 vols., 1961 [1909]).

10. See Michael de la Bedoyere, *The Meddlesome Friar: the Story of the Conflict between Savonarola and Alexander VI* (London: Collins, 1957); Pierre Van Paassen, *A Crown of Fire: the Life and Times of Girolamo Savonarola* (London: Hutchinson, 1961); and John O'Connor, *Jerome Savonarola* (Oxford: Blackfriars Publications, 1946). For his writings, see Bernard McGinn, trans., *Apocalyptic Spirituality: Treatises and Letters of Lactantius, Adso of Montier-en-Der, Joachim of Fiore, the Franciscan Spirituals, Savonarola* (New York: Paulist Press, 1979).

# Fracture                    *17*

ELIGIOUS TENSIONS that had increased to the break-
ing point in the fifteenth century erupted violent-
ly in the early years of the sixteenth. From that
moment until the present, the history of Christian
spirituality, of the extraordinary quest by ordinary
people for an abiding sense of God's presence in
their daily lives, is a story of fragmentation and
conflict, but also one instilled with the enduring hope of reunion.

Already sundered from the Eastern (Orthodox) Church for
almost five hundred years, in the sixteenth century the Western
(Catholic) branch began to ramify prolifically. Lutheran, Anabaptist, Reformed and Calvinist, Anglican, Puritan, Quaker, Methodist, and Baptist churches represent only the principal European
offshoots. Moreover, each separated tradition developed its own
agenda and history, its own character, tensions, and further sub-
divisions, as well as distinctive spiritualities.

Because the varying traditions retained a share in the more
holistic vision of the pre-Reformation era, it remains possible to
render a synoptic account of Christian spirituality, if a greatly
simplified one, by tracing the theme of divine presence that lies at
the heart of every authentic Christian spirituality. For each of the
major Christian traditions continued to affirm that God was present
within human experience and could be recognized, loved, and
conjoined through Word, sacrament, and service in the world.
And no matter how much they disagreed as to *how* to realize the
presence of God in daily life, in some form, meditation and contemplation survived in every tradition, and the mystical impulse,

which responds to the felt awareness of the divine presence, emerged in new and characteristic ways.

*Revolt and Revolution*     The Protestant Reformation did not occur suddenly in 1517 when Martin Luther tacked his Ninety-five Theses to the church door in Wittenberg. Urged from within by leaders such as Nicholas of Cusa and Desiderius Erasmus and even popes such as Martin V and Nicholas V, the movement towards reform had a long history in the late medieval Church.

Vital efforts at moral and structural transformation had begun in the fourteenth century within the major mendicant orders, especially the Franciscans and Dominicans, by way of a return to the strict observance of apostolic life practiced by their Founders. But while mendicant reform would have deep and lasting effects within the Catholic Church, even within the orders themselves such movements met with strenuous resistance. And, weighed down as it was by two centuries of political alliances with competing royal houses and internal schisms, the inability of the Church as an institution to respond adequately to the demand for fundamental renewal was effectively expressed in the executions of John Hus and Savonarola.

Thorough reform came, therefore, as a shock but also as a continuation. Within a single generation, the Church was transformed radically, often violently. Yet neither Luther, Zwingli, Calvin, nor Henry VIII understood themselves to be rejecting authentic Church teaching, morality, or spirituality. Rather, they saw themselves as recovering the ancient and fundamental form of all Christian life.

In many respects, the early Reformers remained as medievally Catholic as their Spanish counterparts, Ignatius of Loyola, Teresa of Avila, and Philip Neri. Not surprisingly, what all the major reformers shared, both Catholic and Protestant, was a vital sense of the presence and action of God in their own experience, guiding and guarding their efforts at renewal against the wiles of Satan and the guile of their opponents. To one degree or another, they were all mystics.[1]

*The Righteousness of God* The son of a miner, Martin Luther was born at Eisleben in Thuringia in 1483.[2] As a boy, he was educated by the Brethren of the Common Life at Magdeburg, where he, like so many reformers of the past, was imbued with the ideals of the *devotio moderna*. In 1501, he matriculated at Erfurt, and, four years later, entered the monastery there of the Augustinian Hermits. Ordained in 1507, in 1510 he was sent to Rome, where he was scandalized by its ostentation and laxity.

Tormented by doubts about the efficacy of good works, indulgences, and other "dispensations," Luther was supported by the Vicar-General of the Augustinians, Johannes von Staupitz, who sent him to the new University of Wittenberg to pursue higher theological studies and lecture. In 1512, Luther received the doctorate and had already begun his great commentaries on scripture.

Between 1513 and 1518, and now vicar of eleven Augustinian monasteries, Luther finally found the "breakthrough" he sought in his sudden insight into justification — that God's grace alone justifies the human soul through faith, and, as St. Paul and St. Augustine had insisted, good works do not "earn" God's favor but demonstrate it. The semi-Pelagianism of the nominalistic theology he had received at Erfurt and Wittenberg was revealed to him at once in all its shallow defectiveness.

Luther turned sharply against the decadent scholasticism of the period, rejecting Aristotelian logic and metaphysics for the profound Gospel spirituality of Augustine, Bernard of Clairvaux, Hugh of St. Victor, Johannes Tauler, and the mysticism of the *Theologia Germanica*.[3] He also rejected the works-oriented religiosity of late medieval Catholicism — indulgences, pilgrimages, votive masses, intercession by the saints, the use of relics, and other "means of salvation." Gradually, he came to deny the necessity of the Church and its priesthood to mediate between God and humankind.

At a chapter of his order at Heidelberg, Luther succeeded in winning over several Augustinians as well as a Dominican, Martin Bucer, who later became the leader of the Reformed Churches in Switzerland and southern Germany. Condemned in Rome for teaching heresy, Luther met fruitlessly with Cardinal Cajetan at Augsburg. Fearful for his life, he then sought refuge with the Elector of Saxony, Frederick III.

Challenged by the Dominican theologian Johannes Eck, Luther and Andreas Bodenstein of Carlstadt debated with him at Leipzig in 1519. There Luther denied the primacy of the pope and the infallibility of General Councils. Formerly on good terms with Luther, Eck now became instrumental in having the Reformer censured by Rome in 1520 and fought strenuously against the Reformation for the rest of his life. In 1537, Eck produced his own German translation of the Bible.

Refusing to submit, Luther was excommunicated in 1521. At the Imperial diet at Worms the following year, he again refused to recant. His writings were condemned and he was placed under the ban. Rescued by Frederick, he took refuge in Wartburg, where he began his translation of the Bible and developed further the theology and discipline of reform. In pamphlets distributed throughout Germany, Luther attacked celibacy, religious orders and vows, and the sacrificial character of the mass. Influenced by his powerful arguments, many priests married, nuns and monks left their monasteries, and radicals such as Bodenstein mounted an iconoclastic campaign at Wittenberg. Alarmed by such extremes, Luther returned to restore order.

He resumed his professorship at the University, where he lectured for the rest of his life. Luther then began to simplify the devotional and liturgical life of the church, reducing the number of sacraments to three — baptism, eucharist, and penance. He replaced daily mass with preaching and family prayers at home. In 1524, he left the Augustinians and married a former Cistercian nun, Katherine von Bora, whom he had helped escape from her convent. The following year, Luther sided with the nobility during the bloody Peasants' Revolt, thus earning the favor of the ruling class, but also losing much popular support.

From this point on, the irreversibility of the Reformation was assured. Luther wrote prodigiously, although he never produced a systematic statement of his theology. His works include over 600 titles in some 100 volumes — scriptural commentaries, controversial pamphlets, catechetical writings, liturgical orders including thirty-six hymns, occasional writings, as well as more than 2,600 letters and some 2,300 extant sermons. By 1534, he had translated the entire Bible into German.

Always a controversialist, and still committed to the vision of the integrity of the Church through time, Luther debated more radical reformers such as von Carlstadt, Ulrich Zwingli, and John Oecolampadius. He attacked Erasmus and replied strenuously to Henry VIII, heartily condemning Anabaptists, Anglicans, and Roman Catholics alike for what he perceived as errors of doctrine and practice. A powerful, deeply troubled man of faith, Luther both attracted and repelled those who championed the cause of reform. But his major accomplishments have endured the test of time and can now be considered in many respects to have carried the central work of Christian reform to an inevitable, if tragic, culmination. He died peacefully in 1546, at the age of sixty-three.

*Word and Spirit*

Luther's spirituality, and that of the church he inspired, not only catalyzed the reform movement of the fifteenth century. It was also deeply mystical. Consistently, he affirmed the real and essential unity of Christ and believers, although he rejected the monastic life with its withdrawal from the world and pursuit of the "interior" vision of God as being unbiblical and inhuman. He did not deny the real presence of Christ in the eucharist, but differed strikingly in his understanding of the mode of that Presence.

Even though Luther was in many respects a medieval figure, he was also deeply affected by the ideals of the Renaissance as proposed by Valla and other humanists. He was fascinated by the Word, finding in scripture and especially in preaching the living Presence of God's spirit. His was essentially a biblical, Pauline spirituality, one permeated with pessimism regarding the unaided human condition, but even more obsessed with the effective mercy of God's grace. If profoundly aware of the inescapable centrality of the cross, suffering, and tribulation in human experience, he also looked on the world positively, rejoicing in creation as God's gift, celebrating the body, life, and sexuality.

Luther's mysticism was expressed in his conviction that the believer *feels* the true presence of God in the joyful assurance of salvation. Rejecting the apophatic spirituality of the Dionysian tradition, however, Luther's mysticism was expressed in service to the world rather than flight from it. He took the devil seriously and fought against temptation, building up his faith on his enduring conviction in the sovereign grace of God rather than any human stratagem or power.

*The Swiss Reform: Zwingli and Bullinger*

The leader of the Reformation in Zürich, Ulrich Zwingli (1484-1531), had been pastor of a church in Glarus.[4] For a time, he served as military chaplain to Swiss mercenaries in the papal army. A humanist admirer of Erasmus and the Renaissance emphasis on critical study of Greek and Hebrew scriptural texts, on his return to Switzerland, Zwingli was elected People's Preacher at the Cathedral of Zürich in 1518.

From Zürich, he labored vigorously to disseminate radical reform throughout the Cantons. A definitive break with Rome occurred in 1522, when in public debate Zwingli overcame a former sympathizer, the German theologian Johann Faber, vicar of the Bishop of Constance. Freed from episcopal control, under Zwingli's influence the Reformed church at Zürich abolished the mass in 1525. Celibacy was rejected (Zwingli himself married Anna Meyer in 1524), and pictures and images were removed from the churches. Zwingli was not opposed to singing, however, and, like Luther, composed several hymns.

Early Reformed theologians stressed the doctrines of salvation by grace through faith alone, as well as the infallible power of divine election. Although aware of Luther's views, Zwingli remained independent and even aloof from the German reformation. The two reformers differed greatly on matters of doctrine and practice, particularly regarding the eucharist. Their meeting at Marburg in the autumn of 1529 proved futile, ending any hope of a unified Reformation. Like Luther, however, Zwingli opposed the more radical doctrines of the Anabaptists, whose leaders were persecuted and in some instances executed.

Zwingli's attempt to impose the Reformation on the Catholic Forest Cantons resulted in fierce resistance in 1529. Three years later, war broke out between Protestant and Catholic Cantons, and Zwingli was killed carrying the city's standard at the head of Zürich's militia at the battle of Kappel. He was succeeded as Pastor of Zürich by his associate, Heinrich Bullinger (1504-75).

More moderate than Zwingli, Bullinger cooperated with John Calvin and was later instrumental in supporting the English Reformation. He assisted Elizabeth I in her struggle against both the pope and the more stringent Calvinist Puritans.

*John Calvin: The Mystical Theocrat* French by birth, John Calvin (1509-1564) continued and developed the spirit of Zwingli and the earlier Swiss Reformers, in some instances altering emphases in a manner distinctive of the Reformed tradition ever since.[5] Calvin was first of all a preacher, imbued with a profound devotion to the Word of God. A student of Valla's writings, he was, even more than his predecessors in the Reformation, a Renaissance humanist rather than a late medieval scholastic or pastor. Also unlike most of them, he was never ordained a priest, although he had been a cleric for a number of years when, around 1530, he came under the influence of a group of Protestant thinkers at Bourges.

A powerful religious experience in 1533 convinced him that God had given him a divine mission to restore the Church to its primitive, apostolic simplicity. Fearing persecution from Francis I, Calvin fled to Basle in 1535, where, a year later, he published in Latin his monumental *Institutes of the Christian Religion*, which he nevertheless dedicated to the king.

A trip to Geneva in 1536 led to his accepting a position there as preacher and professor of theology along with the task of helping organize the reformation of the church. There followed the imposition of a virtual theocracy enforced by oath under the threat of excommunication. Reaction forced Calvin to seek refuge in Strassburg, where he was befriended by Martin Bucer.

Calvin was able to return to Geneva in 1541. After a brief struggle, he finally reorganized the city on principles of strict, authoritarian morality. Opposition was squelched by force, including the torture and execution of a number of opposition leaders, including Michael Servetus. After 1555, he was master of Geneva and the principal theoretician of the Reformation. He wrote a number of scriptural commentaries, theological works, and letters to heads of state. His influence spread to France, England, and Scotland and remains the single most potent force in the Reformed tradition.

*Calvin's Spirituality*

Calvin's early and almost obsessive devotion to the Bible as the privileged medium of God's revelation led to a deepened study of texts and refinements of exegesis. Like other reformers, however, he not only rejected the pomp and panoply of the hierarchy — he rejected the hierarchy. He also reduced sacramental practice to baptism and the eucharist, and eliminated private confession of sin.

Despite his own austere manner of life, Calvin's view of the human person was remarkably holistic, including a central role for feelings and emotion and the full bodily expression of worship. He disdained medieval ascetical practices, including celibacy, and held pleasure in high regard. His was a religion of the heart, not the head.

Calvin's Renaissance emphasis on the primacy of feeling led to his position on predestination, which simply removed from concern all the doubts and intellectual cul-de-sacs stemming from intricate debates over grace and free will. Despite his positive regard for human nature and activity, Calvin was a skeptic intellectually, and, like Eckhart and other proponents of apophatic mysticism, denied that the human mind could comprehend the transcendent and ineffable God.

Despite Calvin's differences with Luther, Zwingli, and the Anabaptists, his confidence in the saving power of grace matched or even exceeded that of other Reformers. Moreover, Calvin's spirituality was supremely social. Like Luther, he argued that the Christian's place is in the world, not the cloister. Worship, reform, and morality were for him all inevitably communitarian.

The mystical element in Calvin's life and teaching has largely been overlooked until recent times, eclipsed by other areas of interest, especially his views on predestination. He was certainly wary of much of what passed for mysticism at the time. But the Reformer of Geneva also affirmed the centrality of experiencing God in and through ordinary human encounters in the world of society and nature. Calvin's emphasis was more on God's power than presence, although it could be equally said that for Calvin, one experienced God's presence *as* power.

Calvin also stressed God's tender love and concern in remarkably feminine imagery: "Our Lord... is like a nurse, like a mother. He does not compare himself only to fathers... but he says that he is more than mother, more than nurse" (*Sermon on Job*). Like Eckhart, Calvin also portrayed God as a woman in labor and a mother with a new-born child.

Of course, Calvin did not undervalue the power of sin, which is often interpreted as a belief in the "total depravity" of the human mind and heart. Typically overstated with a preacher's intensity, Calvin's teaching was no more bleak in this regard than that of Augustine or Thomas à Kempis. Moreover, it is the complement of his teaching on the loving power of God's grace which alone saves us from sin and death.

For Calvin, spirituality is ultimately grounded on absolute trust in and total dependence on God. By God's grace, faith comes to expression in works of love and justice. His was a spirituality of the marketplace, a biblical Christianity in, but not of, the world. His vision of the spiritual life was that of a journey from immaturity to adulthood, a process of maturation in which the spirit was purified and refined by daily trials, adversity, and suffering. Sanctification occurred in the midst of active life. Contemplation was not missing from this conception, but Calvin's opposition to monkish withdrawal from the world obscured the role it played throughout his teaching, especially with regard to sacred scripture.

*The Reformation in France*  For a variety of reasons, the Lutheran reform was not successful in France, but Calvinism achieved a powerful if minority status by 1559. It was strenuously opposed by the monarchy and nobility, however. From 1562 to 1594, the nation was racked by civil war between Catholics and Calvinists, who were nicknamed *Huguenots* about 1560. The worst example of Christian bloodletting occurred on the night of 23 August 1572, when a concerted and widespread attack on Calvinists left as many as 10,000 men, women, and children dead or wounded. Attributed to the instigation of Marie de Médicis, the event became known as the St. Bartholomew Day's Massacre.

In 1598, the Huguenots gained a measure of religious freedom under the Edict of Nantes. Calvinist influence continued to vex the monarchy, however. Under the influence of Cardinals Richelieu and Mazarin, it was progressively worn down. By 1685, the concessions of Nantes were abrogated, and hundreds of thousands of Huguenots either sought refuge through immigration or were absorbed back into the Catholic Church.

*The Radical Reformation*  The Anabaptist Movement, the third major tradition of early Protestantism, was actually a welter of different expressions of radical protest which shared several elements — a belief in the inefficacy of infant baptism which demanded rebaptism as an adult; a tendency to denigrate the material expression of Christian faith in almost every area of life; and a heightened, even apocalyptic otherworldliness.[6]

From its beginnings around 1521 in Wittenberg, early Anabaptist teaching resembled that of the Brethren of the Free Spirit a century before. Violent, revolutionary uprisings, such as the anarchical dictatorship at Münster, were rare and soon died out.[7] Mainstream groups such as the Swiss Brethren, the Hutterites, and Mennonites, tended to be evangelical, urging but not imposing what they considered a simple, gospel life. Mystical and contemplative forms led by Hans Denck (d. 1527), Caspar Schwenckfeld (1489-1561), and Sebastian Franck (1499-1542), flourished for a time, but were eventually absorbed into other groups.

To Anabaptists, following Christ was the essential element in radical spirituality and meant total abandonment of self — *Gelassenheit*, the term popularized by Meister Eckhart and his disciples two hundred years earlier.[8] In this respect, the Anabaptists and their modern descendants among the Hutterites and Mennonites, including the Amish Churches in America, are true followers of Rhineland mysticism. Among other leaders, the dissident mystic Caspar Schwenckfeld, who rejected both Lutheran and Calvinist doctrines, was greatly influenced by Tauler's sermons.

Complete fidelity to Christ entailed for the radicals the likelihood of suffering and martyrdom, a fate they eagerly anticipated, much as had the Montanists and other early Christians. Many in fact were severely persecuted and killed by both Catholics and Protestants. Among early Anabaptist martyrs are found the names of Thomas Münzer, beheaded in 1525; Balthasar Hubmeier, who in 1528 was burned in Vienna, and his wife drowned in the Danube; and Jakob Hutter, from whom the Hutterites took their name, who was tortured and beheaded in 1536. At the Imperial diet at Speyer in April, 1529, rebaptism itself was generally proscribed under penalty of death. Michael Servetus, who was burned in Calvinist Geneva in 1553 for his anti-Trinitarian teachings, is sometimes considered an Anabaptist.

Unlike the fifth-century Circumcellions, the radicals did not openly court persecution or demand martyrdom, but were generally non-violent and even pacifist in their public stance, refusing to bear arms, to swear oaths, or to serve in the military. Major exceptions occurred with the involvement of Thomas Münzer in the Peasants' Revolt of 1524 and the seizure of the city of Münster by followers of Melchior Hoffman, notably John of Leyden, which ended in catastrophe.

*Radical Spirituality: The Inner Light*
The mystical element in radical Protestant spirituality, largely the heritage of both orthodox and heterodox Rhineland mysticism of a century earlier, was founded on a belief in the direct, immediate experience of the divine presence. In many respects, the opposition of the "inner" experience of grace was a mystical response to the perceived emphasis on merely "external" elements of Catholic religious practices of the late Middle Ages. In the words of Bodenstein, "I do need the outward witness. I want to have the testimony of the Spirit within me, as it was promised by Christ."

Fundamental to all early Protestant spirituality was the humanist awareness of the immanence of God in the soul. An element common to Anabaptist spirituality and the radical Lutherans was the conviction of having received a special illumination from God which recreated or regenerated the believer. The mystical immediacy of such experiences of the "inner light" led to a consciousness of grace and salvation. But the radicals rejected both the Lutheran notion of extrinsic or "forensic" justification as well as Calvin's absolute predestination, maintaining that the true Christian was thoroughly transformed by the grace of God, but also averring that it was always possible to fall from grace.

*Body and Soul*
Even among the more radical Reformers, few actually denied the real presence of Christ in the eucharist. But they differed, often significantly, with regard to how God effected that Presence and what it meant. Terms such as "impanation" and "consubstantiation" were coined by Lutheran and other moderate Protestants to avoid

what they considered the rudely materialistic or even magical connotations of "transubstantiation."

The 'spiritualists' on the other hand tended towards a wholly immaterial interpretation, whether metaphysical or social. Ordinarily, the Lord's Supper was celebrated only a few times a year. The meaning of the eucharist was also altered. In some cases, the transubstantiation of bread and wine was replaced by the consecration of the community as the Body of Christ.

The radical wing of the Reform movement represented by Zwingli's followers and the Anabaptists tended toward so spiritual a concept of the Church as to disembody it altogether, stripping away the material expression of faith in sacraments, art, and architecture. The Word of God assumed total priority over the flesh, much as had happened in the fourth and fifth centuries among Montanists and Manichees, and again during the Iconoclast crisis in the eighth and ninth centuries. Preaching dominated everything: "The preaching of the Word of God," Heinrich Bullinger wrote, "*is* the Word of God."

The literal emphasis on the Word had constructive results in scriptural study and interpretation, however, especially in Zürich, where a German Bible was produced by Zwingli and his associates several years before Luther's translation appeared. Reformed spirituality was from the first and foremost a biblical spirituality. Strongly "pneumatological," it also affirmed the sovereign freedom of the Holy Spirit, which transcended both the written Word and salvation history itself.

The expression of spirituality in social action was a major element in early Reformed teaching and practice. Both private and public life were the proper arena for the work of the Holy Spirit. The will of God was the transformation of the world, not its destruction or abandonment. As a consequence, the perceived boundaries between civil society and the Church as a universal community of believers, became less rigid than in Lutheran thought and spirituality, or especially as represented in the "flight from the world" element in the *devotio moderna*.

Zwingli and Reformed Protestantism in general effectively affirmed the authority of the state over all institutional aspects of Christian life, a doctrine sometimes called *Erastianism,* for its principal exponent, the Swiss Calvinist theologian Thomas Erastus (1524-83). Ideal in its origins, in later decades the amalgamation of religion and civil government effected by Henry VIII in England, Calvin in Geneva, John Knox in Scotland, and the Puritans both in England and Massachusetts, produced not only Established Churches as rigid as Spanish or Italian Catholicism, but a powerful, almost totalitarian state. The modern world was beginning to take shape.

## NOTES

1. For a comprehensive account of Reformation spirituality, see especially Jill Raitt, ed., *Christian Spirituality: High Middle Ages and Reformation* (New York: Crossroad, 1988) and Frank C. Senn, ed., *Protestant Spiritual Traditions* (New York: Paulist Press, 1986).
2. A brief account of Luther's life and spirituality can be found in Frank C. Senn, "Lutheran Spirituality," in Frank C. Senn, ed., *Protestant Spiritual Traditions,* pp. 9-54. Also see Rowan Williams, *The Wound of Knowledge,* pp. 142-58, Marc Lienhard, "Luther and the Beginnings of the Reformation," in Raitt, *Christian Spirituality,* ed. cit., pp. 268-99, and D. H. Tripp, "Luther," in Jones et al., *The Study of Spirituality,* pp. 343-46.
3. See *The Theologia Germanica of Martin Luther,* trans. by Bengt Hoffman (New York: Paulist Press, 1980).
4. See Fritz Büsser, "The Spirituality of Zwingli and Bullinger in the Reformation of Zurich," in Raitt, *Christian Spirituality,* ed. cit., pp. 300-17.
5. See Alexandre Ganoczy, *The Young Calvin,* trans. by David Foxgrover and Wade Provo (Philadelphia: Westminster Press, 1987); Ronald W. Wallace, *Calvin, Geneva, and the Reformation* (Edinburgh: Scottish Academic Press, 1988); Lucien Joseph Richard, *The Spirituality of John Calvin* (Atlanta: John Knox Press, 1974); D. H. Tripp, "Calvin," in Jones et al., *The Study of Spirituality,* ed. cit., pp. 354-56; and William J. Bouwsma, "The Spirituality of John Calvin," in Raitt, *Christian Spirituality,* ed. cit., pp. 318-33.
6. See Timothy George, "The Spirituality of the Radical Reformation," in Raitt, *Christian Spirituality,* ed. cit., pp. 334-71.
7. See especially E. R. Chamberlain, *Antichrist and the Millennium,* pp. 59-86.
8. See Peter C. Erb, "Anabaptist Spirituality," in Senn, *Protestant Spiritual Traditions,* ed. cit., pp. 80-124.

# Schism and Catholicism: The Cost of Discipleship  *18*

OR OVER A CENTURY, the English church had distanced itself increasingly from Rome. Lollards, the persecuted and now heretical followers of John Wycliffe, had railed against clerical abuses since the mid-fourteenth century. Suspicious and jealous of the monastic orders, the Crown itself had suppressed non-English religious houses during the Hundred Years War, and during the Great Western Schism, papal taxes were often deflected into national coffers.

Thus, a large measure of state control over the Church was already in place when, in 1534, King Henry VIII formally broke relations with Rome following his excommunication in July of that year for divorcing Catherine of Aragon and marrying Anne Boleyn. The same year, Parliament passed the Act of Supremacy, which recognized the king as Supreme Head of the Church of England. Two years before, Henry had exacted submission from the Convocation of Clergy. Perhaps sensing the coming storm, but surely influenced by the widespread Erastian ideas circulating in Europe, the majority of English bishops and abbots also acquiesced.

But among those who refused to sign the Act of Succession, which annulled Henry's marriage to Catherine of Aragon, recognized the claim of Anne Boleyn's heirs to the throne, and repudiated the pope, were Bishop John Fisher of Rochester and Sir Thomas More, Henry's tutor, friend, and former chancellor from 1529 to 1532. Both were imprisoned in the Tower of London.

*Cromwell and the Carthusians*   Also notable for their resistance to the demands of the new state totalitarianism, which they little understood or cared to, were the Carthusians of London, members of the Church's strictest contemplative order.[1] Their plight was not alleviated by the disgrace of More, who had seriously considered entering the order as a young man, and for three years had lived among them. His relations with the monks remained firm after his marriage and rise to prominence as a jurist, theologian, and chancellor of England after Cardinal Wolsey's death in 1529.

The able and crafty Thomas Cromwell, formerly Wolsey's secretary and now secretary to the king, recognized the spiritual authority of the London charterhouse and began applying pressure on the monks to endorse both the Act of Succession and the Act of Supremacy. Unmoved even by the persuasions of the bishops of York and London, the prior, Dom John Haughton, remained as adamant as More and Fisher. He and the procurator were also sent to the Tower.

Released after agreeing to sign an oath of fealty, the monks returned to the charterhouse. But in January of 1535, there came the first of the major blows against English monasticism that would soon destroy it. Significantly, it fell upon the Carthusians.

Benedictine, Cistercian, Carthusian, and other monasteries throughout northern Europe had been attacked and sometimes destroyed during the Hussite uprising, again during the Peasants' Revolt of 1524-25, and occasionally by radical Lutherans and militant Anabaptists. Cautious of their power and envious of their wealth, Henry had also turned his attention to the hundreds of great abbeys and religious houses that dotted the English country-side.

Despite their capitulation to his claims of primacy, remote and smaller houses had been closed as early as 1534. Now, Cromwell was appointed vicar-general and sent to visit the great houses, paramount among which were the Carthusian charterhouses and the great Benedictine Abbey at Glastonbury.

After a fruitless interview with Cromwell on 16 April 1535, Haughton and the priors of Beauville and Axholme were examined on 20 April and confined to the Tower. They were tried and condemned for high treason on 29 April. And on 4 May, the three priors were brutally executed at Tyburn with the abbot of the Brigittine abbey of Sion, and John Hale, the Rector of Isleworth. On 19 June, the vicar, procurator, and a choir monk were similarly martyred. Three days later old Bishop Fisher, who while in prison on 30 May had been raised by Pope Paul III to the cardinalate, was beheaded. Sir Thomas More followed him to the block on 6 July.

*Pilgrimages of Grace*

Enraged by Cromwell's high-handedness in attacking the "old religion," a series of uprisings began in the northern Catholic counties in October, 1536. Led by Robert Aske, a lawyer, the first "Pilgrimage of Grace," as it was called, ended successfully with promises of redress. Granted a general pardon, Aske trustingly disbanded his followers and returned to Yorkshire. Cromwell's failure to end the persecution led to further distur-bances in 1537, however, and the king's forces overwhelmed the rebels. Over two hundred were hanged to discourage dissent, and Aske himself was condemned for treason and hanged at York.

On 12 May of that year, the new prior and twenty members of the London charterhouse signed the Oath of Supremacy. Two of the leaders who had originally resisted were hanged three days later. Four priests and six lay brothers still held out, however. Imprisoned at Newgate, nine were slowly starved to death, and the last, a lay brother, was hanged on 4 August 1540.

In 1538, Cromwell began the final suppression of the monasteries.  Their lands, revenues, and treasuries were confiscated, the monks and nuns dispersed, or, in the face of resistance, executed for high treason.  The majority of those who signed the Oath were pensioned.  By 1539, the last of the eight charterhouses had been surrendered.  In November of that year, the Benedictine abbey at Glastonbury, the richest and perhaps the oldest of Britain's monasteries, was also suppressed.  Its elderly abbot, Blessed Richard Whiting, and two monks were executed upon the Tor, the great hill overlooking the ancient abbey.

Similar measures were being carried out by Lutheran princes and Calvinists in Denmark, Norway, Iceland, Sweden, Germany, and Switzerland.  And although monastic life continued to flourish in Italy, France, and Spain, by 1540 the monastic period of northern European Christianity had come to an end.

**Catholic Continuity**

Despite Henry's schism with Rome over authority, he staunchly refused to tolerate doctrinal divergence. Worship also continued as before.  Queen Catherine's daughter, Mary Tudor, remained wholly loyal to Rome, but Edward, Henry's precocious but delicate son by Anne Boleyn, was raised Protestant and carefully educated by a succession of Protestant tutors.

In 1549, shortly after Edward came to the throne at the age of ten, Thomas Cranmer, made Archbishop of Canterbury by Henry in 1532, issued the Book of Common Prayer.  A weak and in some respects vacillating figure, Cranmer was nevertheless a man of great spiritual sensitivity.  The Book of Common Prayer, which he revised in 1552, remains his masterpiece and greatest monument, one of the foundation stones of Anglican spirituality.

Cranmer also issued a new Ordinal and the "Forty-Two Articles," a doctrinal statement that, under Elizabeth, would become the basis of the fundamental statement of Anglican belief, the Thirty-Nine Articles.  Under Cranmer, Calvinist teachings and practices made serious inroads into the Established Church. Images were suppressed, altars were supplanted by wooden tables, and communion under both species was reintroduced. Most of these changes were obliterated when Mary Tudor succeeded Edward in 1553. And under her reign Cranmer, as well as Bishops Hugh Ridley and Nicholas Latimer, were burned to death at Oxford between 1555 and 1556.

With Elizabeth's accession in 1558, the tables were turned again. She disliked both Catholicism and Calvinism, but was able to steer a course between both and Lutheranism as well. For some time, England remained effectively Catholic in belief and practice, despite increasing Calvinist (Puritan) popularity. Slowly, a national church began to emerge, guided by the scholarly Archbishop of Canterbury, Matthew Parker, who took pains to preserve evident links with the past.

The Book of Common Prayer was reissued in 1559 and Elizabeth ordered the publication of a mitigated version of the Thirty-Nine Articles acceptable in its final form even to most Catholics. In 1570, however, Pope Pius V unwisely excommunicated the Queen, alienating the court and placing loyal English Catholics in a very difficult position. Soon, the anti-Catholic provisions of the Thirty-Nine Articles were restored. Selective persecutions followed, directed especially against Jesuits and members of other religious orders working clandestinely in England not only to nurture the Catholic faithful, but sometimes to subvert Elizabeth's government as well.

Matters were worsened in 1572 by an abortive Catholic uprising in favor of Mary Stuart, the Scottish Queen and Elizabeth's cousin. As a result, Mary was imprisoned for fourteen years. In view of a clumsy Catholic plot to assassinate Elizabeth in 1586, followed by the massing of the Spanish Armada, Elizabeth had Mary executed in 1587.

Between 1535 and 1680, over 350 Catholics died for their faith in England, including in 1539 the entire family of Cardinal Reginald Pole, who was able nevertheless to reconcile England to Rome briefly under Mary Tudor in 1554. Among other martyrs of this period are found the Jesuit poets, Edmund Campion and Robert Southwell, who were executed in 1541 and 1595.

Under Mary's rule, many Protestants were also tried and executed for heresy, including Bishop John Hooper, who in 1556 was burned at the stake like Cranmer, Ridley, and Latimer. Compared to the thousands of Catholics and Protestants who died in mutual persecutions in Europe during that period, however, the number of Christian executions in England remained mercifully low.

*Spiritual Exercises: The New Way*

Catholic spirituality was not moribund during the early Reformation period. Towards the end of the fifteenth century, effective new methods of prayer and meditation often called "spiritual exercises" had begun to replace the simple, organic, and often unstructured practices of classical patristic, monastic, and medieval spiritualities. Rote prayers, the rosary, and the Stations of the Cross were already part of late medieval spirituality. But the new "ways," an outgrowth of the *devotio moderna*, differed even from these practices in their linear, systematic, step-by-step procedures, definite content, tight structure, and undeviating, almost mechanical regularity.

The dominant apophatic bias of the ancient Alexandrian or "Dionysian" tradition, as well as the Augustinian approach to contemplation, had emphasized imageless, non-discursive awareness accompanied by love which ordinarily found expression in spontaneous works of charity and justice. The new exercises employed rich, complex imagery designed to elicit a panoply of intellectual considerations and emotional responses, especially contrition and a firm purpose of amendment. Feeling tended to predominate, culminating in one or several "resolutions" by which the conclusions and sentiments were directed toward specific applications.

Developed by the reformed Franciscans, but promoted as a reform movement within the Benedictine order, such systematic meditation or "mental prayer" was even better suited to the needs of men and women leading active lives in the world. The widespread destruction of religious houses in northern Europe during the Peasants Revolt, Protestant ascendancy, and Anglican schism assured the success of such methods among urban Catholics in the sixteenth and seventeenth centuries, especially in areas torn by sectarian conflict.

Eventually, even Protestant spirituality would be affected by the new methods of prayer and meditation. In Spain and Italy, even in parts of France where sectarian violence was less common, "spiritual exercises" were especially successful in the ministry of the dynamic new order that embodied the spirit of Catholic reform encouraged by the Council of Trent: the Society of Jesus. And while the Spanish Carmelite reform drew heavily on the medieval tradition of contemplation, systematic meditation appears in the teachings of both Sts. Teresa of Avila and John of the Cross. Spiritual writers such as St. Francis de Sales, the bishop of Geneva, also adapted the new practice to the needs and situation of lay persons.

Ignatius of Loyola's spiritual exercises were so effective and so characteristic of the formation of the early Jesuits that his particular version became synonymous with this form of spirituality as a whole. He seems to have encountered the method through his acquaintance with the Benedictines at Valladolid and Montserrat, where it had been introduced by the Spanish reformer Garcia de Cisneros, whose influential *Exercises of the Spiritual Life* were published in 1500.

For Garcia de Cisneros and other monastic reformers of the late fifteenth century, spiritual exercises achieved inwardly what the external practices of religion — chanting, vocal prayers, fasting, pilgrimages, processions, devotion to the saints, the veneration of relics, and various forms of physical asceticism — disposed people for and reflected symbolically. In Ignatius' brilliant formulation, they became a way of life.

*Catholic*  Papal reaction to the Protestant Reformation was
*Response:*  limited at first to piecemeal and largely futile efforts
*The Council*  to amputate offending members through excommuni-
*of Trent*  cation and reliance on civil authority to prosecute
rebels.  Imperial sentiment grew in favor of an Ecumenical Council to address the need for internal
reform, but was at first resisted by the popes.  Finally, after abortive papal efforts to convoke a council in 1537, 1538, and 1542,
delegates convened at Trent in December, 1545.

The Nineteenth Ecumenical Council met on and off for almost
twenty years, sometimes with Protestant representatives present.
Doctrinal and disciplinary issues dominated the proceedings,
during which the Catholic position was carefully articulated with
regard to the interpretation of Scripture, questions of justification
and grace, original sin, papal authority, the number and character
of the sacraments, liturgical practice, devotion to the saints, the
place of relics, indulgences, and pilgrimages.  Administrative
reforms regulated the appointment and residence of bishops,
seminary reform, and preaching.

In the end, however, reconciliation with the Protestant Reformers proved unworkable.  The tragedy of division would be played
out for centuries to come in the form of ideological and often
physical warfare, bloodying the nations of Europe and the New
World, and entrenching often implacable enmities between nations
of differing Christian views.

The character of Roman Catholicism, and much of its subsequent
spirituality, was solidly determined and stabilized for the next
three centuries by the Council of Trent.  Despite the short, frustrat-
ing reign of Hadrian VI (1522-23), a succession of weak and
ineffectual popes had done little to resist Protestantism or promote
internal reform.  Finally, under the pontificates of Pius IV and St.
Pius V (1559-72), the ideals of Trent were put into effect.  But the
Catholic Reformation was not established by conciliar decree or
papal efforts alone.  In particular, the spiritual reformation of the
Roman church was achieved by a host of zealous mystics and
missionaries whose origins lay mainly in Spain.

Catholic
Reform in
Spain

After centuries of slow struggle towards reform, late medieval Spain saw the beginning of a truly golden age. The year in which Columbus set sail towards a new world, the united forces of Queen Isabella and King Ferdinand finally expelled the Moors after the fall of their stronghold at Granada. In the relative peace that followed, there began a spectacular flowering of cultural and political life made possible by the influx of new wealth from the "Indies."

Spiritually and theologically, Spain prospered even more, especially under the guidance of the brilliant Cardinal Francisco Ximénez de Cisneros, who rose from being a simple and austerely devout Franciscan to become confessor of Queen Isabella and finally Cardinal Archbishop of Toledo, and regent of Castile.

But the spiritual renaissance also had its dark side. In 1478 the joint monarchy had established an Inquisition to enforce the "purity" of the Christian faith, especially from feigned conversions by persecuted Moors and Jews, who were also brutally expelled in 1492. For centuries, Inquisitors such as the Dominican Tomás de Torquemada, as well as members drawn from other religious orders, would exert the full power of state terrorism to assure conformity in doctrine and practice.

Among the chief targets of such fervor were the *Alumbrados* or "Illuminati," a semi-secret mystical sect which first appeared in Toledo around 1510, spread throughout Spain, and eventually reached the Netherlands and France. Like German Anabaptists, the Alumbrados were strongly influenced by the Rhineland mysticism of Eckhart, Tauler, and Ruysbroeck, whose works had been translated into Spanish a generation before.

Believing themselves directly enlightened by the Spirit of God, these illuminists disdained the efficacy of "works," largely rejecting the sacraments and other religious "externals," as well as the common morality of ordinary Christians. Their influence was pronounced on later expressions of unorthodox mysticism, including the Quietism of Miguel de Molinos (condemned in 1687) and that of Archbishop Fénelon and Madame Guyon (condemned in 1694 and 1699).

Among other victims of the Spanish Inquisition were Juan de Valdés (d. 1541), author of the *Dialogue of Christian Doctrine* and the *Christian Alphabet*; Luis de León (d. 1591), the first editor of the writings of St. Teresa and author of the *Names of Christ*, who was imprisoned for over four years;[2] and St. John of Avila (d. 1569), a diocesan priest who was an advisor to St. Teresa and responsible for the conversion of St. Francis Borgia and St. John of God. Arrested and acquitted by the Inquisition in 1531, his book, *Audi, filia* was published in 1556 and placed on the Index in 1559. The major objection to his doctrine seems to have been that he, like Teresa of Avila, was of Jewish ancestry.

Other outstanding Spanish spiritual writers of the early sixteenth century were Francisco de Osuna (1492-1540) and his Franciscan disciple, St. Bernardino of Laredo, whose *Ascent of Mount Sion* had a profound influence later in the century on St. Teresa.[3] Like many Spanish mystics, Osuna was strongly affected by the writings of the Rhineland mystics as well as St. Bernard, the Victorines, and Jean Gerson. His major works were the six *Alphabets*, so called from the arrangements of their chapters. The *Third* or *Spiritual Alphabet* deals with mystical contemplation and had great influence on St. John of the Cross as well as Teresa of Avila. Although clearly orthodox, the closeness of Osuna's doctrine to that of the Alumbrados attracted a cloud of Inquisitorial suspicion over them and all subsequent Spanish mysticism and brought both Ignatius and Teresa themselves before the Tribunal.

Bernardino of Laredo's little book was less indebted to the Dionysian spirituality of the Rhineland, but concentrates on the art of contemplation in terms reminiscent of Richard Rolle and Walter Hilton. He was also influenced by the thirteenth-century Carthusian writer Hugh of Balma and the Flemish Franciscan Henry Herp (d. 1478), whose *Mirror of Perfection* had appeared in Latin translation.

The Benedictine reform movement in Spain, led by the Abbot of Montserrat, García Jimenez de Cisneros (1455-1510), contributed significantly to the development of Spanish mysticism in the sixteenth century. His compilation of spiritual theology, *Exercises of the Spiritual Life*, combined the classical "ways" of purgation, illumination, and union with the methodical practices of the *devotio moderna* that had developed in Germany and the Netherlands.

The movement towards stricter observance among the mendicant orders was the last and perhaps the major influence on the revival of spirituality in Spain at this time. The Franciscan Observantist movement led by St. Peter of Alcántara, a friend and close advisor of St. Teresa, was matched by the preaching and writings of the Dominican St. Luis of Granada (d. 1588), several of whose works were placed on the Index before he was exonerated by the Council of Trent.

St. Peter is credited with inaugurating the "discalced" ("unshod") Franciscans, whose return to bare feet or sandals symbolized the strict simplicity of their life. Through Peter's influence on a somewhat frustrated middle-aged nun named Teresa of Jesus, the discalced reform soon spread to the Carmelite Order and produced two Doctors of the Church. Outstanding among the Spanish reformers of the early sixteenth century, however, was the blond, idealistic young knight from the Basque country, Eneco Lopez de Oñaz y Loyola, called Iñigo by his parents and known to the world as Ignatius.

*Mortal Honor and the Glory of God*
The man the world would come to know as Ignatius of Loyola was born about the year 1491 to a noble family where he absorbed as a child the romantic idealism of late medieval chivalry.[4] Sent in his youth to the court of the royal treasurer, Juan Velásguez de Cuéllar, a relative, he trained as a knight, occasionally landing in jail with his brother, Pedro, for engaging in adolescent pranks and brawls.

In 1517, Iñigo entered the service under the Duke of Navarre. Four years later, at the battle of Pamplona, where he distinguished himself rallying vastly outnumbered Spanish defenders against the French, his legs were blasted by a cannonball, one of them so severely that even with resetting and an extended recuperation, he was permanently lamed.

During his recovery at his family's castle at Loyola, Iñigo asked for reading material. Instead of the courtly romances he desired, all that were found were the *Life of Christ* by the Carthusian, Ludolf of Saxony, and the Dominican James of Voragine's *Golden Legend*, a compilation of saints' lives organized according to the liturgical calendar. Deeply moved by the heroic stories, especially the lives of Francis of Assisi and Dominic, the young knight underwent a steady conversion.

His idealism, chivalrous generosity, and courage were turned towards the glory of God rather than military honor and the courtly dalliance that had delighted him before his injury. He experienced visions of Jesus and Mary and began to contemplate a pilgrimage to the Holy Land. In 1522, he traveled to the abbey of Montserrat where he laid his sword and dagger before the statue of the Black Madonna and after three days of preparation, made a general confession.

He next exchanged clothes with a beggar and settled for what he thought would be a few days at the nearby village of Manresa to record some of his observations in a notebook he always carried with him. He emerged a year later, transformed by an extraordinary experience of spiritual purgation and illumination and having completed at least the initial version of his *Spiritual Exercises*, the form of which he probably encountered at Montserrat.[5] The culmination of this period came at the River Chardonner, when in a few moments, "the eyes of his mind were opened," and the meaning of his life and destiny, as well as profound insights into the deepest mysteries of faith, were conveyed to him with astonishing clarity.

The knight had become the mystic and visionary, an aspect of his spirituality and that of his early followers too easily overlooked. His visions continued as he traveled first to Rome, where he obtained the blessing of the reforming Pope Hadrian VI, and then to the Holy Land. Transformed again by the sense of closeness to God, Iñigo was nevertheless forced to leave Palestine by the Franciscan provincial because of the danger present to Christians.

Realizing that his vocation lay elsewhere, Iñigo returned to Spain, where he took classes and began instructing people in the faith, some of whom became his companions. Soon, the little band was arrested by the Inquisition on suspicion of being Alumbrados. After their release the company went to Salamanca to continue their studies and teaching. Imprisoned again and released after examination, Iñigo and his friends took themselves to the University of Paris, where his studies in theology under the Dominicans led to his receiving the Master of Arts degree. There, too, he began to use the name Ignatius.

In 1534, Ignatius and his first six companions, including Peter Faber and Francis Xavier, took private vows of poverty and chastity, dedicating themselves to the service of the Church. Unable to return to the Holy Land, they resolved to go to Rome and offer their services to the pope.

*The Society of Jesus*
In June, 1537, Ignatius and five of his companions were ordained to the priesthood, although he deferred his first mass until Christmas of 1538 in Rome, where the Knight of Christ would spend the remainder of his life. As the journey to the City had neared its end thirteen months earlier, Ignatius stopped to visit a chapel of La Storta to pray. As had happened at Manresa, he experienced a powerful trinitarian vision, in which God promised to favor his cause, confirming forever the now middle-aged priest in his mission.

In September, 1540, a new order was born, approved by Pope Paul III. Six months later, Ignatius and ten companions pronounced their public and solemn vows. In July, 1550, the Society of Jesus was solemnly established by decree of Pope Julius III. Ignatius died six years later, after spending himself tirelessly preaching, teaching, organizing, and governing the Society, promoting the *Spiritual Exercises*, and instructing novices. He was canonized in 1622. By then, the number of Iñigo's companions had increased to almost 9,000.[6]

The mystical, romantic character of Ignatius was to a large extent shared by the early Jesuits, especially St. Francis Xavier, the Apostle of the Indies, who died in 1552 off the coast of China, having exhausted himself preaching and baptizing in India, Ceylon, Molucca, and Japan. But under Everard Mercurian, Master General from 1573-80, and the first non-Spaniard to hold this office, a drift away from the mystical elements in early Jesuit spirituality was severely enforced to the great detriment of spiritual leaders such as the provincial of Aragon, Antonio Cordeses, and Balthasár Alvarez, who was for a time the spiritual director of St. Teresa of Avila.[7]

Although the mystical charism of the Society of Jesus survived Mercurian's condemnations, especially in the writings of St. Alphonsus Rodríguez (1532-1617) and, two centuries later, Jean Pierre de Caussade, the spirituality of the Jesuits was from the first strongly committed to action. Contemplation was seen, not as a complement to or preparation for action, but concomitant with it. Ignatius' elimination of the choral office, distinctive garb, and other monastic observances completed the process begun by Francis and Dominic of freeing vowed religious from the cloister for work in the world.

In addition to missionary work in Asia and the Americas, the Society of Jesus pledged itself to internal reform of the Church, its members undertaking often dangerous tasks of ministering to Catholics in Protestant areas and England. No area of endeavor seemed alien to Jesuits, who quickly distinguished themselves in the sciences and humanities, education, law, and diplomacy as well as business and politics. In them, the Renaissance, which had begun in faith and ended largely in a return to cultured paganism, was itself reborn as a vital Christian humanism.

*Teresa of Jesus and the Carmelite Reform*

Although three hundred years separate them in time, St. Teresa of Avila and St. Therese of Lisieux, named for her Spanish forebear, are the alpha and omega of the Carmelite Reform — Big Teresa and Little Teresa. Between them are ranged a procession of saints and mystics, beginning with St. John of the Cross, and including Brother Lawrence of the Resurrection and Edith Stein. Teresa towers over all the members of Carmel, however, as the Mother of the Reform, mystic, and Doctor of the Church.

Born in 1515 to a wealthy Castillian family of partial Jewish descent, Teresa de Cepeda y Ahumada was a charming, imaginative, and headstrong child who once attempted to run away from home with her brother, Rodrigo, to be martyred by the Moors — not so much for love of God as for the glory of such a death.[8]

Educated by Augustinian nuns, after a brief return to her home Teresa entered the Carmelite Convent at Avila in 1535. Although only a mitigated rule was observed there, Teresa's initial ardor soon led to a mysterious illness which left her paralyzed for a year. She recovered at home, owing to her father's intervention, and returned to convent life where for a time she accepted the relative laxity. But a few years later, while praying before an image of the suffering Christ, she was suddenly converted to a life of stricter observance and truly mystical fervor.

Visions and revelations followed, culminating in a conviction that she had been called by God to reform the Carmelites. Guided by St. Peter of Alcántara and the young Jesuit Balthasár Alvarez, and supported by her provincial, Teresa overcame strenuous opposition within the convent and community, and founded a "discalced" house in 1562. With *the Way of Perfection*, she also resumed her writing career, which had begun a year earlier with an autobiography written under obedience, her *Life*.[9] She also began to found more reformed houses and met, as a result, the young Carmelite Juan de San Matia, whom she quickly attracted as a disciple and ally.

Sent to the Convent of the Incarnation in Avila to reform the 130 nuns there, Teresa met strong resistance and called for Fray Juan to assist her. He also became her spiritual director, and under his guidance Teresa advanced to the highest stages of union with God.

Teresa's writings continued as she once again took to the roads to found more Reformed houses — seventeen in all. *The Way of Perfection*, composed for the sisters at her first foundation, was finished around 1567. The *Foundations*, which continues her autobiography until shortly before her death, was not completed until 1582. From 1570 to 1575, she wrote two short works, *The Soul's Exclamations to God* and *Conceptions of the Love of God*. Her masterpiece, *The Interior Castle*, was written between June and late November of 1577, being interrupted for three months by the most vigorous persecution of the Reform movement yet mounted by the Carmelites of the mitigated rule and their allies.[10]

Teresa's *Spiritual Relations*, short jottings on the life of prayer, were finished in 1581. In 1582, exhausted from her labors, aged and ill, the great mystic died at Alba de Tormes on 4 October, the feast of St. Francis of Assisi.

Although not systematic, Teresa's spiritual teaching articulated the developmental stages of the spiritual life in a manner never excelled in depth or brilliance. Having experienced God's presence in her own life with growing intensity until her "mystical marriage" in 1572, she insisted that mystical union is the goal of all Christian spirituality. The chief obstacles to contemplative union are discouragement, fear, and laziness. Scaling heaven, she realized, requires bravery, dedication, and persistence, as well (she would undoubtedly add) as a sense of humor.

Her doctrine is aptly summarized on a little bookmark found in her breviary after her death:

Let nothing disturb thee;
Let nothing dismay thee;
All things pass;
God never changes.

Patience attains
All that it strives for.
He who has God
Finds he lacks nothing:
God alone suffices.

Canonized in 1622 with Ignatius of Loyola, Francis Xavier, and Philip Neri, in 1970 Teresa was declared a Doctor of the Church together with St. Catherine of Siena, the first women to be so recognized. Although intended for cloistered nuns, her writings were as warm and human as she herself was, and as a result have found their way into the spiritual literature of the world.

*Little John and the Cross*
Juan de Yepes y Alvarez was the youngest of three sons of Gonzalo Yepes, a member of a wealthy family of silk merchants, and Catalina Alvarez, a poor weaver. The marriage had been bitterly opposed by Gonzalo's proud family, who promptly disowned him. He was obliged to learn to be a weaver like his beloved wife. Thus Juan, who was born on the feast of the Nativity of St. John the Baptist in 1542, was reared in poverty with his two brothers.

The family's hardships were multiplied when Gonzalo died after a long and costly illness. Catalina appealed in vain to the Yepes family for assistance but was left to fend for herself and her sons as best she could. As a result, Juan received his primary education in a school for the poor. But as an apprentice to tradesmen in the area he also learned several crafts, including painting and sculpture, artistic skills which would serve him later as a member of the Carmelite reform and one of the great Spanish poets of all time.

At seventeen, Juan began work in the Plague Hospital in Medina del Campo and was also allowed to enroll in the Jesuit

College there. There, from 1559 to 1563, he received a classical education in Latin, Greek, grammar, rhetoric, and theology. His patron, Don Alonso Alvarez, also supported Juan's studies for the priesthood, intending him for work as a chaplain in the hospital. Drawn to the Carmelite Order, however, he entered the novitiate in Medina del Campo in 1563, and on making profession received the name Juan de Santo Matia.

Juan's studies took him to the Order's college at Salamanca, where he attended classes at the university, one of the greatest in Europe. In tribute to his outstanding abilities, Juan was appointed Prefect of Studies for the Carmelites. Ordained in 1567, he was, however, considering transferring to the Carthusian Order because of his deep desire for prayer and solitude. But on the occasion of a visit to Medina del Campo for his first mass, he met St. Teresa, who had come there to consolidate the second foundation of monasteries of the Reform. She was then fifty-two.

Reassuring him that he did not need to leave the Carmelites to deepen his life of prayer, Teresa attracted him as an ally in extending the Reform to the friars. Appointed assistant professor in Medina, Juan benefitted from her proximity, as "Mother Teresa" instructed him in the ideals of the Reform and even pointed out the availability of a small farmhouse nearby where he could establish the first community of discalced friars.

In October, 1568, Juan and a companion set out to transform the farmhouse into a monastery. Soon they were joined by three Carmelite friars, and by 28 November, Teresa's dream was realized with the provincial's dedication. Adopting the Primitive Rule, Juan changed his name to Fray Juan de la Cruz — Friar John of the Cross.

By 1569, the house was a priory. So quickly did the community grow that it was necessary by 1570 to move it to Mancera de Abajo. At that time, Juan was sub-prior and novice master. A year later, he was made Master of the Carmelite College at Alcala, where young members of the Reform movement were sent for initial studies. It was then that St. Teresa was sent to Avila to reform the Convent of the Incarnation and sent for Fray Juan to assist her.

Misunderstanding and opposition arose between the
*Holy*
*Fray*
*Juan*
Calced and Discalced Carmelites in 1574-75, leading
to a series of drastic efforts to suppress the reform
movement. As a result, Juan was arrested and carried off by force in 1576. He was returned to the
Incarnation at the nuns' request and because of the
direct intervention of the papal nuncio, Nicolas Ormaneto, who
strove to protect the beleaguered reformers. But when Ormaneto
died a year later, Juan was again seized and imprisoned at a
Calced monastery in Toledo.

For nine months, he was confined in a cell small even for him
— he stood only five feet tall and was very thin. Juan suffered
severely from winter cold and summer heat. Fed a meager diet,
often on his knees, he was scourged by the community three times
a week for refusing to renounce the reform. Such treatment in-
flicted lasting injury on his frail health. It also produced some of
the greatest poetry in the Spanish language when, six months after
his imprisonment began, a new warder secretly provided him with
paper and ink, as well as a clean habit when possible.

Thus, not only were "The Spiritual Canticle" and three other
immortal poems written in prison, but the foundations for his great
commentaries were laid. And on the night of 16 August 1578, as
later described in his poem "The Dark Night," Juan escaped and
was able to reach the safety of a convent of Discalced nuns in
Toledo, who hid him from the searchers.

Finally arriving at El Calvario in Andalusia, Juan was elected
prior there. However, the new papal nuncio was hostile to the
reform, and soon placed the Discalced friars under the jurisdiction
of the Calced. Juan and other leaders were also excommunicated,
although he did not know of this.

In 1580, King Philip II personally intervened in the quarrel,
having been won over by the insistence of Mother Teresa. The
Reformed Friars obtained recognition and a measure of indepen-
dence, although full autonomy would not be granted until 1593.
Two years later, the great Founder of the Reform herself died at
Alba de Tormes. Teresa's "holy little Fray Juan," "little Seneca,"

the "half friar," wept uncontrollably for hours, it is said. But the great struggle was over, if Fray Juan's final conflict was only beginning.

For some years, the little friar managed the offices of rector of the Carmelite College at Baeza, which he founded in 1579, vicar general of Andalusia, prior at Granada and also at Segovia, as well as electoral positions in the Reformed province. In 1590, however, Juan found himself at odds with the vicar general of the Discalced friars, Nicolas Doria, who wished to relinquish jurisdiction over the nuns and expel the great Reform leader and Teresa's favorite ally, Jeronimo Gratian.

Doria banished Juan to Andalusia, and also targeted him for expulsion from the Order. The little friar was now forty-nine, and his health had begun to fail. Sent to Ubeda for medical treatment, Juan was treated harshly by the jealous prior, who assigned him the worst cell in the house and complained bitterly at the expense of his treatments. Juan's condition worsened, and on 13 December 1591, he called the prior to his cell, asked forgiveness for the difficulties he caused, and died peacefully, having received his wish not to die a superior, to die in a place where he was not known, and to suffer much.

**The Spiritual Doctor**

Canonized in 1726, St. John of the Cross was declared a Doctor of the Church by Pope Pius XI in 1926. His writings, which are largely commentaries on his mystical poems, "The Ascent of Mt. Carmel," "The Dark Night," "The Spiritual Canticle," and "The Living Flame of Love," do not comprise a systematic theology, but rather a complex, organic treatment of the whole process of spiritual development.

An apophatic or 'negative' theologian like Meister Eckhart and the Rhineland mystics, John of the Cross was nevertheless independent and original in many of his syntheses of the great tradition of Christian mysticism and more sweeping in his vision of the whole. All of his writings are directed at greater union with the unimaginable God at the summit of spiritual development. This, he believed, would not be achieved without passing through the "dark nights" of physical and spiritual suffering that conform us to the crucified Christ and prepare the heart for enlightenment and union.

Like Eckhart and the author of *the Cloud of Unknowing*, St. John rejected reliance on ascetical practices as anything more than a remote preparation for growth in grace. For him, accepting sufferings that come unbidden is far more effective in removing the distractions and attachments that occlude our awareness of God's presence. With the *Cloud* author, John also saw love as the sovereign means and expression of union with God, which surpasses all objective knowledge. He did not disparage the mind, however, recognizing with St. Teresa the primacy of pure intellectual communication as the highest form of mystical experience.

## NOTES

1. See David Mathew and Gervase Mathew, O.P., *The Reformation and the Contemplative Life: A Study of the Conflict between the Carthusians and the State* (London: Sheed and Ward, 1934).
2. See Luis de León, *The Names of Christ*, trans. by Manuel Duran and William Kluback (New York: Paulist Press, 1981).
3. See Francisco de Osuna, *The Third Spiritual Alphabet*, trans. by Mary E. Giles (New York and London: Paulist Press/S.P.C.K., 1981) and Bernardino of Laredo, *The Ascent of Mount Sion*, trans. by E. Allison Peers (London: Faber and Faber, 1952).
4. See *The Autobiography of St. Ignatius of Loyola*, Joseph O'Callaghan, trans. (New York: Harper and Row, 1974). For a recent account of Ignatius' life and spirituality, see Harvey Egan, S.J., *Ignatius Loyola the Mystic* (Wilmington, DE: Michael Glazier, 1987).
5. For the Spiritual Exercises, see Louis J. Puhl, S.J., *The Spiritual Exercises of St. Ignatius of Loyola* (Chicago: Loyola University Press [Newman], 1951).
6. For an account of the spirituality of the early Jesuits and their history, see Joseph de Guibert, S. J., *The Jesuits: Their Doctrine and Practice* (Chicago: Loyola University Press, 1964).
7. On Alvarez and the reaction against mystical spirituality, see Scott Lewis, "Balthasar Alvarez and the Prayer of Silence," *Spirituality Today* 41 (June, 1989): 150-75.
8. A still-valuable account of St. Teresa's life can be found in E. Allison Peers' *Mother of Carmel* (Wilton, CT: Morehouse-Barlow Co., Inc., 1979 [1944]).

9. The collected writings of St. Teresa are available in two editions, E. Allison Peers, trans., *The Complete Works of St. Teresa of Jesus*, 3 vols. (London: Sheed and Ward, 1946), and Kieran Kavanagh, O.C.D. and Otilio Rodriguez, O.C.D., trans., *The Collected Works of St. Teresa of Avila* (Washington, D.C.: I.C.S. Publications, 1980).

10. See *The Interior Castle*, trans. by Kieran Kavanagh, O.C.D. and Otilio Rodriguez, O.C.D. (New York: Paulist Press, 1979). An earlier translation by E. Allison Peers is still available from Doubleday Image Books.

# Houses Divided: From Glory to Enlightenment  19

ETWEEN 1492 AND 1600, the advent of the modern world, the paths of Christian spirituality multiply boundlessly. Sects and cults spring up and die off, sometimes gradually, often violently. The main lines of Catholic and Protestant spirituality also begin to ramify prolifically. And with the discovery and exploration of the New World, events in the Americas and even in Asia soon reflect and alter the European situation.

*Protestant and Catholic*

Following the Diet of Speyer in 1529, six Lutheran princes and fourteen German cities protested against the withdrawal of imperial toleration of dissenting Christians and in favor of freedom of conscience. Thereafter, Christians who rejected the primacy of the pope, the authority of the hierarchy, the efficacy of good works, and who differed (even among themselves) with the

Roman church with regard to biblical interpretation, the number of the sacraments, celibacy, and other significant doctrinal and disciplinary matters, were called *Protestant*. Those who stood with the church of Rome would be known as Roman Catholics.

It is not a satisfactory nomenclature, since Anabaptists, Anglicans, and later, Mormons, among others, do not fit comfortably within the dichotomy. In several respects, the French or "Gallican" Church, although Catholic, was also less (or more) than "Roman." But common usage prevailed and still avoids the early polemics that in one way or another identified the opposed branches of Christianity as the devil's disciples.

The fragmentation of western Christianity, like the break between the eastern and western Churches five centuries earlier, was the consequence of human fallibility and historical development. Perhaps inevitable, surely tragic, in both instances the fission of the Christian Body nevertheless contributed to the survival of the whole. Moreover, it ushered in an era of reform within both principal factions and, with that, new and vigorous varieties of spirituality.

As developments in Germany and Spain had dominated spirituality in the turbulent sixteenth century, similar currents in French Catholicism surfaced in the seventeenth. New forms of Protestant piety also appeared in Germany, England, and the American colonies. During the period of the most severe conflict, even Catholic spiritualities remained sharply divided between liberal and reformed (i.e., Calvinist) influences. Still the potential for unity survived as men and women of great holiness of life sought under the guidance of the Holy Spirit to reintegrate their own lives and that of the Christian people as a whole.

Alert in new ways to the presence and movement of God in history and the hearts of ordinary men and women, such Catholics and Protestants sought to live, move, and work in that presence. Often, they articulated the sense of God with brilliant and passionate fidelity, at other times, they expressed themselves clumsily and interpreted their experience in terms inescapably suggestive of illusion and excess.

The New
World:
Conquest and
Expansion
Throughout the sixteenth and seventeenth centuries, Central, South, and southern parts of North America were colonized by Spain and Portugal, while England and France concentrated on the northeast coast. The Christian faith was spread by missionaries of various denominations, and often imposed by force on native populations. Thus both Protestant and Catholic Christianity preserved its European character in the New World.

Beginning in 1542, India, China, and Japan were also evangelized by Jesuit, Franciscan, and Dominican missionaries. India would remain open to both Catholic and Protestant Europeans. But in Japan, after a series of persecutions starting in 1596, all Europeans were expelled in 1640. In China, conversely, after intermittent generations of modest success and sporadic persecution, "Gregory Lopez," or to give him his Chinese name, Lo Wen Tsao (1617-1691), was consecrated the first native bishop in 1685.

Although a Dominican priest, Gregory nevertheless sided with the Jesuits, Matteo Ricci and Roberto de Nobile, in proposing that the Church adopt Chinese ritual and language. Opposed by his own order and eventually by Rome, however, "Chinese rites" were officially prohibited in 1742, greatly inhibiting the further spread of Christianity, which slowly fell into decay. China would have to wait until 1918 before another bishop would be ordained from among her own people.

Europe
Divided:
Gallicanism
Early in the seventeenth century, still exhausted by the convulsions of the Reformation and Counter-Reformation, European Christians faced increasing religious diversity and conflict, new international tensions, rapid economic and social transformation, and profound intellectual ferment. In sum, the disintegration of the organically unified world of medieval Christendom into a welter of competing national states, churches, and systems

of thought was complete. This was true even in France, which had remained nominally Catholic.

Dominated politically before Louis XIV reached his majority by Cardinals Richelieu and Mazarin, in the early seventeenth century France experienced a series of dramatic upheavals similar to those in Germany and England and even, to some degree, in Spain. Puritan rigorism, a kind of Catholic Calvinism with origins in Belgium, appeared among the nuns of the Cistercian convent at Port-Royal, a few miles from Paris. Called Jansenism because of its main proponent, a professor at the University of Louvain named Cornelius Jansen (1585-1638), this stark and uncompromisingly pessimistic spirituality would exert far-reaching influence despite its repeated condemnation in Paris and Rome.

Mainstream Catholicism was well represented by a host of remarkable saints and mystics, including Francis de Sales, Jeanne Françoise de Chantal, Vincent de Paul, Louise de Marillac, and John Eudes. Other, non-mystical currents were set in motion by the French Oratorians, Cardinal Bérulle, Jean-Jacques Olier (the founder of the seminary of St. Sulpice), and Charles de Condren.

Towards the end of the century, the severely anti-mystical stance of the Jansenists was opposed by the moderate Quietism of Madame Guyon and Archbishop Fénelon. Their teaching met its downfall, however, in the brilliant preacher and author, the Bishop of Meaux, Jacques-Bénigne Bossuet, whose spiritual leanings, like those of the Dominicans, favored Jansenism.[1] Throughout Europe, mysticism had fallen on bad times because of the utopian excesses at Münster, the appearance of the Alumbrados in Spain, and now the development of an ostensibly heretical form of passive contemplation and the disinterested love of God in the teaching of Miguel de Molinos and Madame Guyon.[2]

In reaction, orthodoxy veered again toward an asceticism that fell short of its natural development into mystical experience. The felt and habitual sense of the presence of God that had animated the great mystics of the fourteenth century and the Spanish Reformation was displaced by the conscious cultivation of sentiments of human unworthiness, a recognition of the supreme holiness of

God, and a preoccupation with acquiring religious virtues, especially humility and obedience. The practice of "abandonment" to the will of God came increasingly to the fore.

It is no wonder that the term *spiritualité* also came to prominence at this time, a word sufficiently vague and encompassing to capture the widely disparate movements of the time — and our day as well. Safe from the implications of mystical prayer and contemplation, *spiritualité* came to suggest what had been known as "devotion," a life of methodical prayer and active service distinct both from "mere" theology or doctrine and also from fanaticism.

**Madame Acarie and Her Circle** One of the earliest figures in the sixteenth-century spiritual revival was Barbe Jeanne Avrillot, or Madame Acarie (1566-1618), the mystic, mother, and widow who introduced the Carmelite reform into France. Having shown signs of a contemplative vocation as a child, her wealthy and ambitious family quickly arranged for a suitable marriage for her at sixteen. Although devoted to her husband and children, Madame Acarie continued to nourish her spiritual life and fostered its development in others.

Deeply impressed by the writings of St. Teresa, with the assistance of Pierre Bérulle, a young priest in a circle of influence that included a number of brilliant spiritual writers, she persuaded the king to authorize a Discalced Carmelite convent in Paris in 1603. In turn, she aided Bérulle in founding the Oratory in France, and also supported the foundation of the Ursuline Order. Among others, St. Francis de Sales came to consider her a spiritual mother.

When Madame Acarie's husband died in 1613, she sought admission to the Carmelite monastery in Amiens as a lay sister. Professed in 1615 as Marie de l'Incarnation, she continued her work of spiritual direction and support until her death at the age of fifty-two. A developed mystic, Soeur Marie's ecstatic experiences of union with God greatly resembled those of her model, St. Teresa of Avila. She left no writings, however, having expressed her spirituality in active service. Marie de l'Incarnation was beatified in 1791.

*Bérulle: The Other Cardinal*  Educated by the Jesuits, and known even as a teenager for his wisdom and sanctity, Pierre Bérulle (1575-1629) become advisor to the Queen, Marie de Médicis, and in 1620, was able to achieve a reconciliation between her and Louis XIII, much to the displeasure of Cardinal Richelieu.[3] A contemplative by disposition and mystical in his spirituality, Bérulle was a skilled diplomat as well as religious writer. In 1625, he arranged the marriage of Louis' sister, Henrietta Marie, to the Prince of Wales, the future King Charles I.

Made cardinal in 1627, Bérulle died two years later at the age of fifty-four, having failed in his opposition to an alliance with England against Spain and facing exile at the hands of Richelieu, from whom he differed in almost every respect. Although Richelieu was also a spiritual writer of note and succeeded in reforming the Benedictine Order in France, Bérulle's spiritual influence was nevertheless far greater, determining the tone of much French spirituality for several centuries.

Veering away from the ecstatic mysticism of Madame Acarie, Bérulle and his followers, particularly Jean-Jacques Olier (1608-57), founder of the seminary of Saint Sulpice, Charles de Condren (1588-1647), Bérulle's disciple and successor, St. John Eudes (1601-80), and Louis Grignion de Montfort (1673-1716), developed a spirituality of devotion based on an almost Jansenistic view of human unworthiness and God's majesty.

Based more on the sense of absolute sovereignty developing in France, England, and Spain of the period than a sound Christology, the focus of Bérulle's spirituality was the Incarnation, in which God was now seen to have "abased" himself to redeem sinful human nature. The apt response to God's condescension was human abjection, expressed as total servitude to the divine will. Mystical friendship leading to union with God as spouse of the soul was displaced by sentiments of servile fear and humility.

The vow of spiritual "servility" or "slavery" to Jesus and Mary central to Bérulle's doctrine led to his estrangement from Madame Acarie's circle and the Carmelites. Nonetheless, it became a popular idiom. His strong devotion to Mary, long characteristic of Catholic spirituality, was elevated to unsurpassed heights by Grignion de Montfort in particular. Similarly, despite its sentimentality and inherent limitations, the theme of "spiritual infancy" or "holy childhood" reached a remarkable culmination in the spirituality of St. Therese of Lisieux two hundred years later.

*Francis de Sales and Jane-Frances de Chantal*
Despite Bérulle's lasting influence, the most powerful spiritual force in Post-Reformation France was St. François de Sales (1567-1622), whose influence has endured even longer than that of the Oratorian.[4] Born to a noble family of the Savoy, Francis gave up a promising career in law to enter the priesthood. Shortly after his ordination, he was sent as provost to Geneva, where he would achieve fame as Bishop and immortality as a spiritual writer and saint.

Despite resistance and even attempted assassination, Francis' preaching and teaching won numbers of Calvinists back to the Roman faith. Nominated bishop in 1599, he was consecrated in 1602. Although a brilliant administrator, his success would rest on his ability as a spiritual director. It was in that capacity that, in 1603, he met Jeanne-Françoise de Chantal (1572-1641), with whom he developed a profound friendship.

A widow like Madame Acarie, Jeanne-Françoise had dedicated her life to God by a vow of perpetual chastity after her husband's death in 1601. Together, the two saints founded the Congregation of Visitation nuns at Annecy in 1610. Although cloistered, the "Visitandines" accepted young women and widows who did not feel called to a life of strict seclusion. They also devoted themselves to the care of the poor and sick. Francis de Sales was never to realize his vision of a wholly active order, however.

Francis de Sales' most enduring achievement lay in writing, particularly his masterworks, *An Introduction to the Devout Life* (1609), and his lesser known *Treatise on the Love of God*, published in 1616.[5] Despite his concern for the religious women of the Visitation and his own clergy,[6] de Sales' teaching is directed primarily toward laymen and women intent on developing a vital spirituality while remaining in the world, "people who live in crowded cities within their families, in the midst of domestic cares or the press of public affairs... soldiers, workers, the court...." Consonant with the tenor of the era, he stressed humility as the foundation of holiness, but unlike Bérulle and others, his doctrine never descends into spiritual "servility" or sentimentality.

Francis de Sales' influence was profound on both Catholic and Protestant spirituality — among his early readers were James I of England, Jeremy Taylor, and the Jesuits Jean-Nicholas Grou and Jean-Pierre de Caussade.[7] Canonized in 1665, St. Francis de Sales was declared a Doctor of the Church in 1877. Because of his skill in writing, he was also declared Patron of the Catholic Press in 1923. St. Jeanne-Françoise de Chantal was canonized in 1767.

*Monsieur Vincent*

For those with eyes to see, the life and work of St. Vincent de Paul uncovered the destitution underlying the extravagance of courtly life in the era of the early Bourbon monarchy.[8] His most powerful patron, ironically, was the Queen Regent herself, Anne of Austria, mother of the Sun King, Louis XIV.

Born in 1580 into an impoverished family near Dax, Vincent's father recognized the boy's unusual intelligence and urged him towards the only career in which a poor peasant could advance — the priesthood. Ordained at nineteen, at twenty-eight he had become chaplain to Queen Marguerite, the wife of the convert king, Henri IV. Soon Vincent secured an adequate benefice and retired to the Abbey of St. Leonard de Chaumes aiming to devote the rest of his life to the pursuit of comfort and the support of his family.

A series of misadventures, including being captured by pirates and accused of theft and hypocrisy by his companions, brought Vincent into increasing contact with the inner suffering of truly dedicated priests as well as the physical suffering of the poor. His faith in God's providence and mercy began to develop. He preached missions, counseled, and sought relief for the sick and poor, especially orphans, galley-slaves, and war-victims.

In many respects an apostle of direct action like Ignatius of Loyola, Vincent established Confraternities of Charity, companies of lay men and women pledged to aid the destitute. In 1625, he founded the Congregation of the Priests of the Mission (also known as Lazarists or, today, Vincentians), and in 1633 with St. Louise de Marillac (1591-1660), a well-to-do widow, co-founded the Daughters of Charity, the first congregation of women intended to care for the poor and sick in the world beyond the cloister.

Like Francis of Assisi, Vincent found union with Christ in serving the poor. "You serve Jesus Christ in the person of the poor," he said in one of his famous conferences. "That is as true as the fact that we are here. A sister will go ten times a day to visit the sick, and ten times a day she will find God there.... Go and visit the poor convicts in the galleys, you will find God there.... Look after the little foundlings and you will find God there.... God accepts the service you give to the sick and takes it as done to himself...."

Vincent chose St. Louise de Marillac to become the first superior of the Daughters of Charity. A close friendship had developed between them while he was her spiritual director. Each supported the other in the many trials they faced as founders, missionaries, and, in her case, a worried mother. She even mothered Vincent, admonishing him in a letter of 1640 that he should show his own ailing body the same charity he that he did toward the bodies of other poor persons. Similarly, she insisted that he combat a cold by getting more sleep.

Appointed in 1643 to the Council of Conscience by the Queen, Anne of Austria, Vincent organized relief work among those suffering continual devastation during the Wars of the Fronde from 1648-53. Resolutely opposed to Jansenism, he exercised a moderating influence on the stormy religious situation by offering spiritual direction to an entire generation of dedicated priests. Vincent died in 1660 and was canonized in 1737.

*The Jansenist Controversy*   Admirers and students of St. Augustine from their student days together at Paris and Bayonne, Cornelius Jansen and Jean Duvergier (1581-1643) developed a very pessimistic view of human nature and the world, including the state of Christianity in Europe.[9] Predestination came to play an exaggerated role in their theology, as it did in the Calvinism their doctrine closely resembled. Rigorists, they targeted the Jesuits in particular for contributing to moral and spiritual laxity in France, especially with regard to their encouragement to receive the eucharist frequently. They and their followers were similarly opposed to play, games, and pleasure.

In 1620, Duvergier was made Abbé of Saint-Cyran and, a few years later came into contact with the powerful Arnauld family. In 1625, he met Jacqueline Arnauld, who as Mère Angélique, was prioress of the recently reformed convent of Cistercian nuns at Port-Royal, a few miles from Versailles, where a sister of Blaise Pascal was a also a member of the community. In 1633, Saint-Cyran became spiritual director of the convent, which was soon the center of Jansenist influence.

Jansen himself died in 1638, two years after becoming Bishop of Ypres. A crisis ensued when five propositions from his posthumously published work *Augustinus* were censured first by the Sorbonne and then, in 1653, by Pope Innocent X. Antoine Arnauld, a Jansenist professor at the Sorbonne, was deprived of his chair. In 1656, Blaise Pascal defended Arnauld in his *Lettres Provinciales*, blaming the Jesuits for the persecution.

Louis XIV was nevertheless determined to exterminate Jansenism as a divisive influence in what he planned to be a harmonious, if by contemporary standards, totalitarian state. An attempt was made to force the Cistercian nuns at Port-Royal to abjure Saint-Cyran's teaching. Adamantly refusing, they were sent to Port-Royal-les Champs. Mollified by the new pope, Clement IX, the nuns finally relented, but Jansenism resurfaced a decade later when Arnauld attempted to rehabilitate Jansen's theses.

For decades, the debates rolled on, for despite repeated condemnations, Jansenist doctrine survived, enhanced by the undoubtedly staunch morality of its proponents. By the mid eighteenth-century, however, Jansenism no longer presented a doctrinal threat. But its influence on morality and spirituality had infected most Catholic countries, including the United States, through the formation of priests educated in France and Belgium.

*Germany:*
*The Rise of*
*Pietism*

In Lutheran Germany, the Puritan impulse towards a simple, apostolic form of life surfaced in Pietism, a movement inspired by Johann Arndt (1555-1621) and first developed by Philipp Jakob Spener (1635-1705).[10] Pietists emphasized the real presence of God in the experience of everyday life rather than the remote zones of academic, often polemical, theology or the set structures of monasticism. Like Puritanism elsewhere, Pietism was idealistic, democratic, and voluntarist — a religion of the heart, not the head.

After conflicting Lutheran bodies had achieved a measure of reconciliation with the Formula of Concord (1577) and *the Book of Concord* (1580), a period of stability followed. Within a generation, however, Arndt, a pastor trained in medicine, perceived the onset of tepidity and complacency among once fervent believers in justification by faith alone.

Also a writer and editor, Arndt had been forced to move from Switzerland to Brunswick because of Calvinist pressure. His masterpiece, *True Christianity* (1606), exhorted his coreligionists to reappropriate their Lutheran heritage by a recovery of the experiential dimension of the Christian faith.[11]

Arndt was a disciple of Luther's friend, the gentle Philip Melancthon, whose irenic views toward the papacy were rejected by the Formula of Concord. Like his master, Arndt proposed a mystical spirituality. Having studied the works of Tauler and Thomas à Kempis as a youth, he advocated a transformation of the heart and holiness of life above mere doctrinal orthodoxy.

Arndt's views were developed by Johann Bengel (1687-1752) then by Spener, the publication of whose *Pia Desideria* in 1666 as an introduction to an edition of Arndt's sermons marks the real beginning of Pietism as a movement in Lutheran spirituality. Republished in 1675 as a separate work, *Pia Desideria* ("Pious Desires") emphasizes the necessity of a deep conversion to God experienced in the whole of life and realized in good works.

Pietism was thus overtly social in its expression as well as radically experiential, avoiding theological controversies and even sectarian disputes. Its central theme was the "Second Birth," a total rededication to Christ which leads to steady growth in holiness. At the hands of Spener's friend, August Francke (1663-1727), Pietism became a true movement, as groups ("conventicles") resembling today's base communities were formed to pray together, study scripture, and offer mutual support.

Count Ludwig von Zinzendorf (1700-60) continued the development and expansion of Pietism into Germany as a whole and beyond. Although his expression of spirituality was often couched in terms similar to the sentimentality of the Sulpician school of French spirituality, his influence on the revival of German spirituality in the eighteenth century was generally beneficial. Similarly, Bengel's influence on Cotton Mather and that of Francke on John Wesley testify to the importance of Pietism in the development of evangelical religion throughout the Protestant world.

The Survival
of Mysticism
The more explicitly mystical element in seventeenth-century German spirituality was realized with paradoxical brilliance and obscurity in Jakob Boehme (1575-1624) and Angelus Silesius (1624-77). Boehme, a Lutheran, was the son of a farmer and for a time worked as a shepherd before becoming a shoemaker. While plying that trade, he experienced the first of several mystical revelations.

Censured then persecuted by Lutheran authorities for his views, Boehme travelled from place to place until his death in Silesia at the age of forty-nine. A voluminous writer, Boehme's most influential work was *The Way to Christ*, published in 1623.[12] All of his works are deep, difficult, and pervaded with allegorical symbolism derived from alchemy and astrology.

Despite the heterodox expression of his mysticism, Boehme's works were studied by John Milton, William Law, Isaac Newton, and, later, by the German idealists from Schelling to Hegel. His influence on William Blake was also pronounced. The impact of Boehme's mysticism was particularly strong on Johannes Scheffler, the son of a Polish Lutheran nobleman who had immigrated to Silesia. Having studied medicine at Strassburg, Scheffler transferred to Leyden, Holland, where he came under the influence of Abraham von Frankenberg, Boehme's disciple and editor.

In 1653, Scheffler converted to Catholicism under the influence of the Jesuits, adopting the name Angelus Silesius ("The Silesian Angel" or "Messenger"), under which he published several religious books. His great work, *Der Cherubinischer Wandersmann* (*"The Cherubic Wanderer"*), expressed in rhymed quatrains the teaching not only of Boehme, but especially of Meister Eckhart, whose spirit he absorbed with astonishing accuracy.[13] Its 302 verses were composed in four days of ecstatic inspiration. Ordained in 1661, from 1663 Scheffler devoted his remaining years to literary debate with a variety of Protestant groups.

*The
Anglican
Inheritance*

Because England's ties with its Catholic past were not severed so completely as in Lutheran and Calvinist Europe, English spirituality retained a greater measure of the rich spiritual tradition of the "old religion."[14] The episcopacy was preserved, along with the splendid inheritance of the English cathedrals, with their transcendent architecture and chant, which began its own characteristic development.

Despite the suppression of the monasteries, Benedictine influence remained strong, while the mysticism of Rolle, Hilton, Julian of Norwich, and the *Cloud* author survived both in Anglican and, among expatriates in Belgium, Holland, and France, Catholic forms. The most influential Benedictines abroad were at Cambrai — Dom Augustine Baker (1575-1641) and Dame Gertrude More (1603-33), his spiritual disciple and a descendent of St. Thomas More. Baker's *Holy Wisdom* is a prolonged discourse on the art of contemplation much in the spirit of the *Cloud*.[15] Gertrude More died of smallpox while still young, but even before her election as abbess at the age of twenty-three, she had earned a wide reputation for holiness of life.[16]

The English Capuchin William Fitch, known as Benet of Canfield (1562-1610), also exercised remarkable influence on the development of French spirituality through his contacts with the circle of Madame Acarie. A convert from Puritanism, Fitch emphasized death to self and complete abandonment to the will of God.

In England itself, the revival of patristic influence that produced the Jansenist reaction in France had similar results. Among Anglican theologians and scholars, the more mystical and literate Platonic and Neoplatonic elements came to predominate, laying the groundwork for the development of mystical spirituality, particularly among a group of scholars at Cambridge University between 1633 and 1688, the "Cambridge Platonists."[17]

An even more remarkable upsurge of mystical fervor had already occurred among several English poets of the period, notably John Donne (1571-1631), George Herbert (1593-1633),[18]

Henry Vaughan (1622-95) and Thomas Traherne (1636-74). Other writers and figures of note include Herbert's friend, the scholar and preacher Lancelot Andrewes (1555-1626) and Nicholas Ferrar (1592-1637), a member of the Virginia Company and member of Parliament, whose retirement to a semi-monastic community at Little Gidding in 1625 foreshadowed the reappearance of monastic life in England at the end of the nineteenth century.

The mystical heritage of English spirituality was not confined to the cathedrals and universities, however. The lives of ordinary people in villages and farming communities remained rooted in the power and beauties of nature in forest, countryside, and sea, as well as the celebration of agricultural festival and the liturgical year. The sense of divine presence pervaded life as a whole.

Opposed, however, to the rich, mystical spirituality of the Cambridge Platonists and Caroline divines, Calvinism found its most strenuous expression in the triumph of the Commonwealth over the Stuart kings, leaving a heritage of non-conformist simplicity of life announced in the teachings of George Fox and, later, John Wesley.

*Puritan Reaction*

In England, the tension between the Reformed and Established Churches that seriously divided seventeenth-century France exploded in civil war, the overthrow of the monarchy, including the execution of King Charles I in 1649, the abolition of parliament, and the imposition of a Protectorate under Oliver Cromwell in 1653.

Although never representing more than a sizable minority of the English people, Calvinist (Presbyterian) influence was disproportionate to the number of its adherents and had increased steadily since the reign of Edward VI. The accession of Charles Stuart in 1625 saw an often heavy-handed attempt to suppress Calvinism, especially under the Archbishop of Canterbury, William Laud (1573-1645), who, presiding over the Star Chamber, passed sentence on many Dissenters. Impeached by Parliament, Laud preceded Charles to the headsman's block by ten days. Both came to be considered martyrs by the Church of England.

Cromwell, Lord Protector from 1653 to 1658, bridged the Congregationalist and Presbyterian tendency in English Calvinism, and proved to be a more tolerant ruler than might have otherwise been expected, especially given his brutal treatment of the Catholic Irish following the rebellion of 1641. Something of a mystic mixed with the self-righteous intransigence of an Old Testament Judge, Cromwell believed that God had appointed him to transform England into a model theocracy. Buried at Westminster Abbey, after the restoration of the monarchy and the Church of England in 1660 his body was disinterred and hung at Tyburn.

*The Puritan Spirit*

Inheritors of the long tradition of evangelical Christianity that had animated the Celtic monks, Benedict, Francis, Dominic, and Ignatius of Loyola, English Presbyterians or Puritans, as they were called, sought union with God in the marketplace, the halls of government, and especially the home rather than in the cloistered sanctuary of monastic or even semi-monastic seclusion from the world.[19] Repelled by courtly ostentation and ecclesiastical panoply, Puritans shunned ornate ceremony of all kinds, including the festive costume affected by the wealthy, and adopted a simple, ultimately severe style of life based squarely on a rigid, encompassing morality.

Calvinist and therefore fundamentally Augustinian, Puritan spirituality emphasized human depravity and helplessness in the face of sin, but also the richness of God's mercy and the power of grace, with stress on predestination. Divine election in Christ, conversion and firm repentance, being "born again," "covenanting" with Christ and the true Christian community, and final perseverance comprised the major moments of the "Pilgrim's Progress" toward the heavenly city, the New Jerusalem.

Otherworldly and highly interiorized, Puritan spirituality did not favor spiritual direction, but rather immediate communion of the soul with God. Such individualism tended to reduce the spiritual life to the privacy of personal consciousness, often, like John Bunyan's, isolated and tortured by dread of damnation. Thus also the public realm was increasingly abandoned to the judgment of strict, often unbending external norms among which the seeds of hypocrisy could also take root.

In most respects, however, authentic Puritans were sincere Protestant counterparts of the medieval reformers and Carmelite nuns and friars in Spain, if more Franciscan and Teresian than Thomist and "sanjuanist." Essential elements of Puritan spirituality were derived from medieval practice, the *devotio moderna*, and even Jesuit teaching. These included methods of regular prayer, biblical study, spiritual reading and writing (especially diaries), and meditation. Daily examination of conscience and both public and private confession of sin were an integral part of the Puritan's spiritual exercises.

Ejaculatory prayer such as promoted by the author of the *Cloud of Unknowing* was a favorite practice, and many Puritan theologians such as Richard Baxter extolled the virtues of meditation and contemplation. Although mainly ascetical in character, Puritan spirituality also led to exalted states of rapture in the felt presence of God that, as described for instance by Cotton Mather, can only be called mystical. In addition to public worship, which centered on preaching and the Lord's Supper, communal spiritual practices included public fasting, the strict observance of the sabbath, and a strict code of business ethics, encompassing a stewardship of resources for the sake of the poor.

Among outstanding English Puritan writers and pastors are found Lewis Bayly, John Bunyan, Richard Baxter, and John Milton. Puritanism also flourished in the Massachusetts Bay Colony, where the names of John Winthrop, Increase and Cotton Mather, and Jonathan Edwards gained undying fame.[20]

Doomed as much by its almost utopian idealism, which ended (like Calvin's and Augustine's) in coercion, as by the revitalization of the established churches, Puritanism died out in England and the colonies within a century. Richard Cromwell (1626-1712),

Oliver's son and successor in 1658, abdicated after a year to pursue God's blessings first in exile, then in his rural retreat, by means of meditation, reading, and prayer.

Many Puritan contributions to Christian spirituality were constructive, especially the conviction of God's presence in the events of everyday life. Because of later excesses, however, in the popular mind the Puritan legacy consisted of blue laws, witchcraft persecutions, and an unrelenting animosity towards the theater, games, dancing, festival, and liturgical ritual — elements deeper in the English tradition than either idealism or evangelism, whatever their enduring appeal.

Despite the stress placed on sermons by the Puritan tradition, moreover, English preaching would not achieve the status it enjoyed in Protestant Europe for another two centuries. The Reformation emphasis on the Word of God was not lacking, however, and English Bibles were published widely.

Catholics were also provided their bible, however. The New Testament had been published by expatriate Oxford scholars of the English College at Douai, Belgium, in 1582, and the Old Testament in 1609. Both the Catholic version and the Geneva Bible of 1560 were extensively consulted when the Authorized (King James) Version was produced by a committee of scholars in 1609 and published two years later.

*Radical Dissent: Baptists and Quakers*
Among several extreme Puritan sects appearing in sixteenth century England, foremost were the Baptists and Quakers. An offshoot of the Anabaptist movement of the previous era, the Baptist Church had its origins among English Mennonites under the influence of John Smyth (1554-1612), a Puritan preacher exiled to Amsterdam in 1608. There, a year later, he rebaptized himself and his followers, who, after his death in 1612, established themselves in London.

Radical separatists, the General and Calvinistic Baptists became advocates of freedom of conscience and religious liberty in England

and America, where Roger Williams established a church at Providence, Rhode Island, in 1639. Among Baptist figures of the period, the writer John Bunyan (1628-88) remains outstanding for his great epic, *The Pilgrim's Progress* (1678) and other works, many of which he wrote while in prison for his beliefs.

Known later as the Religious Society of Friends, the Quakers arose from the prophetic inspiration and teaching of George Fox (1624-91), an apocalyptic, mystical figure who wandered from town to town in mid-seventeenth century England. Like the Illuminists and Alumbrados, Fox was advocate of the "Inner Light of Christ," an immediate and joyful assurance of salvation. Preaching total reliance on the guidance of the "Inner Voice of God," he traveled throughout the country and undertook missionary journeys to Ireland, the West Indies, North America, and Holland, preaching personal holiness, non-violence, and simplicity of life. Frequently imprisoned, as were his followers, Fox was one of the most charismatic figures of his time, a man without guile or ambition, patient under persecution, and possessed of considerable organizational abilities. His most famous work is his *Journal*, which was published three years after his death.[21]

After years of persecution under both Cromwell's Commonwealth and the Stuart Restoration, Fox's "Friends of Truth" were finally accorded toleration in 1687. In later years, their original vehemence in worship and preaching, from which they received the epithet "Quakers," was tempered by the influence of Quietistic doctrine.

*The Emergence of Methodism*

The final development in English spirituality during this period was a movement within Anglicanism known as Methodism, among other names. Currents of popular devotion similar to those flowing in German Pietism surfaced in the work of John Wesley (1703-91), an Anglican priest who in 1726 was offered a fellowship at Lincoln College, Oxford. There he gathered together a community of friends dedicated to a more intense spiritual life.

Influenced greatly by the teachings of Jeremy Taylor (1613-67) and William Law (1686-1761), early Methodism cultivated a somewhat mystical approach to prayer and personal holiness, although Wesley himself resisted what he perceived as erroneous mystical tendencies such as those emanating from the influence of Jacob Boehme which had affected William Law. After a disappointing missionary venture in Georgia with his brother Charles, Wesley came into contact with Pietism in Germany. Soon the evangelical element in his ministry was refined and fired by a new effort directed at the working class.

Often at odds with the Established Church, Wesley turned increasingly to the people themselves. Beginning in 1742, he traveled tirelessly on horseback throughout Britain, Scotland, Wales, and Ireland preaching and establishing centers of evangelism. In 1768, Methodism reached New York, and in 1771 Wesley sent Francis Asbury to supervise the evangelical movement in America.

Wesley himself remained within the Church of England and wished that Methodism would also remain an Anglican movement. Pietistic and Calvinistic tendencies among many of his disciples soon led to a break with the Anglicans, however, and Methodism became a distinct Protestant congregation.[22]

*The Light of Reason*

With the rise of Methodism in England and its spread to America, and the continuing proliferation of ever-smaller Protestant sects, by the beginning of the eighteenth century the configuration of the religious map of the West was set for the coming three centuries. Exhausted by the previous two centuries of mostly religious warfare which in some areas of Germany and France had more than halved the population, Europe settled into an era of political and philosophical development.

As the smoke cleared away, Enlightenment filled the air. Wars of religion gave way to wars of national dominance, culminating at the end of the century in revolutions intent on establishing the reign of Reason rather than the arbitrary will of kings, popes, and prince-bishops. Aiming to steer clear of religious factionalism, intellectuals expressed their belief in God as "deism." Piety was interpreted in terms of moral obligation.

Calvinistic pessimism was replaced by faith in the goodness of human nature advocated with particular force by Wilhelm Leibniz (1646-1716) and Jean-Jacques Rousseau (1712-78). Scientific achievement escalated, spurred by the achievements of Francis Bacon, Copernicus, Kepler, Galileo, and, above all, Sir Isaac Newton. But the Spirit of Enlightenment was articulated most persuasively if, on occasion, perversely, in the essays and letters of François Arouet (1694-1778), known forever as Voltaire, whose faith in reason was overmatched by his confidence in human fallibility, arrogance, and greed. Witty and agnostic, Voltaire was a biting critic of both the Catholic Church and atheists such as the younger *philosophes*, but an even stronger supporter of moral reform and social justice.

Voltaire's religious skepticism found calmer expression in the pietistic agnosticism of Immanuel Kant (1724-1804), who envisioned a "religion without revelation" based on the conviction of moral obligation emanating from the heart of the universe. A true rationalist, Kant rejected all intrusions into the world of fact by the supernatural, lampooning the psychic and mystical elements of religion that had begun to surface in the preaching and writings of "the Swedish Seer" and scientist, Emanuel Swedenborg (1688-1772).[23] Swedenborgianism nevertheless survived and still exists today.

Theologically, Kant's influence was less powerful among Catholic than Protestant and Anglican scholars. Spiritually, however, his writings were the occasion of a massive and reactionary revival of fideism in the nineteenth century, a recovery of the element of feeling in religious experience, and ultimately of the appearance of fundamentalism.

## NOTES

1. See E. E. Reynolds, *Bossuet* (Garden City, NY: Doubleday and Co., 1963). Few of Bossuet's writings are available in English. Among them, see *Letters of Spiritual Direction*, trans. by Geoffrey Webb and Adrian Walker (London: Mowbray and Co., 1958).

2. On Miguel de Molinos, see Ronald Knox, *Enthusiasm*, pp. 295-318. Molinos' main work, *The Spiritual Guide*, long considered a spiritual classic by Protestants and many Catholics, can still be found in various editions (see Michael Molinos, *The Spiritual Guide* [Gardiner, Maine: Christian Books, 1987]). On Madame Guyon and Archbishop Fenélon, see Elfrieda Dubois, "Fénelon and Quietism," in Jones et al., *The Study of Spirituality*, pp. 408-15. For a detailed but favorably biased account, see Phyllis Thompson, *Madame Guyon: Martyr of the Holy Spirit* (London: Hodder and Stoughton, 1986). A more negative appraisal is given by Knox, *Enthusiasm*, pp. 319-55.

3. See John Saward, "Bérulle and the French School," in Jones et al., *The Study of Spirituality*, pp. 386-96, and William M. Thompson, ed., *Bérulle and the French School*, trans.by Lowell M. Glendon (New York: Paulist Press, 1989).

4. See Elizabeth Stopp, "François de Sales," in Jones, et al., *Christian Spirituality*, pp. 379-85.

5. *Introduction to the Devout Life*, trans. and ed. by John K. Ryan (New York: Harper and Row, 1952), and *The Treatise on the Love of God*, 2. vols., trans by John K. Ryan (Garden City, NY: Doubleday Image Books, 1963).

6. See especially Francis de Sales, Jane de Chantal, *Letters of Spiritual Direction*, trans. by Péronne Marie Thibert, ed. by Wendy Wright and Joseph F. Power (New York: Paulist Press, 1988).

7. For the teachings of Caussade, see Jean-Pierre de Caussade, S.J., *Self-Abandonment to Divine Providence*, trans. by Algar Thorold, revised by John Joyce, S.J. (London: Collins, 1971), also translated by Kitty Muggeridge as *The Sacrament of the Present Moment*, (London: Collins, 1981). See also Kitty Muggeridge, ed., *Spiritual Letters of Jean-Pierre de Caussade* (London: Collins, 1986) and Jean-Pierre de Caussade, S.J., *The Workings of the Divine Will* (London: Burns and Oates, 1958 [1875]). On Caussade, see Mark Gibbard, "Jean Pierre de Caussade," in Jones et al., *The Study of Spirituality*, pp. 415-19.

8. See St. Vincent de Paul, *Correspondence, Conferences, Documents*, Vol. 1, trans. by Pierre Costé (Brooklyn: New City Press, 1985.) On the life and teaching of St. Vincent de Paul, see Mary Purcell, *The World of Monsieur Vincent* (Chicago: Loyola University Press, 1963 and 1989).

9. For a thorough discussion of Jansen and Jansenism, see Ronald Knox, *Enthusiasm*, pp. 176-230. See also Elfrieda Dubois, "Jansenism" and "Pascal" in Jones et al., *The Study of Spirituality*, pp. 396-08.

10. See John Weborg, "Pietism: The Fire of God which... Flames in the Heart of Germany," in Senn, *Protestant Spiritual Traditions*, pp. 183-216, and David W. Lotz, "Continental Pietism," in Jones et al., *The Study of Spirituality*, pp. 448-52.

11. Johann Arndt, *True Christianity*, trans. by Peter Erb (New York: Paulist Press, 1979).

12. Jacob Boehme, *The Way to Christ*, ed. and trans. by Peter Erb (New York: Paulist Press, 1978).

13. Angelus Silesius, *The Cherubic Wanderer*, trans. by Maria Shrady (New York: Paulist Press, 1986).
14. See Martin Thornton, *English Spirituality* (Cowley Publications, 1986). See also Paul V. Marshall, "Anglican Spirituality," in Senn, ed., *Protestant Spiritual Traditions*, pp. 125-64.
15. Augustine Baker, O.S.B., *Holy Wisdom or Directions for the Prayer of Contemplation*, intro. by Dom Gerard Sitwell, O.S.B. (Wheathamstead, Harts: Anthony Clarke Books, 1972). See also Abbot Justin McCann, O.S.B., *The Cloud of Unknowing and Other Treatises by an English Mystic of the Fourteenth Century, with a Commentary on the Cloud by Fr. Augustine Baker, O.S.B.* (Westminster, MD: Newman Press, 1952 ed.).
16. See Benedict Weld-Blundell, O.S.B., ed., *The Inner Life and Writings of Dame Gertrude More*, 2. vols. (London: R. and T. Washbourne, 1910), and Fr. H. Collins, *The Life of Dame Gertrude More* (London: Thomas Richardson and Sons, c. 1890).
17. See Martin Thornton, "The Caroline Divines and the Cambridge Platonists," in Jones et al., *The Study of Spirituality*, pp. 431-37 and also his *English Spirituality*, pp. 230-81.
18. George Herbert, *The Country Parson* and *The Temple*, ed. by John Nelson Wall (New York: Paulist Press, 1981).
19. See E. Glen Hinson, "Puritan Spirituality," in Senn, ed., *Protestant Spiritual Traditions*, pp. 165-82 and Gordon Wakefield, "The Puritans," in Jones et al., *The Study of Spirituality*, pp. 437-45.
20. See Edwin Scott Gaustad, *The Great Awakening in New England* (Chicago: Quadrangle Books, 1957).
21. See Douglas V. Steere, ed., *Quaker Spirituality: Selected Writings* (New York: Paulist Press, 1984) and Gordon S. Wakefield, "The Quakers," in Jones et al., *The Study of Spirituality*, pp. 445-48.
22. See John and Charles Wesley, *Selected Prayers, Hymns, Journal Notes, Sermons, Letters, and Treatises*, ed. by Frank Whaling (New York: Paulist Press, 1981). Ronald Knox devoted a large part of *Enthusiasm* to a study of Wesley and Methodism. See pp. 422-548. See also A. Raymond George, "John Wesley and the Methodist Movement," in Jones et al., *The Study of Spirituality*, pp. 455-59, and David Lowes Watson, "Methodist Spirituality," in Senn, ed., *Protestant Spiritual Traditions*, pp. 217-73.
23. See Emmanuel Swedenborg, *The Universal Human* and *Soul-Body Interaction*, ed. and trans. by George F. Dole, New York: Paulist Press, 1984. A summary may be found in Slater Brown, *The Heyday of Spiritualism* (New York: Pocket Books ed., 1972, pp. 50-64).

# Progress and Reaction    20

 T THE END OF THE EIGHTEENTH CENTURY, both Europe and the New World were convulsed by a series of revolutionary attempts to shake off the last vestiges of the ancient and oppressive regimes of the late Middle Ages. In the name of freedom, equality, and justice, the rights of common people were asserted in violent and often bloody uprisings against empire, monarchies, aristocracy, and established religion.

From the American Revolution to the final defeat of Napoleon, the struggles lasted for more than fifty years. Eventually, a conservative coalition of monarchical, imperial, and ecclesiastical forces triumphed, although the republican ideal severely tempered the surviving representatives. Constitutions and limited powers came to replace the "divine right" of kings, the Holy Roman Empire was reduced to a shadow, and religious disestablishment moved slowly forward.

Although European and Latin American revolutionary struggles were largely over by mid-century, the quest for popular liberation would continue well into the twentieth century, as Imperial Russia fell before the republican ideal, along with Ireland, Italy, Greece, and Spain, among other nations. Inspired by such examples, the quest continues today in Latin America, Africa, and Southeast Asia.

*Revolution and the Decline of Religion*  Catholic spirituality was profoundly disturbed by the revolutionary fervor of the early nineteenth century, especially because of the suppression of orders and monasteries, as well as other institutions of religion, including universities. In 1773, the Jesuit Order underwent suppression for forty-one years, except, ironically, in Orthodox Russia and Protestant Prussia. But for the first time in history, during the French Revolution religion itself came under attack as one of the principal bastions of power and privilege. Churches, monasteries, and convents were closed, their revenues confiscated, and, during the Reign of Terror, hundreds of bishops, priests, and women religious were executed.

The temporal power of the papacy had also come under serious attack by German bishops as early as 1742. From 1778, the policies of Emperor Joseph II in Austria and Tuscany further reduced papal authority. But the triumph of French republican secularism in Germany, Austria, Italy, and Spain led to much more extensive restrictions on organized religion, especially monastic life.

In 1795, religious liberty was technically restored, but a year later, Napoleon led his troops into Rome, where they seized a third of the papal estates and many church treasures from Pius VI. Rome was declared a republic and the aged pope himself was arrested and subjected to a series of moves which ended with his death in Valence in 1799. Concordats by Pius VII in 1801 and 1803 eased tensions, but Napoleon reserved the nomination of bishops to himself. Further disputes led to another invasion of Rome in 1808. The pope was taken prisoner once more and deported to France, where he was forced to make sweeping concessions to Bonaparte. After Napoleon's defeat in 1814, Pius VII was returned to Rome, where he reestablished the Society of Jesus. In 1815, the Congress of Vienna restored the Papal States, and new concordats were reached with the liberated nations of Europe.

*Recovery and Outreach*

With the attempted restoration of the old order after 1815 and again following the revolutionary disturbances of 1848, new orders and congregations as well as old ones began to rise from the ashes of the past. A recovery of essential elements of traditional Christian spirituality accompanied the reappearance of monastic life. New forms of both Catholic and Protestant spirituality also flourished, as evangelization and missionary work began to channel the restless energies of idealistic, courageous men and women into areas only recently opened by exploration.

During the eighteenth century, Catholic and Protestant missionary activity in the Americas had spread from coast to coast, dividing the continents along linguistic and credal lines between Spain, Portugal, France, and England. In Central and South America, however, evangelical extension was limited and, with the short-lived exception of the Jesuit Reductions in Paraguay from 1610 to 1768, remained complacently and paternalistically Old-World European in character.

The suppression of the Society of Jesus from 1773 to 1814 profoundly hindered the missionary work of the Catholic Church. Meanwhile, Protestant missionaries such as David Brainerd (1718-47), and the Baptist William Carey (1761-1834) in India continued the tradition of John Wesley and George Whitefield.

In 1795, the London Missionary Society was founded by a league of Presbyterian, Anglican, and Congregationalist churches. The following year, thirty missionaries were sent to the South Pacific. Hundreds more went to India, China, Africa, and the West Indies. Among them was the famous explorer, David Livingstone. In 1799, the Church Missionary Society was founded by the Church of England, and began world-wide activities.

Throughout the nineteenth century, European and American missionaries, both Catholic and Protestant, continued to evangelize the newly reopened lands of the Western Pacific and southeast Asia. There, on occasion, they encountered representatives of an even more ancient tradition.

After hundreds of years slow development, Russian
and Greek spirituality underwent a series of revivals
*Orthodox*
*Spirituality*
in the eighteenth and nineteenth centuries, culminating in a flowering of classical studies and holiness.
As before, monasticism occupied the center of the
spiritual recovery. The influence of St. Nicodemos
the Hagiorite (1748-1809), a monk of Athos canonized as late as
1955, was the primary factor in the nineteenth-century revolution.[1]

Open to Western spiritual influences as well as the richness of
the Byzantine past, St. Nicodemos collected passages from the
Greek Fathers on the prayer of the heart — the Jesus Prayer —
which were published in Venice in 1782 as the *Philokalia*, "the love
of beauty."[2] Through this work, the hesychast tradition was
reintroduced in Russia by Paissy Velitchkhovsky. From the Var-
laam and especially the Optina monasteries, generations of holy
men (*startzy*) extended the sway of this powerful spirituality into
the world of ordinary lay people in cities and towns throughout
Russia.

On the intellectual front, Alexis Khomiakoff (1804-60), a liberal
theologian and mystic, joined forces with Ivan Kireevksy to found
the Slavophile Movement, with the aim of strengthening Orthodoxy without returning to the isolationism of the past. His attacks
on Christian "modernism" in the form of rationalism and idealism
resembled that of his younger contemporary, Soren Kierkegaard.
Khomiakoff's insistence on the inclusive and inward holiness of the
Church (*sobornost*), which supercedes all institutional bonds and
sanctions, put him at odds with the official church, but also identified him more closely with the radical movement represented by
Kierkegaard and others in the West. It also contributed to contemporary developments in both church doctrine and ecumenical
exchange.

Other outstanding figures in the Russian renaissance were
Bishop Theophane the Recluse (1815-94), who translated the
*Philokalia* into Russian, St. Seraphim of Sarov (1759-1833), and a
host of lay figures, many of whom were novelists and writers of
great power, including Feodor Dostoievksy (1821-81), Leo Tolstoy

(1828-1910), Constantin Leontev (1831-91), and Vladimir Soloviev (1853-1900).

Shortly before the Bolshevik revolution was to overthrow the ancient empire and reduce the influence of Church to virtual negligibility, the anonymous "tales of the Pilgrim" became popular in Russia and eventually in France and the Western world. Filled with the spirit of St. Seraphim of Sarov and the tradition of the wandering *startzy* and "Fools for Christ," these stories, now known as *The Way of a Pilgrim* and *The Pilgrim Continues His Way* enshrined the genius and holiness of the more fundamental "Russian Revolution" in trust for a later generation.[3]

*The Liberal Spirit*

Throughout Europe, the rationalist attack on religion in the eighteenth century had legitimated atheism in the nineteenth. Thinking men and women were expected to disdain claims of supernatural intervention, whether revelation, miracles, or grace. Life was to be guided by reason and ordered by demonstrable and accepted moral principles, which also found expression in enlightened civil law. Traditional religion, whether Catholic or Protestant, was relegated to rustics, fanatics, and the credulous. Priests and ministers were scorned.

Scientific empiricism, academic historicism, literary criticism, and economic industrialism further eroded the religious authority of the churches. In France and Germany especially, state totalitarianism continued to advance into the void left by the decline of organized religion. Even after the defeat of Napoleon and the restoration of the French monarchy, ecclesiastical rights and privilege were steadily engulfed in the wake of secularism.

Nonetheless, new life was breathed into the Church by a generation of young romantics who believed it possible to bridge the gap between the ancient faith and the modern world. The effort to reconcile Catholicism with historical and literary scholarship, science, and political progress was led by Joseph de Maistre

(1753-1821), Félicité de Lammenais (1782-1854), Henri Lacordaire (1802-61), and Charles de Montalembert (1810-70).

The condemnation of liberalism by Pope Gregory XVI in 1832 and a subsequent falling-out between de Lammenais and Lacordaire, brought the new movement to a halt. De Lammenais eventually left the Church entirely, but under the influence of the Benedictine Dom Prosper Guéranger, Lacordaire went on to reestablish the Dominican Order in France.

Ordained in 1827, Guéranger had revived the Benedictine Order by purchasing and refurbishing the priory of Solesmes, which soon became a center of monastic and liturgical reform. Both Guéranger and Lacordaire introduced uniform, Roman customs into their orders at the expense of local rites and practices, and many of their efforts at revival were merely antiquarian conceits. On the whole, however, their influence prepared the way for both the liturgical movement of the twentieth century and the ultimate affirmation of the relevance of authentic Christian witness in the modern world.

*Germany: the Return to Orthodoxy*

Nineteenth-century spirituality was revitalized for a time, especially in Germany, by liberal romantics such as Johann Herder, Friedrich Schlegel, and Johann Görres, who reacted to the arid rationalism of the preceding era. Friedrich Schleiermacher (1768-1834) had already emphasized the positive role of feeling in religion, returning to an almost mystical sense of total dependence on God as the heart of religious experience.

Considered the father of modern theology, Schleiermacher had been reared in a Pietist environment, but rejected a religion of feeling alone in favor of a holistic, more deeply thoughtful approach to experience. But in his classic works, *Speeches to the Cultured Despisers of Religion* (1799) and *The Christian Faith* (1822), reason clearly remained at the service of experience, not its master.

Christian reaction against romantic liberalism began with Albrecht Ritschl (1822-1889), a professor of theology at Tübingen and Göttingen. Although committed to liberal ideals, Ritschl opposed the "irrationalism" latent in the influence of Schleiermacher, but also held out firmly against any incursion of philosophy into Christian doctrine. He was followed in this by the great patristic scholar, Adolf Harnack (1851-1930).

Much stronger opposition to liberal theology came from the Danish writer, Soren Kierkegaard (1813-55).[4] Considered to be the founder of Existentialism, his writings would deeply influence German Protestant theology in the twentieth century. Among the most influential are *Either-Or, Concluding Unscientific Postscript, The Concept of Dread*, and *The Sickness unto Death*. The infinite gulf between God and humanity grounded Kierkegaard's teaching, especially in terms of the moral and spiritual tension, even the anguish, which human beings experience in the quest for salvation.

Although Kierkegaard launched his major attack on conventional Christianity in 1854, his message would not be widely heard for several generations. Even then his influence would be far greater in philosophy than in theology and spirituality. But long after his death Kierkegaard nevertheless succeeded in reestablishing faith as the central tenet of the evangelical tradition, especially in the work of Karl Barth, Paul Tillich, and Rudolf Bultmann.

*England: Retreat and Revival*

In both England and America, traditional and evangelical spirituality also reacted against the rationalism and secularism of the preceding era. The Anglican Church remained firmly established, but progressively lost influence in both the political realm and ordinary life, particularly where industrialism drew masses of the rural poor and destitute villagers to large cities and their factory jobs.

Official religion was increasingly relegated to the private world of individual conscience. Non-conforming evangelical traditions, however, especially Methodism and, from 1865, the Salvation Army of William Booth, attempted with some success to counter the trend towards de-Christianization.

For Catholics in England, three events in the nineteenth century profoundly altered their status both publicly and as members of the Church: the passage of a series of "Catholic Relief Acts" in Parliament, culminating in the reestablishment of the hierarchy in 1850; the Oxford Movement; and the influx of Catholic Irish during and after the great famine of 1848.

Partly because of the immigration of large numbers of French refugees during the Terror, Catholic Relief Acts were passed by Parliament in 1778, 1791, 1793, and 1829. These removed many of the legal and social penalties that had disenfranchised Roman Catholics since the time of Queen Elizabeth I. The appointment of Cardinal Nicholas Wiseman as first Archbishop of Westminster effectively ended the exile of the Roman Catholic Church, but it was not until 1926 that the remaining civil disabilities were repealed.

Scotland was also affected by the improved situation of Catholics, who at the end of the eighteenth century were represented by only a handful of communities in the Western Highlands, the outer islands, and remote parts of the northeast. The urban church began to recover largely because of the massive immigration of Irish refugees to Glasgow and the strenuous efforts of lay leaders who were converted to Catholicism early in the century. Most notable among the latter were Robert Montief, David Urquhart, Sir Kenelm Digby, and Robert Campbell of Skerrington.

*The Oxford Movement and the Road to Rome*

Conservative Anglican reaction to the skepticism and rationalism of the previous era, as well as the liberalism affecting contemporary religiosity, motivated a group of young Anglican priests and laymen, among them John Keble, Richard Fronde, W. G. Ward, Hugh Rose, Edward Pusey, and John Henry Newman, to reaffirm the ancient patristic and Catholic heritage of English theology and spirituality.

Keble effectively launched the Movement with his dramatic 1833 sermon in which he accused England of "national apostasy." A series of pamphlets, *Tracts for the Times*, publicized the effort to recover the "Catholic" character of the Church of England and thus reduce the appeal of Roman Catholicism itself. Reaction was swift by many who considered themselves happily Protestant. Nevertheless, the "Anglo-Catholic" movement within the Church of England survived and ultimately led to the adoption of many formerly proscribed elements of worship and discipline. It also produced a wave of converts to the Roman Church, including W. G. Ward, Henry Manning, Frederick Faber, and especially John Henry Newman (1801-90).

Because of his preeminence in the Oxford Movement, Newman's decision to enter the Roman Church in 1845 had a profound impact on both Anglican and Catholic communions. It was felt not least in the area of spirituality. For although not a spiritual writer, Newman's pastoral and literary achievements, and even his plans to reintroduce Catholics into Oxford and Cambridge, which alienated him from Ward and Manning, created a solid base from which a new sense of Catholic spirituality could emerge.

It did not emerge during his lifetime, however. Newman also failed to reestablish Catholicism on a firm intellectual foundation in the universities. But despite the hierarchy's repudiation of his progressive attitudes towards church discipline and teaching, Newman was universally esteemed by both Catholics and Anglicans for the greatness of his thought and the beauty of his character. In 1877, he was elected Honorary Fellow of Trinity College, Oxford, and Pope Leo XIII created him cardinal in 1879.

Newman's thought gained rather than lost influence after his death in 1890, and without doubt determined the tone and direction of much of the Second Vatican Council. Among his great works, the *Apologia pro Vita Sua*, *The Idea of a University*, *A Grammar of Assent*, and the long poem *The Dream of Gerontius* have achieved classic status in Christian literature.[5]

Churches
in the
Wilderness
In America, popular religion prospered in the early nineteenth century as waves of revival rippled from New England to the Midwest and the ever-receding frontier. The development of ecclesiastical power and privilege were restricted, however, by grass-roots suspicion of European ways. The gradual arrival of Catholic bishops from Europe was thus met with unbridled hostility from Protestants and wary suspicion by many Catholics.

The spirituality of early nineteenth-century America was as varied as it is today. As Jacksonian politics carried the day, Anglican aristocracy gave way to Methodist and Baptist evangelical democracy. Despite its excesses and crudeness, such egalitarianism was more successful in the U.S. than in Republican or Imperial France, and appealed in particular to the pioneer impulse.

Poets and novelists also influenced the shape of American spirituality. In New England, the Transcendentalist movement led by Ralph Waldo Emerson (1803-82) admitted the influence of Hinduism, while the nature mysticism of Henry Thoreau sowed seeds for a future generation. Nathaniel Hawthorne examined the strengths and weaknesses of the Puritan establishment. Above all, perhaps, Walt Whitman (1819-92) discovered and revealed the genius of the American spirit.

New Catholic religious communities such as the Sisters of Charity and the Paulists embodied much of the budding American spirit. Significantly, like Newman and Faber, St. Elizabeth Ann Seton (1774-1821) and Isaac Hecker (1819-1888) came to Catholicism from Americanized Anglican and Methodist churches. Among other notable converts was Rose Hawthorne, the daughter of Nathaniel, whose foundation of a congregation of Dominican sisters to tend dying victims of cancer continues its work today.

American evangelical spirituality also reacted against the rationalism of the eighteenth and early nineteenth century. Charles Finney (1792-1875) turned from the practice of law to become an itinerant Presbyterian preacher. His "revival" meetings brought about an awakening of Protestantism second only to the "Great Awakening" by Jonathan Edwards a century earlier, but in fact more extensive and influential. Finney himself became a professor of theology at Oberlin College in 1835, and its president in 1851. A vocal opponent of slavery, he promoted social reform as well as personal holiness. His revival moment continued to enliven Protestantism well into the twentieth century.

The classic era of American preaching occurred between 1840-90. During the Great Revival of 1857-60, over a million conversions were reported. As the American renewal reached Ulster, England, and Scotland, another million were added. One of the greatest of the American evangelists, Dwight L. Moody (1837-99), was the son of a bricklayer from Northfield, Massachusetts. Received into Congregational Church in 1856, Moody moved to Chicago, where he experienced a profound conversion the following year. He eventually abandoned his successful business interests to become a catechist and itinerant preacher.

During the Civil War, Moody worked as a nurse with the YMCA. Returning to evangelism, in 1870 he met Ira D. Sankey, a singer and organist with whom he formed a productive partnership. Moody's visits to England in 1867 and 1881 included a special mission to university students. Evangelical associations formed at Oxford and Cambridge eventually formed the British College Christian Union, later known as the Student Christian Movement.

*The Millennial Spirit*

In both America and England, the apocalyptic fever present in George Fox's vision and much evangelical preaching found new expression in both liberal and Adventist sects long after it had disappeared from the Society of Friends. In the late eighteenth and early nineteenth centuries, a variety of utopian communities appeared in England, Germany, and especially the United States. Most were founded by enthusiastic Protestant Christians embued with an eschatological fervor to see the perfect society on earth, if not the Second Coming of Christ. Among the more famous were those at Oneida, New York; the Amana Colonies of

Iowa; and the Shakers, whose origins lay in the English Quaker revival of 1747. Led by Mother Ann Lee, the Shakers, "the United Society of Believers in Christ's Second Appearance," immigrated to New York in 1774.[6]

Communities of Hutterite Anabaptists that settled in the United States and Canada, as well as Mennonites and Amish groups, shared some characteristics of the more apocalyptic and perfectionist societies. Robert Owen's Indiana commune, New Harmony, and others in Scotland and England embodied the ideal of social perfectionism without a pronounced eschatological spirituality. But expectations of the Second Coming and the immanent end of the world animated the spirituality and activity of many other sects, the most important being the Seventh Day Adventists, founded by William Miller in 1831 in Dresden, New York; the International Bible Students Association (Jehovah's Witnesses), founded in 1874; and in England, the Irvingites or Catholic Apostolic Church, founded by Edward Irving in 1832.

Despite miscalculations and false alarms, Adventist sects have survived to the present and in some instances even expanded. Millennial expectations also surfaced in new forms of Pentecostalism. Tongue-speaking and other charisms had appeared at intervals throughout the Christian era, but the Pentecostal movement would reach a height of popularity, especially among Black Americans, following the San Francisco earthquake in 1906.

*More Signs and Wonders*

Revivalism and evangelical enthusiasm continued to enliven Protestant churches throughout the century. Partially as a result of awe-inspiring conversion experiences, healings, and other manifestations of grace, a strong interest in miracles and other supernatural occurrences developed towards mid-century, particularly at the "grass-roots" level.[7]

In the United States, table-tapping, apparitions, voices, material "apports," and a variety of other manifestations of "departed spirits" at seances became a highly popular enthusiasm. Those connected with Margaret Fox and her sisters in 1848 eventually led to the formation of the Spiritualist Church. Other dramatic "supernatural" abilities appeared in the career of Daniel Dunglas Home, whose feats of levitation and fire-handling, among others, baffled scientists of his own day and have never been disproved.

Reverberations of the American supernaturalism were felt in Europe. In England, spiritualism prospered and stimulated research into psychic phenomena. In the more Catholic areas of the Continent, paranormal events were paralleled by reports of visions and a flood of interest in stigmatization.

Apparitions of the Virgin Mary to St. Catherine Labouré in 1830, at La Salette in 1846, and Lourdes in 1858 polarized Catholic and secular opinion. Miracles of healing followed in each instance and continue to the present. Visions of other saints were prevalent. In addition, a number of stigmatics began to attract attention, including Louise Lateau, Catherine Emmerich, and St. Gemma Galgani (1878-1903). Twentieth-century figures, such as Therese Neumann and Padre Pio, have exhibited many similarities.

The upsurge of interest in the physical phenomena of mysticism produced volumes of both learned commentary and pious twaddle. The positive effect on the faith of millions of Christians cannot be denied, however. It was accompanied, moreover, by a serious renewal of mystical spirituality at the turn of the century which had a lasting impact on all Christians.

*The Rise and Fall of Modernism* — For Catholics in general, the nineteenth century began spiritually with an individualistic resistance to secularism and ended in the triumphalistic wake of the First Vatican Council (1869-70), which rejected the modern world as a whole. Although cut short by the outbreak of the Franco-Prussian war, the council reasserted centralized institutional authority throughout the Church, culminating in the promulgation of papal infallibility, a move which alienated many Catholics as well as Protestants.

Defections by religious figures such as the priest-historian, Johann von Döllinger, produced crises in Germany and Austria. Dissenters formed "Old Catholic" bodies, which eventually established relations with the Church of England and various Protestant denominations. Some survive today. But despite the intervening pontificate of Leo XIII, which (despite his condemnation of "Americanism") was marked by greater social sensitivity and openness to the world, the opposition of Popes Pius IX (1792-1878) and Pius X (1835-1914) to all liberal trends in the Church (now known generically as "modernism") firmly established the Catholic Church as a major conservative force.

Towards the end of the century, developments in scriptural scholarship based on new forms of literary analysis, as well as progress in the social and natural sciences, had been rejected by conservative Christians as serious concessions to the modern world. But Catholic "Modernists" such as the Jesuit George Tyrrell, Alfred Loisy, and Maurice Blondel, sought to incorporate the new approaches in theology and devotional writing. Reaction was severe, resulting in alienation and excommunication for some modernists. Others, such as Lord Acton and Baron von Hügel, remained within the Church, but labored under a lingering cloud of suspicion. Pope Pius X eventually condemned the entire modernist movement in the decree *"Lamentabili"* and his encyclical *"Pascendi"* (1907). Many of the major tenets of modernism nevertheless found their way into Catholic as well as Protestant scholarship during the next century, especially after the Second Vatican Council.

*The Achievement*     Catholic spiritual writing, especially of a mystical character, had reached low ebb by the mid-nineteenth century. The controversies over Jansenism and Quietism had taken their toll, followed by the catastrophes of the French Revolution. When published in 1864 and 1889, the works of St. John of the Cross were heavily expurgated, as would be the autobiography of St. Thérèse of Lisieux published in 1899.[8]

Thérèse, who died in 1897 at the age of twenty-four, was basically unknown outside her own convent until well into the twentieth century. By contrast, many of the most attractive saints of the nineteenth century, such as Jean Vianney (the Curé of Ars), Antonio Claret, Dom Bosco, Isaac Hecker, and Mother Cabrini, left little or no writings other than letters and collections of their favorite devotional passages.

While enduring, the achievements of the period — youth work, missionary endeavor, education of the poor, and health care — were concrete and practical. But the best literature of the period tended to be apologetic or expository, as in the case of Newman and Lord Acton, or homiletic, as in the sermons of Lacordaire. What spiritual writing there was, especially in English, veered frequently into sentimentality.

As the century drew to a close, the spiritual climate changed. The monastic revival produced writers of depth as well as warmth, such as the Irish Benedictine, Dom Columba Marmion (1858-1923). Baron Friedrich von Hügel's 1908 study of the spiritual circle of St. Catherine of Genoa, *The Mystical Element of Religion*, remains a classic.[9] It appeared in the midst of a number of scholarly treatments of mysticism, beginning, perhaps, with Dean William Inge's *Christian Mysticism* (1899), and included William James' classic Gifford Lectures, *The Varieties of Religious Experience* (1902). A new era was beginning.

Protestant contributions to spirituality were also largely concrete examples of evangelism and missionary work. Outstanding achievements in the area of medical care and social welfare were made by Clara Barton, Florence Nightingale, and General William Booth, among others. The late nineteenth century was also the era of Darwin, Marx, and Freud, however. The flowering of the physical and social sciences quickly diminished the luster of the new supernaturalism. Modernism threatened many basic tenets of orthodox belief. Traditional religion remained defensive.

In the meantime, heralded by the World's Columbian Exposition of 1893 in Chicago, the twentieth century began in relative peace and the confidence that science and the progress of civilization would continue to extend the blessings of European culture to the rest of the waiting world. The ominous misgivings of Kierkegaard, the anxieties of Thérèse of Lisieux, the fevered harangues of Friedrich Nietzsche, along with the fears of Pius X, would be recalled only in the aftermath of the terrible conflict of 1914-18 — the first "World War."

## NOTES

1. See Nicodemos of the Holy Mountain, *A Handbook of Spiritual Counsel*, trans. by Peter A. Chamberas (New York: Paulist Press, 1989), and Serge Bolshakoff, *Russian Mystics* (Kalamazoo: Cistercian Publications, 1977).
2. English translations: *The Philokalia: Complete Text*, compiled by St. Nikodemos of the Holy Mountain and St. Makarios of Corinth, trans. by G. E. H. Palmer, Philip Sherrard, and Kallistos Ware, 5 vols., London: Faber and Faber, 1979 –. See also *Early Fathers from the Philokalia*, trans. by E. Kadloubovsky and G. E. H. Palmer (London: Faber and Faber, 1954), and *Writings from the Philokalia on Prayer of the Heart*, trans. by E. Kadloubovsky and G. E. H. Palmer (London: Faber and Faber, 1951).
3. In English translation, see R. M. French, trans., *The Way of a Pilgrim and A Pilgrim Continues His Way* (New York: Seabury, 1965) or Helen Bacovcin, trans., *The Way of a Pilgrim and A Pilgrim Continues His Way* (Garden City, NY: Image Books, 1978).
4. For a summary of Kierkegaard's life and influence, see D. A. Hart, "Kierkegaard," in Jones, et al., *The Study of Spirituality*, pp. 469-73.
5. One of the few recent works on Newman's spirituality is Charles Dessain's *The Spirituality of John Henry Newman* (Minneapolis: Winston Press, and Dublin: Veritas, 1977).
6. See Robley Edward Whitson, ed., *The Shakers: Two Centuries of Spiritual Reflection* (New York: Paulist Press,1983) and Edward Andrews, *The People Called Shakers: a Search for the Perfect Society* (New York: 1963 ed.).
7. For an interesting and highly readable account of nineteenth-century enthusiasm for the "supernatural," see Slater Brown's *The Heyday of Spiritualism*, op. cit.
8. See Patricia O'Connor, *In Search of Thérèse* (Wilmington, DE: Michael Glazier, 1987), p. 189. The most reliable English translation of the autobiography is that by John Clarke, O.C.D., *Story of a Soul* (Washington: Institute of Carmelite Studies, 1976).
9. Friedrich von Hügel, *The Mystical Element of Religion as Studied in St. Catherine of Genoa and Her Friends* (London: J. M. Dent and Sons and James Clarke and Co., 2 vols., 1961 [1909]). On Von Hügel himself, who exercised a powerful influence on Evelyn Underhill and other important spiritual writers, see Joseph Whelan, S. J., *The Spirituality of Friedrich von Hügel* (London: Collins, 1971).

# The Twentieth Century: Crisis and Renewal  *21*

THE EMERGENCE OF TRENDS and patterns is best seen in hindsight. Events only a few decades away from us still appear complex and variable, enmeshed as they were in webs of social, cultural, and historical factors which change and develop even as they continue to influence our lives today. Thus, as we end our pilgrimage through the centuries of Christian spirituality with a tour of our own era, we can at most identify some of the main movements, indicate their antecedents, glance at a few of the more striking personalities, and try to discern directions of development and future consequences. A deeper and more definitive understanding must await the work of future historians (whose own era will probably be as opaque to them as ours is to us).

By way of preliminary observation, I consider it curiously characteristic of the twentieth century that every major tendency in the development of Christian spirituality seems to have become manifest in one way or another, as if the entire history were being recapitulated prior to the beginning of the third millennium. Viewed in terms of their original appearance rather than recent chronology, the first and most dramatic of these tendencies was a return to the deepest *apostolic roots* of service and ministry effected in the Roman Catholic Church by the Second Vatican Council, much as Protestantism was being invigorated by the "Back to the Bible" movement and the ecumenical energy of the World Council of Churches.

At the same time, even as a new wave of biblical scholarship emerged at the heart of Catholic renewal, *ecstatic spirituality* appeared at the grass-roots level in the form of the "charismatic movement," continuing the impulse begun in Protestant Christianity at the turn of the century. *Jewish Christianity* also found new expression in the 1960s and 1970s with the "Jews for Jesus" movement, elements of which were still extant in 1989. *Gnosticism* recurred in forms of Christian hermeticism, Kabbalism, New Age enthusiasms, the use of arcane approaches such as the *I Xing*, Tarot Cards,[1] and numerological spiritualities such as the "Enneagram" developed by Oscar Ichazo, all of which became popular in Catholic circles in the 1980s.

The *pastoral romanticism* of Paulinus of Nola and the spirituality of *alienatio* of the fifth century found new expression in Distributism and Catholic Worker houses during the late 1920s and early 1930s and again in the early 1970s, when new communes sprang up throughout the United States as if the ghost of Mother Ann Lee and Robert Owen had appeared to focus the spiritual restlessness of young enthusiasts eager to experiment with a wide variety of shared living situations.

After the Second World War, a revival of the *monastic life*, especially in the United States, found thousands of men and women retiring to solitude either under private vows or joining eremitical communities such as the Camaldolese or Carthusians. The coenobitic tradition found popular vocal expression in the lectures and writings of Columba Marmion, Hubert Van Zeller, John Main, and above all in Thomas Merton, as well as more recently in David Steindlrast, Basil Pennington, and Thomas Keating. The ecumenical dimension of Roger Schutz' Taizé monastery as well as Anglican and Orthodox monasticism are especially noteworthy.

Following the Second Vatican Council, a strong recurrence of interest in *medieval mysticism* led to the popular rediscovery of Meister Eckhart, Hildegard of Bingen, and other mystics of the

apophatic tradition, including the *Cloud* author, and in the kata-
phatic tradition, Bernard of Clairvaux, Francis of Assisi, Catherine
of Siena, and Julian of Norwich, among others. Even Celtic spirituality enjoyed a season of popularity.[2] Ignatian spirituality also
underwent a profound revitalization. Similarly, the mysticism of
Carmel, embodied in the writings of Teresa of Avila, John of the
Cross, Brother Lawrence of the Resurrection, and St. Thérèse of
Lisieux came to the fore again in Europe, North America, and
elsewhere.

A gradual revival of *Orthodox spirituality* in France, England,
and the United States, marked emblematically by the reappearance
of the "prayer of the heart," was paralleled towards the end of the
century by a resurgence of religion in the Soviet Union and some
of its satellites. Similarly, the great evangelical traditions of the
fifteenth and sixteenth centuries found new voices in Aimee
Semple McPherson, Fr. Charles Coughlin, Billy Graham, Bishop
Fulton J. Sheen, and a later generation of "tele-evangelists."

*Social action* and *pacifism* were represented by Walter Rauschenbusch's Social Gospel Movement at the turn of the century and,
from the 1930s on, the communal mysticism of Dorothy Day and
Peter Maurin of the Catholic Worker Movement and forms of
Catholic Action, including the "Priest-worker" Movement of the
late 1940s. During the Nazi era and afterwards, spiritualities of
*resistance and liberation* were represented by Simone Weil, Franz
Jaggerstetter, Dietrich Bonhoeffer, and Christian movements such
as the White Rose in Nazi Germany, France, Holland, and Belgium;
the struggle for civil rights led by Martin Luther King, Jr.; the peace
movement, with Philip and Daniel Berrigan, Elizabeth McAlister,
William Sloan Coffin, Benjamin Spock, and others; and the struggle
against Latin American oppression — from Camillo Torres to
Leonardo Boff, amid a growing number of activists and theological
writers from Russia to South Africa.

The extraordinary *missionary outreach* of the sixteenth and
seventeenth centuries was resumed at the beginning of the twentieth century in the Catholic Church by the foundation of the
Maryknoll Mission Society of priests and sisters and extensive

evangelization in Latin America, Africa, and Asia. Protestant missionary work similarly flourished, especially in the Far East. New forms of inter-religious encounter appeared. Emigré monks such as Dom Bede Griffiths actually established Christian ashrams in India.[3] Conversely, Asian forms of religious belief and practice, especially forms of yoga and Zen Buddhism, found much more successful expression in the West than had happened in previous centuries. The conferences and writings of Fr. Anthony de Mello, S. J., are worth particular note in this regard.[4]

The *rationalism* of the Enlightenment and the *skeptical empiricism* of the era of Darwin, Marx, and Freud were echoed briefly in the "God is Dead" theology of the late 1960s, while mid nineteenth-century enthusiasm for *paranormal experience and pursuits* resurfaced in forms of occultism, flying saucer cults, spiritualism, even new forms of witchcraft and satanism. In some respects evocative of the manias of the fifteenth, sixteenth, and seventeenth centuries, such contemporary heterodox movements often differ significantly in both character and function from earlier varieties, however.

Whatever else might be said of this jumble of often competing spiritualities (and anti-spiritualities), one thing is certain: twentieth-century men and women have not lost the instinct for religious meaning and purpose, even when institutionalism on one hand and enthusiasm on the other obscure the traditional paths followed by generations of Christians. But, lacking the clarifying perspective of time and distance, what are we to make of this seemingly chaotic resumé?

*An Ambiguous Inheritance*

To begin with, for both Catholics and Protestants, the legacy of the nineteenth century was a mixture of positive and negative elements. Materialism, secularism, and atheistic humanism had led to a recession of the sense of God's presence in life, one often of crushing poverty for the masses of European humanity. New forms of political oppression and totalitarianism were emerging, most of them united eventually under the umbrella of antagonistic forms of socialism — Marxist-Leninist communism on one hand, and, on the other, the pathological National Socialism of Germany's "Third Reich" and other kinds of Fascism.

Not surprisingly, in the early years of the century, many church leaders were uncomfortable with the modern world and seemed bent on a return to the Middle Ages or the Reformation. Pope Pius X attempted to eradicate every trace of modernism in the Catholic Church. Conservative Protestantism, reawakened by the accomplishments of evangelists such as Dwight Moody and the theological reactions to modernism of Ritschl and his school, found expression in "Neo-orthodoxy." In Europe, the most influential of these movements was led by the Swiss pastor and theologian, Karl Barth (1886-1968). In the United States, Protestant reaction to nineteenth-century liberalism culminated with the appearance of "Fundamentalism."

*The Fundamentals*

Today, Fundamentalism implies a strictly literal interpretation of the Bible, the rejection of the modern world in favor of an idealized past, moral puritanism, and an antagonism towards liberal Christianity often allied with political and social conservatism. Originally, however, the term referred to a series of twelve tracts called "The Fundamentals." The first was issued in 1909. Composed by a group of evangelical theologians, the tracts proposed as a minimum for Christian belief the literal truth (inerrancy) of the Bible, the divinity of Christ, the Virgin Birth, the physical resurrection of Jesus, and the return of Christ in glory to judge the living and the dead.

Promoted throughout the English-speaking world, the fundamentalistic tracts led to a sharp division in most Protestant churches between liberals (or Modernists) and conservatives (Fundamentalists). Apart from the anti-Catholic tone of much mainstream Protestantism of the time, the basic position of the early fundamentalists did not differ in many respects from that of the attitude of Pope Pius X and conservative Catholics until the Second Vatican Council.

The inherited spiritualities of most Christian traditions were largely individualistic, moreover, placing major emphasis on particular rather than communal salvation.[5]   Although often otherworldly and pessimistic as well, such ways of life nevertheless exhibited genuine humanitarian sympathies and expressed them actively in generous efforts for the poor, ignorant, ill, refugees, "pagans," and other lost souls.  But these spiritualities could not recognize and therefore did not address the social conditions that created such situations and thus provided only sporadic relief rather than real alternatives or lasting solutions.

Thus for much of Europe and North America, the long era called "Victorian" ended ambivalently, first in the disillusionment and pessimism of the First World War (1914-18), and then in the reactionary exuberance of "the roaring twenties," itself to end only in the great economic depression of 1929 and the following decade.

*New Beginnings*

Positive factors also characterized Christian spiritualities of the early part of this century.  The prolific multiplication of Catholic religious congregations in the nineteenth and early twentieth centuries had been paralleled by the appearance of a host of new Protestant sects, denominations, and organizations.   As noted before, missionary activity assumed particular importance with most of them, as the Great Powers of Europe, as well as Russia and the United States, threw open the last regions of Asia, the South Pacific, and the southern hemisphere for colonization and exploitation.

During earlier phases of the missionary renewal, competition among denominations was sharp as Catholics and Protestants rivaled each other in the race for souls.  But as the labors of missionaries changed from simple and direct evangelization to humanitarian and social assistance on behalf of developing peoples, cooperation slowly replaced competition.

Meanwhile, faced at home by extremes of wealth and poverty that divided parishes, denominations, and churches, some liberal Protestants attempted to cope by means of innovative programs of social action. Washington Gladden (1836-1918) of Columbus, Ohio, and Walter Rauschenbusch (1861-1918), a New York Baptist pastor, became leading exponents of the "Social Gospel" movement at the turn of the century, which embodied many modernist principles later incorporated into civic and national legislation.

Similarly, lay-centered "Catholic Action" was put into practice by groups such as Abbé Cardijn's Young Christian Workers (the "Jocists") in Belgium and France, the Legion of Mary in Ireland, and the Grail Movement in Holland. In the United States, the Catholic Youth Organization was founded by Chicago Bishop Bernard Sheil in 1930 as an alternative to the mainly Protestant Young Men's Christian Association (YMCA) and the Young Women's Christian Association (YWCA). The Christian Family Movement also originated there as late as 1947, which, with the Young Christian Students, formed a nucleus of social action until the Second Vatican Council. The latter's Protestant counterpart, Campus Crusade for Christ, was even more successful in reaching hundreds of thousands of students with its evangelical programs.

The growth of lay-centered spirituality among Catholics was accelerated further during this time by the spread of the Cursillo movement from Spanish-speaking to "Anglo" settings, the development of Marriage Encounter programs, and the appearance of less socially-conscious movements such as the Charismatic Renewal and secular institutes.

*From Cooperation to Ecumenism* Nurtured by constructive missionary encounters and social action efforts, ecumenical cooperation among various Protestant churches increased dramatically in the period after the First World War. Catholics remained wary, but a reunion of the Christian body was at last becoming more of a real possibility than the dream of starry-eyed idealists.

As the century progressed, inter-denominational spiritual writing of a very high order began to appear. Here, as elsewhere, the voice of women was increasingly heard, as universal suffrage became the target of demonstrations and appeals following the Great War of 1914-18. By mid-century, a number of women spiritual writers had left their mark on both Catholic and Protestant spirituality — Thérèse of Lisieux, Evelyn Underhill, Caryll Houselander, Maisie Ward, Simone Weil, Dorothy Day, Raissa Maritain, Hilda Graef, Anne Morrow Lindbergh, and Catherine de Hueck Doherty among them.

*War, Peace, and Aggiornamento*

Many of the promising projects of the 'twenties and 'thirties, such as nascent ecumenism, universal suffrage, the relief of the poor, and missionary breakthroughs in Asia and Africa, were curtailed by the outbreak of a new and more terrible World War in 1939. The advent of the atomic age in 1945 which ended the war, also brought with it a new awareness of the unity of humankind, and the urgency of achieving lasting peace and international cooperation.

In Europe, cooperation among Protestants, Catholics, and Jews continued and even increased during and after the harrowing experiences of the Hitler era. As the rebuilding of the great cities of Europe engendered a new hope for a world of United Nations in 1945, so a major step towards a common Christian faith also occurred in 1948, when the World Council of Churches was formed from several existing inter-faith organizations. Tragically for both enterprises, the emergence of Soviet power resulted in post-war tensions that once again threatened to end in world conflagration.

Unexpectedly, at the height of the Cold War, the unfinished business of the First Vatican Council was taken up with astonishing results by the Second from 1962 to 1965. Seen as the occasion of "a new Pentecost" by Pope John XXIII, and attended in great numbers by bishops from Third World Nations as well as Protestant and Orthodox observers, the Council may well prove to have been the turning point of the century. Among many accomplishments, it affirmed in terms congenial to most Protestants the sense of the Church as "the people of God" envisioned by John Henry Newman a century earlier.

Many other liberal tenets of nineteenth-century church leaders in France, Germany, and England found conciliar expression in terms of greater freedom of conscience, increased lay participation and ministry, liturgical renewal, the value and validity of non-Christian religious, and, above all, commitment to rather than flight from the modern world. Possibly the Council's greatest impact on Christian spirituality in the future will come from the critical shift from an essentially clerical model to an inclusive, even lay-centered spirituality.

Despite important and initially exciting post-conciliar developments, however, by the early 'seventies, rival elements in both Catholic and Protestant communities were becoming polarized by reforms in liturgy, doctrine, and discipline. Factionalism began to erode the real achievements of both the World Council of Churches and the Second Vatican Council. Bolstered by the continuing hostilities between East and West as well as a world-wide economic decline, a vocal "new conservatism" appeared. But in most respects, the reaction against modern reform looked back only to the nineteenth and early twentieth centuries — the anti-Modernist retrenchment of Popes Pius IX and Pius X, and the emergence of Protestant Fundamentalism in America.

As a result, the issues in contention tended to be dated and even superficial, compared to perennial problems of theological and spiritual divergence. "Creationism," a literalist interpretation of the first chapters of Genesis, countered the inroads of "evolutionism" among evangelical Protestants. Ecumenism was likewise rejected, along with what was perceived to be a "softening" of moral orthodoxy with regard to abortion, sexual liberation, and capital punishment. While linked to Protestant resistance to abortion, conservative Catholic reaction focused more on liturgy and discipline, in extreme cases (such as that of Archbishop Marcel Le-Febvre and his followers), rejecting all reforms resulting from Conciliar and post-conciliar decrees. Many upper-class American

Catholics, including scholars and well-known public figures, also rejected the social teachings of conciliar bishops, particularly those regarding nuclear deterrence and social and economic justice. Once again, however, the clock could not be set back.

Post-
Conciliar
Spiritual
Trends
Given the upheavals of the first half of the century, it is not surprising that post-conciliar spiritual currents consist of diverse and sometimes divisive influences at work within the Christian community as well as outside it. While *ecumenism* has remained a powerful undercurrent, emphasis has shifted in the northern hemisphere from reunion among Christians and inter-religious dialogue to forms of *protest against war and social injustice* in the peace and human rights movements. Church documents and popular conviction now strongly stress the explosive potential of deepening poverty among an increasing majority of the world's peoples, versus the aggregation of wealth and power among ruling elites. Similarly, among both people of color and developing nations in the southern hemisphere, the *struggle against political and economic oppression* is substantially transforming the sense of the presence of God and the role of the Church in historical process and personal experience.

Other developments in contemporary spirituality include a *resurgence of traditional mysticism* as well as the *emergence of new religious movements*. Recent years have also witnessed the *growth of holistic and ecologically concerned ("green") spiritualities* and the *renaissance of Orthodox spirituality* in the nations of the Soviet Union and its satellites.

Emancipation
and
Liberation
In Europe and the United States, the situation of women in both civil society and the Church had been improved by the suffragette movement and augmented by their role in the Second World War effort. Women's rights and those of other minorities were also advanced by the bitter struggle for civil rights and

racial equality identified with the work of Dr. Martin Luther King, Jr., and other prophetic figures.

In many respects, the contemporary peace movement, which combines efforts at reducing hostilities between national and religious opponents with a general campaign for nuclear disarmament, similarly continues the earlier pacifism of Dorothy Day and Evelyn Underhill.[6] Still broadly ecumenical, the struggle for civil liberation and racial justice, like the struggle for peace, embraces women and men of every class, ethnic origin, age, and political position. It is, moreover, now world-wide.

*Latin America: The Sleeping Giant*
Nowhere has this shift in spiritual consciousness been felt with such force than in the struggle for basic human rights as well as civil liberties in Central and South America. Following the Second Vatican Council, the emergence in Latin America of a vital and in many respects new Christian spirituality culminated in the meetings of the bishops' conferences (CELAM) in Bogotá and Medellin, Colombia, in 1968, and in Puebla, Mexico, in 1975. God's "preferential option for the poor" was clearly enunciated as the heart of evangelization — a realization that is transforming the sense of Christian presence throughout the world.

Popes Paul VI and John Paul II themselves declared openly that the economic imperialism of the nations of the northern hemisphere could no longer dominate the peoples of the so-called "Third World." Out of such an awareness, and specifically in view of the suffering and struggle of oppressed peoples for political, economic, and cultural freedom grew the school of "liberation theology" and its entailed or even underlying spirituality, especially through the writings of Gustavo Gutiérrez, Leonardo Boff, Jon Sobrino, and Segundo Galilea.[7]

Tensions in Central and South America generated by the struggle for liberation, including the development of "base communities," has erupted periodically in violence, such as the assassination of Bishop Oscar Romero in El Salvador and ruthless murders and assaults on scores of sisters, priests, lay ministers, and hundreds of thousands of peasants, workers, Indians, students, and political dissidents. Uneasy relations among competing forms of Christian mission also sometimes pit liberationists against more conservative, middle-class evangelicals, Pentecostals, and traditional upper-class elites sympathetic to oppressive regimes such as those long dominant in Argentina, Chile, El Salvador, Guatemala, Paraguay, and, until recent times, in Brazil, Cuba, Nicaragua, and elsewhere. Gradually, however, throughout Latin America, the spirit of gospel liberation is infusing the hierarchy and clergy as well as the people with an openness to democratic reform and religious inclusiveness, an attitude that will inevitably transform Christian spirituality also in the North.

*Witnesses to Change: Merton and Teilhard*

Postconciliar developments in Catholic spirituality included a new interest in mystical spirituality and a greater appreciation of the contributions of Asian religions, emphases associated with the teachings of two of the most influential religious writers of the century, Pierre Teilhard de Chardin (1881-1955) and Thomas Merton (1915-1968).

Early in the present century, a vital new current of spirituality began to emerge from the scientific speculations and devotional, indeed mystical, writings of Teilhard de Chardin, the Jesuit paleontologist and mystic, although it was not until after his death that his influence was truly felt.[8] In the years immediately prior to the Second Vatican Council, Teilhard's endorsement of the evolutionary hypothesis as a universal cosmological principle, together with his wide-ranging concern for human social development, reawakened the spirit of scientific humanism dormant among Catholics since the Reformation. But it had already earned him the suspicion and then hostility of Roman authorities, who banned publication of his non-scientific works. After his death, however, Teilhard's teachings were disseminated by the secular press and achieved instant popular recognition. The contemporary growing fascination with "the new cosmology," associated with so-called "New Age" spiritualities, is no less a direct consequence of Teilhard's teaching than their relative freedom from adherence to a creationist view of the origin of the universe.

Almost every element in modern Christian spirituality also found expression in one or another aspect of Thomas Merton's life, writings, and activity.[9] As a relatively young man, Merton turned from a life of worldly skepticism and indulgence, abandoning a possibly brilliant career as a writer to embrace the solitary discipline of the Cistercian Order. At Gethsemani Abbey, near Louisville, Kentucky, Merton slowly developed a solid, mystical spirituality based on Scripture as well as the Fathers and Doctors of the Church that issued forth in a steady stream of often best-selling books. But at the same time, he was nurturing a social sensitivity which found eventual expression in resistance against nuclear war, racial discrimination, and even the War in Vietnam, culminating in an embracing outreach towards Asian religions which took him to Bangkok and his death in tragic circumstances in December, 1968.

*A Kind of Pentecost*      At first widely identified with the "new Pentecost" Pope John XXIII prayed for at the beginning of the Second Vatican Council, the important spiritual movement known as Neo-Pentecostalism in Protestant circles and the "Charismatic Renewal" by many Catholics was more the outgrowth of grass-roots ecumenical activities before and during the 'sixties. In many respects, charismatic Catholicism represents a resurgence of fundamentalism and otherworldliness rather than the progressive reforms emanating from the council, especially its emphasis on social justice. Even so, as a contemporary manifestation of the ecstatic spiritualities present in the Church from its earliest days, the Pentecostal-Charismatic movement occupies a significant position in the spiritual history of the twentieth century.

Long dormant in most Protestant and all Catholic spiritualities, ecstatic devotion, especially in public settings, reappeared at the turn of the century among Black evangelical denominations in the United States.[10] Merging with the Holiness tradition of original Anabaptist and Pietistic origin, it became an interracial (but segregated) movement, eventually spreading to Europe, Central and South America, Indonesia, and Africa. An entire denomination, the Assembly of God, soon grew out of this confluence of traditions.[11]

Unlike conciliar Catholicism and the intellectual Protestantism of Neo-Orthodoxy and the World Council of Churches, Pentecostalism has remained a fundamentally popular movement. Endorsed by many bishops and favored by the Vatican itself, the Catholic Charismatic Renewal has been characterized in general by strong loyalty to traditional values such as obedience to ecclesiastical and civil authority, strong devotion to Jesus, belief in miracles, reliance on prayer, and a confident expectation of God's immediate and particular assistance in every area of life. Catholic charismatics are strongly opposed to abortion, contraception, homosexuality, the ordination of women, and other 'liberal' trends. Many Pentecostals are also strongly millennialist, considering the present age to be the final, apocalyptic era heralding the Parousia.

Of special importance with respect to the Presence of God, pentecostal Christians are committed to the real and direct experience of that Presence as manifested in the "gifts" of the Holy Spirit. Supreme among the charisms is *glossolalia* or "speaking in tongues," a form of ecstatic speech or singing claimed to approximate the miracle of languages described in Acts 2:4 and elsewhere. While emblematic of pentecostal spirituality, tongue-speaking is associated with healing, interpretation of tongues, prophecy (see 1 Cor. 14), and other less scripturally warranted but characteristic rituals such as "slaying in the spirit" — a temporary catatonic seizure accompanied by a sense of rapture — and routine exorcism (deliverance).

Although now declining somewhat in numbers and influence, pentecostal Christianity remains a vital spiritual element in the contemporary Church, a positive, communal, strongly ecclesial development with important ecumenical roots and promise.[12]

*Sacred vs. Secular: New Religious Movements*

As in other creative eras of Christian spirituality, in the declining years of the twentieth century, new communities and congregations began to multiply. Like the variety of groups that arose in the twelfth, fourteenth, and sixteenth centuries, some of them, such as the Missionaries of Charity of Mother Teresa of Calcutta, are traditional in function, if not also in form. Others differ considerably from conventional religious congregations — "secular" institutes such as Opus Dei and Caritas Christi, the Neo-Catechumenate and strongly reactionary networks like Catholics United for the Faith in the U.S.

Often, these communities have no canonical status. Some, such as the monastery at Taizé, France, are ecumenical. Pax Christi, the international Catholic peace movement, like the Catholic Worker movement, does not claim to be more than that. Most other groups are allied to no church and yet are animated by a profound Christian spirituality, one largely inarticulate but nonetheless operative. Their scope of activity encompasses the most critical areas of contemporary life, especially on a global scale. Like medieval mendicants, they are supported by voluntary contributions. Their membership consists of many of the brightest, most dedicated, and creative women and men of this generation, people seriously committed to saving the world.

Truly secular communities, and thus generally unrecognized as forces of a vital new spirituality, these include, among others, Amnesty International, Bread for the World, Earthwatch, Food First, Friends of the Earth, Greenpeace, Infact, Oxfam, and the Worldwatch Institute, and a host of smaller voluntary organizations throughout the world. Wholly characteristic of the modern age, these new agents of change have passed beyond the lure of individualism and private salvation, electing to work for a better world in ways that nevertheless incarnate the ideals and values of Christian spirituality at its best.

Since the late 1960s, new religious cults of both the "left" and "right" have also been perceived as a threat to conventional churches, which have tended to react in consternation and in some cases angry opposition.[13] Such new religious movements are more highly structured than New Age spiritualities. Moreover, they are not restricted to Europe and North America, but have affected every part of the world, including Japan, Korea, India, Africa, and Latin America.

*Religious Alienation and the "New" Mysticism*    Beginning in the late 1960s, what can best be described as gnostic expectations of a "new age" of peace, prosperity, and enlightenment, the "Age of Aquarius" heralded by the popular musical *Hair* and based on a loose reading of Eastern religious texts and the writings of C. G. Jung, began to filter into mainstream consciousness. Suddenly a host of archaic, arcane, and occult practices as well as a new interest in reincarnation, psychic phenomena, and esoteric mysticism (including a resurgence of witchcraft and Satanism in a variety of manifestations) became the preoccupation of the younger generation. While sometimes more vicious and destructive than the imagined crimes of the late Middle Ages and Renaissance, as noted earlier, Satanist groups today are often more pretentious than dangerous, as in the case of Anton LaVey and his Church of Satan. The Earth-mysticism of neo-pagan "witches" like Starhawk and others is not only more serious but far more constructive in its preoccupation with healing the planet and advancing the rights of women and minorities.[14]

The considerable psychological and cultural energy of this shift in consciousness was deflected for a decade by the Vietnam War and worsened economic conditions in the United States and elsewhere. But in the prosperous mid-1980s it erupted again as New Age spirituality. Rather than a coherent body of thought and practice, the New Age movement is still an inconsistent and highly diverse array which philosopher Christopher Lasch satirized as a melange of "Meditation, positive thinking, faith healing, rolfing, dietary reform, environmentalism, mysticism, yoga, water cures, acupuncture, incense, astrology, Jungian psychology, biofeedback, extrasensory perception, spiritualism, vegetarianism, organic gardening, theory of evolution, Reichian sex therapy, ancient mythologies, archaic nature cults, Sufism, Freemasonry, cabalistic lore, chiropractic, herbal medicine, hypnosis, and any number of other techniques designed to heighten awareness, including elements borrowed from the major religious traditions."[15]

Although highly exaggerated, Lasch's characterization is not inaccurate.  But more noteworthy is the fact that this wild upsurge of spiritual enthusiasm is meeting the felt needs of a growing number of people in the United States and Europe and doing so outside the margins of organized religion.  In the long run, that may be its strength as well as value, as increasing numbers of young adults continue to drop out of mainstream denominations but in a direction opposite that of the new Fundamentalism.  Like ultra-liberal congregations of the first half of the century, such intentional associations serve as cultural and spiritual "lifeboats" as the religious ship of state encounters rough seas and high winds.[16]

As the end of the century nears, the rift between increasingly authoritarian forms of religion (whether in doctrine or discipline — or both), and individualistic, antinomian, and "free" movements of religious consciousness is likely to widen.  As a result, the mystical potential of the "New Age" spiritualities may be channeled into ancient blind alleys of elitism, estrangement, and excess, while the vital sense of the presence of God in traditional religion could wither and harden into greater formalism.  On the other hand, emerging forms of dialogue might also lead to a recognition of mutual concern for spiritual deepening and growth and with that, a truly New Age of openness and collaboration.

*The Quest for Wholeness*

Another element in late twentieth-century spirituality, the emphasis on holism and health, has precedents in the formation of the Red Cross and other relief agencies in the nineteenth century as well as efforts towards conservation and simpler ways of living in a rapidly industrializing society.  Today's ecological spiritualities, now focused on the meaning and value of creation,[17] were likewise presaged by the romantic agrarianism of the "back to the earth" movement earlier in the century, including the "Distributism" of G. K. Chesterton and Hilaire Belloc, which was based in many respects on the social teaching of Leo XIII's encyclical *Rerum Novarum*.[18]

Chesterton in particular "was asking for a return to the sanity of field and workshop, of craftsman and peasant, from the insanity of trusts and machinery, of unemployment, over-production and starvation."[19] He found support from a variety of quarters, including George Bernard Shaw, Eric Gill, and Fr. Vincent McNabb, the Dominican preacher and pamphleteer. Opposed to the concentration of wealth and power in the hands of capitalists as well as their dehumanizing appropriation in socialism, this radical approach to widespread, but not collective, ownership of property and the means of production was taken up in the United States by the Catholic Worker Movement under Dorothy Day and Peter Maurin.[20] It was also espoused by the National Catholic Rural Life Conference and enjoyed support among both Catholic and Protestant groups in England, France, Belgium, Canada, and Australia.

While successful among many well-educated and even influential persons, such ideas were neither immediately understood nor ultimately popular among the masses. The disastrous effects of the Great Depression and the Second World War made them seem even more impossibly remote. Recently, however, worsening economic conditions and the commitment of Catholic and Protestant religious leaders to alleviating the disparities between the rich and poor as well as the devastation of the natural environment have reawakened interest in such prophetic, alternative approaches.

*Glasnost and Sobornost*

Perhaps the most surprising example of such creative "breakthrough" in late twentieth-century spirituality has been the apparently sudden revival of religion in Russia and other nations of the Soviet Union. As humankind stands poised on the edge of space exploration, and backs away from the brink of nuclear war, few events could be more hopeful.

The Communist Revolution of 1917 and the First World War had plunged Russia into a mad whirlwind of cultural transformation and destruction. Religion was officially and actively suppressed throughout the Soviet Union, sometimes ruthlessly. Emigré theologians and spiritual writers such as Nicholas Berdyaev (1874-1948), Sergius Bulgakov (1871-1944), Vladimir Lossky (1903-58),[21] and the saintly Nicholas Arseniev (1888-1977),[22] were able, however, to continue the spiritual renaissance begun a century earlier, nurturing the faith of their compatriots and instructing the Western church in the mystical theology of the East.

In this line must be included Metropolitan Anthony (Bloom) of Sourozh, who presides over the Russian Orthodox Patriarchy of Great Britain. The nephew of the pianist and composer Alexander Scriabin, Bloom himself holds a degree in medicine. His works and talks on the life of prayer have greatly enriched contemporary spiritual life.[23] In North America, similarly, the work and writings of Baroness Catherine de Hueck Doherty have tutored two generations of Christians open to the mystical heritage of Russian spirituality.[24]

Such figures, together with their counterparts behind the Iron Curtain, undoubtedly prepared the way for the promising events of the present spiritual renaissance behind the "Iron Curtain." In different ways, all embody the mystical quality of *sobornost*. Often translated "catholicity," this character, so integral to the ecclesial vision of Alexis Khomiakoff a century ago, signifies the organic unity of different persons in the Church, combining full individuality with full incorporation into community.

In the new openness of *glasnost* and *perestroika* (restructuring) associated with Soviet leader Michail Gorbachev, the thawing of official Soviet rigidity towards religion and other "counter-revolutionary" attitudes, *sobornost* may well be the long-awaited gift from the mystical heritage of ancient Byzantium. If so, it is not only rich with promise for the reunion of the Body of Christ on earth, but represents one of the world's best chances for a humanly possible future.

*Transition* For all its confusion and conflict, the twentieth century witnessed true cultural and social progress, including promising developments in the sciences, arts, communication, technology, and commerce. Spiritually, it likewise marked a period of decline and recovery, during which, after centuries of antagonism, Christians drew closer together, recognizing more clearly their corporate destiny as brothers and sisters, people of One God present in both history and immediate, personal experience.

Of course, immense challenges lie ahead, including meeting a bewildering host of problems created by the very scientific and technological progress of the previous ninety years. But the last decade of the twentieth century has opened onto a future of hope. After almost fifty years of living under the threat of a nuclear war that would devastate the entire planet for generations, the American and Soviet superpowers are earnestly seeking a lasting peace. Whether as cause or effect, the reunion between Eastern and Western churches may also be nearer than anyone dreamed possible for almost a millennium.

Exhausted after two World Wars and the prolonged Cold War, Europe still awaits a spiritual reawakening from the materialistic preoccupations of economic and political rebuilding. But the new liveliness of the Catholic Church in Poland, Hungary, Czechoslovakia, and Yugoslavia may presage a breakthrough from the East. In Germany, England, and the United States, ecumenical discussion continues to draw the separated members of the Western church into a firm and lasting communion. Dialogue with Buddhism and Hinduism continues on a much smaller scale in Japan and India, but progress in mutual understanding is slowly growing.

In all likelihood, the future success of ecumenism will largely depend on events in North America and the Third World. In these areas, evangelical spirituality continues to exert a powerful force on both Catholics and Protestants, with preachers such as Billy Graham reaching vast audiences through personal crusades and the electronic media. In the last decade, however, the "Third Great

Awakening" may have taken a fatal turn into the superficial and passing excitement of "tele-evangelism."

The American Catholic Church, swelling with the influx of Spanish-speaking immigrants, is also discovering a host of new problems and opportunities, among them large-scale defections to evangelical denominations in North, Central, and South America. In the United States, after more than a century of clerical domination, lay leadership is assuming an importance rivaling that of the early nineteenth century, when the Church was guided by lay trustees. Residual clericalism and conflicts among influential figures allied with right- and left-wing political movements may hinder progress in this critical area. But a rapidly developing sense of solidarity among the dispossessed — women, the poor, people of color, and other minorities — may succeed in forming the nucleus of a new consensus, one united in a spiritual rather than ideological vision of commitment, service, and witness.

As the Christian faith spreads and develops in Latin America, Africa, Oceania, and Asia, such a spiritual transformation is inevitable. But the contours it will assume will be the result more of inspiration among the native leadership in these young churches than of the guidance of missionary forces. Similarly, the evolution of base communities will inevitably play a major role in future spiritualities, as groups replace individuals as agents ("doers") of the Word. A deep biblical orientation and continual faith-reflection together with effective programs of bodily, mental, and spiritual liberation from all forms of oppression and destruction will undoubtedly characterize these communities and their work. They will also be endowed with a sense of God's presence among and within them, directing and sustaining them, and through them transforming the course of world history itself.

# NOTES

1. See in particular *Meditations on the Tarot: A Journey into Christian Hermeticism*, trans. by Robert Powell (Amity, NY: Amity House, 1985).
2. See, for instance, Shirley Toulson, *The Celtic Alternative* (London and Melbourne: Century Hutchinson, 1987) and Esther de Waal, ed., *The Celtic Vision: Prayers and Blessings from the Outer Hebrides* (London: Darton, Longman and Todd, 1988).
3. See Bede Griffiths, O.S.B., *Christian Ashram* (1966), *Return to the Center* (1976), *The Golden String* (1979), *The Marriage of East and West* (1982), all published by Collins, London, and *River of Compassion: A Christian Commentary on the Bhagavad-Gita* (Warwick, NY: Amity House, 1987). The movement is not limited, of course, to immigrants. Sister Vandana, a Indian Catholic religious has also founded a Christian ashram on the banks of the Ganges in Rishikesh. See Sister Vandana, *Waters of Fire* (Warwick, NY: Amity House, 1988).
4. See Anthony de Mello, S.J., *Sadhana: A Way to God* (1984), *Song of the Bird* (1982), *Wellsprings* (1984), *One Minute Wisdom* (1988), and *Taking Flight* (1988), all published by Doubleday Image Books, Garden City, NY.
5. A classic example of the codification of such attitudes in a rigidly systematic spirituality can be found in Adolphe Tanquerey's handbook, *The Spiritual Life: A Treatise on Ascetical and Mystical Theology* (Tournai: Desclée and Co., 1923).
6. On Underhill, see Dana Greene, ed., *Evelyn Underhill: Modern Guide to the Ancient Quest for the Holy* (Albany: State University of New York Press, 1988). On Dorothy Day, see note 15 below.
7. Some important recent contributions to an emerging spirituality of liberation include Leonardo Boff and Clodovis Boff, *Introducing Liberation Theology* (Maryknoll, NY: Orbis, 1988); José Comblin, *The Holy Spirit and Liberation* (Maryknoll, NY: Orbis, 1989); Segundo Galilea, *The Way of Living Faith: A Spirituality of Liberation* (San Francisco: Harper and Row, 1988) and *The Beatitudes: To Evangelize as Jesus Did* (Maryknoll, NY: Orbis, 1987); Gustavo Gutiérrez, *A Theology of Liberation* (Maryknoll, NY: Orbis, 1989 ed.) and *We Drink from Our Own Wells* (Maryknoll, NY: Orbis, 1985); and Jon Sobrino, *Spirituality of Liberation: Toward Political Holiness* (Maryknoll, NY: Orbis, 1987).
8. Pierre Teilhard de Chardin, *The Phenomenon of Man* (San Francisco and London: Harper and Row/Collins, 1959). For an important overview of Teilhard's spirituality, see Thomas M. King, S.J., *Teilhard de Chardin* (Wilmington, DE: Michael Glazier, 1988), and Ursula King, *Towards a New Mysticism: Teilhard de Chardin and Eastern Religions* (New York: Seabury Press, 1980).
9. Some of Merton's most enduring works include *The Seven Storey Mountain* (New York: Harcourt, Brace and World, 1948), *Seeds of Contemplation* (New York: New Directions, 1949), *Conjectures of a Guilty Bystander* (Garden City, NY: Doubleday, 1966), *Contemplation in a World of Action* (Garden City, NY: Doubleday, 1971) and *A Vow of Conversation: Journals 1964-1965*, ed. by Naomi Burton Stone (New York: Farrar, Straus, Giroux, 1988). See also Michael Mott, *The Seven Mountains of Thomas Merton* (Boston: Houghton Mifflin, 1984), and Raymond Bailey, *Thomas Merton on Mysticism*, (Garden City, NY: Doubleday, 1975).
10. See Iain MacRobert, *The Black Roots and White Racism of Early Pentecostalism in the U.S.A.* (London: Macmillan Press, 1988) and Vincent Synan, *The Holiness Pentecostal Movement in the United States* (Grand Rapids: Eerdmans, 1971).

11. See Walter J. Hollenweger, *The Pentecostals: the Charismatic Movement in the Churches,* trans. by R. A. Wilson (Minneapolis: Augsburg, 1972), and Vincent Synan, op. cit.

12. See Kilian McDonnell, O.S.B., *Charismatic Renewal and Ecumenism* (New York: Paulist Press, 1978), and Kilian McDonnell, O.S.B., ed., *Presence, Power, Praise: Documents on the Charismatic Renewal* (Collegeville, MN: Liturgical Press, 1980).

13. For a balanced perspective, see J. Gordon Melton and Robert L. Moore, *The Cult Experience: Responding to the New Religious Pluralism* (New York: The Pilgrim Press, 1982). For a historical overview and careful assessment, see Charles Y. Glock and Robert N. Bellah, eds., *The New Religious Consciousness* (Berkeley: University of California Press, 1976), Jacob Needleman and George Baker, *Understanding the New Religions* (New York: Seabury, 1978), and Jacob Needleman, *The New Religions* (New York: Pocket Books ed., 1972).

14. See Starhawk, *Dreaming the Dark: Magic, Sex, and Politics* (Boston: Beacon Press, 1982).

15. "Soul of a New Age," *Omni,* October, 1987.

16. The secular, even scientific spirituality of much New Age enthusiasm is perhaps most carefully articulated in Marilyn Ferguson's *The Aquarian Conspiracy: Personal and Social Transformation in Our Time* (Los Angeles: J. P. Tarcher, Inc. 1987 ed.). For a thoughtful appraisal, see David Toolan, S.J., *Facing West from California's Shores* (New York: Crossroad, 1987).

17. See, among recent works from a variety of perspectives, John Carmody, *Ecology and Religion: Toward a New Christian Theology of Nature* (New York: Paulist Press, 1984), Matthew Fox, O.P., *The Coming of the Cosmic Christ: The Healing of Mother Earth and the Birth of a Global Renaissance* (San Francisco: Harper and Row, 1988), Wesley Granberg-Michaelson, *A Worldly Spirituality: The Call to Take Care of the Earth* (New York: Harper and Row, 1984), Paulos Mar Gregorios, *The Human Presence: Ecological Spirituality and the Age of the Spirit* (Amity, NY: Amity House, 1987), Philip Joranson and Ken Butigan, *Cry of the Environment: Rebuilding the Christian Creation Tradition* (Santa Fe, NM: Bear and Co., 1984), Anne Lonergan and Caroline Richards, *Thomas Berry and the New Cosmology* (Mystic, CT: Twenty-third Publications, 1987), Robert Muller, *New Genesis: Shaping a Global Spirituality* (Garden City, NY: Doubleday Image, 1984), Charlene Spretnak, *The Spiritual Dimension of Green Politics* (Santa Fe, NM: Bear and Co., 1986), and Richard Woods, O.P., *Symbion: Spirituality for a Possible Future* (Santa Fe, NM: Bear and Co., 1984).

18. See Maisie Ward, *Gilbert Keith Chesterton* (New York: Sheed and Ward, 1943) pp. 509-28 and passim.

19. Ibid., p. 511.

20. On her life and work, see Dorothy Day, *The Long Loneliness: An Autobiography,* intro. by Daniel Berrigan (San Francisco: Harper and Row, 1988), Robert Coles, *Dorothy Day: A Radical Development* (Reading, MA: Addison-Wesley Pub. Co. 1987), Robert Ellsberg, ed., *By Little and by Little: The Selected Writings of Dorothy Day* (New York: Knopf, 1988), William D. Miller, *All is Grace: The Spirituality of Dorothy Day* (Garden City, NY: Doubleday, 1987), and William D. Miller, *Dorothy Day: A Biography* (San Francisco: Harper and Row, 1982).

21. For perhaps the most accessible Russian theologians to Western Christians, see Lossky's *The Mystical Theology of the Eastern Church* (Cambridge: James Clarke, 1957), *The Vision of God,* trans. by Asheleigh Moorhouse (Crestwood NJ: St. Vladimir Seminary Press, 1963 and Bedfordshire: The Faith Press and the American Orthodox Book Service, 1972 ed.), and *In the Image and Likeness of God* (Crestwood, NJ: St. Vladimir Seminary Press, 1985).

22. See especially Nicholas Arseniev, *Mysticism and the Eastern Church*, trans. by Arthur Chambers (London and Oxford: Mowbrays, 1979) and *Revelation of Life Eternal* (Crestwood, NJ: St. Vladimir Seminary Press, 1982).
23. Bloom's earlier works, *Living Prayer* (1966), *School of Prayer* (1970), *God and Man* (with Marghanita Laski, 1971), and *Courage to Pray* (with George Lefebvre, 1973), have been published in a single volume, *The Essence of Prayer* (London: Darton, Longman and Todd, 1986).
24. See especially *Poustinia: Christian Spirituality of the East for Western Man* (Notre Dame and London: Ave Maria Press, 1975/Collins 1976).

# Epilogue: Towards the Third Millennium

URVEYING THE SPIRITUAL HISTORY of the Christian people in a single, sweeping glance poses a daunting task for writer and reader alike. But the spectacle provided by such a synopsis also reveals, I believe, evidence that from their mustard-seed beginnings, corporate and individual ways of living based on the recognition of God's abiding presence continued to animate the personalities and lives of a remarkably vital assembly of women and men. It also shows, I feel, that their spiritualities in turn supplied the power and resilience to renew the often all-too-fallible structures of the Church as an institution. I doubt if closer scrutiny will belie these convictions.

It is important here to note that both dimensions of Christian spirituality are important and, in fact, inseparable. Institutions and structures are necessary components of all enduring human enterprise. But they are never sufficient to satisfy the longing of the human spirit for ultimate personal value and significance. Nor can they adequately channel the incomprehensible radiance of divine energy and love. Conversely, personal spiritual experience alone can never be the whole of Christian life or history. It is the heart, soul, and life of faith, the privileged and necessary zone where freedom, grace, and love are born within the Church. But without structure and discipline, spirituality dissipates its energy into a multiplicity of disconnected and idiosyncratic enthusiasms.

Over the long haul, it is only in the interplay of freedom and structure that life and grace flourish – the life of each of us, and the life of all of us, branches and vine. And that is *sobornost*, order, catholicity. Thus the lure of Holiness calls the human spirit onwards towards full maturity, towards its own future, in continuing intercourse with the divine, elusive Presence at the beginning and end of all history.

*New Frontiers*

History, too, is only an aspect of Christian experience, one which must always look forward in hope to the Day of the Lord. Thus, a spirituality suitable for the probable future must be broad enough to encompass the coming age of space, including the likely colonization of the moon and closer planets within the lifetime of many of us, among yet other undreamed-of technological achievements. At the same time, it must be able to address a world situation of increasing poverty, of likely global catastrophes in the ecological order, and of widespread famine and epidemic, as our ability to cope with political, medical, and economic problems on our home planet is outstripped by the pace of population growth, environmental deterioration, and runaway social change.

A spirituality capable of embracing such wide extremes of human experience can only be one rooted in the depths of human nature itself, one which is not the expression of nor linked to any particular cultural form or value system, and one which expresses the age-old and deepest human longing for communion with the ultimate personal Source of all meaning and value. It must be a form of life that promises and effects human integrity and connection with what is truest, most real, best, most noble, and most beautiful in the universe.

Neither closed to the past nor trapped by it, such a spirituality will therefore have to be creatively open to possibilities yet unfathomed by the human mind. Centered within an ever-expanding consciousness of the loving Presence that is always ahead of us, as well as with us, in us, and before us, only such a spirituality can propel us ever onwards, as it has from the beginning, towards becoming what the human family was created to be: the full image and likeness of that God.  In the last analysis, such a spirituality is what Christian life was undoubtedly meant to be and has sought to become over the past two thousand years.  For Christian spirituality is "only" human spirituality in its most universal, inclusive, and progressive expression.

Here and now, of course, the synoptic vision of the paths we have taken so far should also humble us with the realization that such a spirituality is still evolving, as it must, from its imperfect seed-like origins as it all-too-slowly and too-often painfully matures into fully responsible citizenship in the Realm of God.

We still have a long journey ahead.

# RESOURCES

Jordan Aumann, *Christian Spirituality in the Catholic Tradition*, San Francisco: Ignatius Press, 1985.

A. H. Armstrong, ed., *The Cambridge History of Later Greek and Early Medieval Philosophy*, Cambridge: The University Press, 1970.

Derek Baker, ed., *Medieval Women*, Oxford: Basil Blackwell, 1978.

Louis Bouyer, Jean Leclerq, et al., *A History of Christian Spirituality*, 3 vols., London: Burns and Oates, 1968.

Henry Chadwick, *Early Christian Thought and the Classical Tradition*, Oxford: Clarendon press, 1984 ed.

Henry Chadwick, *The Early Church*, Baltimore: Penguin Books, 1969.

Harvey D. Egan, S.J., *Christian Mysticism: The Future of a Tradition*, New York: Pueblo Publishing Co., 1984.

Anne Fremantle, *The Protestant Mystics*, intro. by W. H. Auden, Boston: Little, Brown, 1964.

W. H. C. Frend, *Martyrdom and Persecution in the Early Church*, Garden City, NY: Doubleday, 1967.

W. H. C. Frend, *The Rise of Christianity*, Philadelphia: Fortress Press, 1984.

W. H. C. Frend, *Saints and Sinners in the Early Church*, Wilmington, DE: Michael Glazier, 1985.

Thomas M. Gannon, S.J. and George W. Traub, S.J., *The Desert and the City: An Interpretation of the History of Christian Spirituality*, New York: Macmillan, 1969.

Reginald Garrigou-LaGrange, O.P., *The Three Ways of the Interior Life*, Rockford: TAN Books, 1977 (orig. London, 1938).

R. M. Grant, *Gnosticism and Early Christianity*, New York: Columbia University Press, 1966.

William Ernest Hocking, *The Meaning of God in Human Experience*, New Haven: Yale University Press, 1963.

Gerald Hughes, S.J., *In Search of a Way*, Garden City, NY: Doubleday, 1980.

Kathleen Hughes and Ann Hamlin, *Celtic Monasticism*, New York: Seabury, 1981.

Cheslyn Jones, Geoffrey Wainwright, Edward Yarnold, S.J., *The Study of Spirituality*, New York: Oxford University Press, 1986.

Richard Kieckhefer, *Unquiet Souls: Fourteenth Century Saints and Their Religious Milieu*, Chicago and London: University of Chicago Press, 1987.

David Knowles, O.S.B., *The English Mystical Tradition*, New York: Harper and Brothers, 1961.

Ronald Knox, *Enthusiasm: A Chapter in the History of Religion*, New York: Oxford University Press, 1961 (1950).

Kenneth Leech, *Soul Friend*, New York: Harper and Row, 1980.

Andrew Louth, *The Origins of the Christian Mystical Tradition from Plato to Denys*, New York: Oxford University Press, 1981.

Bernard McGinn and John Meyendorff, *Christian Spirituality: Origins to the Twelfth Century*, New York: Crossroad, 1985.

John T. McNeill, *The Celtic Churches*, Chicago: The University of Chicago Press, 1974.

Johannes Quasten, *Music and Worship in Pagan and Christian Antiquity*, trans. by Boniface Ramsey, O.P., Washington, DC: National Association of Pastoral Musicians, 1983.

Jill Raitt, ed., in collaboration with Bernard McGinn and John Meyendorff, *Christian Spirituality: High Middle Ages and Reformation*, New York: Crossroad, 1987.

Cyril C. Richardson, ed., *Early Christian Fathers*, New York: Collier Books, 1970.

J. A. T. Robinson, *The Body: A Study in Pauline Theology*, London and Philadelphia: SCM Press/Westminster, 1952.

Frank C. Senn, ed., *Protestant Spiritual Traditions*, New York: Paulist Press, 1986.

Maxwell Staniforth, ed. and trans., *Early Christian Writings*, New York: Penguin Books, 1968.

Samuel Terrien, *The Elusive Presence*, San Francisco: Harper and Row, 1978.

Martin Thornton, *English Spirituality*, Cowley Publications, 1986.

Helen Waddell, *The Desert Fathers*, London: Constable and Co., 1936.

D. S. Wallace-Hadrill, *Christian Antioch: A Study of Early Christian Thought in the East*, London: Cambridge University Press, 1982.

R. T. Wallis, *Neoplatonism*, London: Duckworth, 1972.

Rowan Williams, *The Wound of Knowledge: Christian Spirituality from the New Testament to St. John of the Cross*, London: Darton, Longman and Todd, 1979.

Katharina M. Wilson, ed., *Medieval Women Writers*, Athens: The University of Georgia Press, 1984.

# INDEX